Santa Fe & Taos

Santa Fe & Taos

A Great Destination

Sharon
Niederman

The Countryman Press   •   Woodstock, Vermont

ALSO BY THE AUTHOR:

New Mexico: An Explorer's Guide

New Mexico's Tasty Traditions: Recollections, Recipes, and Photos

Return to Abo: A Novel of the Southwest

*A Quilt of Words: Women's Diaries, Letters,
and Original Accounts of Life in the Southwest 1860–1960*

Signs and Shrines: Spiritual Journeys Across New Mexico

Interior photographs by the author unless otherwise specified
Maps by Erin Greb Cartography, © The Countryman Press
Book design by Bodenweber Design
Composition by Eugenie S. Delaney

Explorer's Guide Santa Fe & Taos
978-1-58157-142-4

Published by The Countryman Press, P.O. Box 748, Woodstock, VT 05091
Distributed by W. W. Norton & Company, Inc., 500 Fifth Avenue, New York, NY 10110
Printed in the United States of America

10 9 8 7 6 5 4 3 2 1

For Charles Henry

WINTER TWILIGHT, CANYON ROAD

Do not say you will come back
When it is warmer
When you have time
When the light is better
When the galleries are open
When the chestnut trees are green
When a woman in red sits on the garden bench
When the blue gate is wide open
When the duende seizes you
When you are not obsessing
When you are not regretting
When you are not counting
Your losses
See the Hunger Moon scale the Sangres
Press the shutter. Now.

—SHARON NIEDERMAN

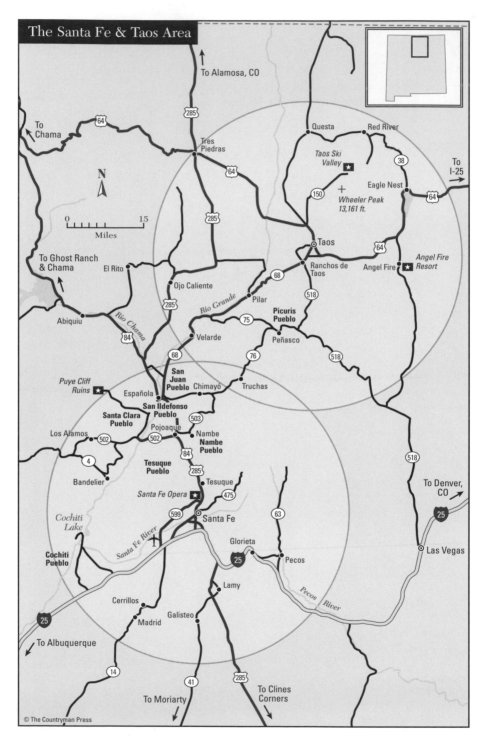

The Santa Fe & Taos Area

To Alamosa, CO

To Chama

Questa

Red River

Tres Piedras

Taos Ski Valley

N

To I-25

Wheeler Peak 13,161 ft.

Eagle Nest

Taos

To Ghost Ranch & Chama

El Rito

Ranchos de Taos

Angel Fire

Angel Fire Resort

Ojo Caliente

Rio Grande

Pilar

Picuris Pueblo

Abiquiu

Rio Chama

Velarde

Peñasco

Puye Cliff Ruins

San Juan Pueblo

Chimayó

Truchas

Española

San Ildefonso Pueblo

Santa Clara Pueblo

Pojoaque

Los Alamos

Nambe

Nambe Pueblo

Tesuque Pueblo

Bandelier

Tesuque

To Denver, CO

Santa Fe Opera

Cochiti Lake

Santa Fe

Las Vegas

Cochiti Pueblo

Santa Fe River

Glorieta

Pecos

Lamy

Pecos River

Cerrillos

Madrid

Galisteo

To Albuquerque

To Moriarty

To Clines Corners

0   15
Miles

© The Countryman Press

6

Contents

Introduction

IN 1881, NEW MEXICO GOVERNOR LEW WALLACE made the observation, "Every calculation based on experience elsewhere fails in New Mexico." While Wallace meant the statement ironically and that is how it is generally understood, this book is all about the celebration of the 47th state's wondrous unique qualities.

The vibrant mix of cultures, the variety of languages spoken, and the respect for time-honored customs makes New Mexico an exciting place to be. However, a happy and successful visit to New Mexico requires the appropriate attitude adjustment. Just as you can go from desert to high mountain environments in an hour, you can shift from adventure to luxurious relaxation faster than you can say *mañana*. This book, based on three decades of living, writing, and traveling here, can guide you toward creating the best possible New Mexico experience—for you. Here's what you need to know:

- Always get precise directions before setting out. Travel with adequate maps. Once on the road, you will find a definite lack of signs, street names, and markers. In addition, many streets are old and winding, not built for automobiles (this is one aspect of "Santa Fe charm"), so travel along them can be disorienting. If you stop to ask directions, you may find they are skimpy and grudgingly given, or given with an assumption of familiarity you do not possess. Locals may be able to tell each other "It's over there, just past the big cottonwood, turn right at the dip and look for the blue mailbox," while, after half a dozen bumps in a dirt road, you may wonder exactly which "dip" was meant.

- Always call in advance to be sure a restaurant or attraction is open. Although definite hours may be advertised, the reality is that hours of operation are often flexible, based on time of year, family demands, and number of visitors.

- Santa Fe and Taos are popular destinations. It is not unusual for favorite lodgings to be booked for the winter holiday season and Indian Market a year in advance; for many other wonderful B&Bs, six months in advance is common. The sooner you can make your travel plans, the more choices you will have, and the less compromise you will have to make.

LEFT: The history of Native people is depicted on Museum Hill in Santa Fe.

Roasting chiles scent the autumn air.

- Remember you are entering another time zone here. We're not just talking about Mountain Time. *Mañana* does not mean "tomorrow." It may be translated as "not today." The room you booked was supposed to be ready at two, yet when you arrive you're told it won't be ready until four. Or the tour you booked is canceled until next week. Patience, courtesy, and flexibility are the best attitudes to maintain. Pressuring, or threats to "talk to the manager" or "call the boss," will be counterproductive. New Mexico is not the place to throw your weight around. Any display of self-importance will only typecast you as an outsider and decrease the chances that you'll get what you want. New Mexicans were isolated for four centuries, and they made up their own rules. Rushing is not efficient here. But you're on vacation anyway, right? So go with the flow. And carry a book with you for times you may have to wait.

- Take care of your health. You've probably heard it before, but here goes: Allow a few days to adjust to the altitude, drink lots of water, wear sunscreen at all times of day, take a hat, dress in layers, give yourself lots of rest stops. The sun is very intense at this altitude, there's less oxygen, and you may very well feel the effects. And whatever the season, it's best to be prepared for sudden changes in weather. When venturing out, be prepared for temperature changes of as much as 40 degrees in a single day—and remember, the weather may change dramatically very suddenly. Dress accordingly.

- In Santa Fe, especially during high season, you may encounter some treatment from restaurant, shop, or hotel personnel that can only be termed rude. This, unfortunately, is as likely to occur at the high end as at the low. Be advised and either let it glide like water off a duck's back or take your business elsewhere. There's no need to take it personally or expect it to change.

- The official state question at restaurants is: Red or green? But you will find that the question most commonly asked by outsiders in New Mexico is: Which is hotter, red or green chile? Regardless of the answer, if you are genuinely concerned, it's best to ask for a small taste of each kind of chile before placing your order. It may take you a little while to become accustomed to the taste sensation of chile, but once you do, you will be addicted, eagerly anticipating your next taste. And the touted health benefits of the chile are for real. Meanwhile, remember you can order any dish containing chile with the chile served on the side.

- Even if you are not by nature a shopper, you will find things here so special, so unique that you'll find yourself frequently reaching for your wallet. Art, jewelry, furniture, clothing, crafts—northern New Mexico is a bazaar of the one-of-a-kind and the exquisitely handmade. In Santa Fe, Spanish Market takes place the last weekend in July, while Indian Market is held the weekend of August closest to the 19th;the wildly popular International Folk Art Festival is the second weekend in July. In fall, artists' studio tours held in the nearby villages of El Rito, Dixon, Abiquiu, and Galisteo offer especially appealing shopping opportunities. Be sure to factor shopping money into your vacation budget. And don't say we didn't warn you.

Santa Fe's International Folk Art Festival has become a must-do shopping occasion.

While people speak of off-season and in-season, there really is no off-season in New Mexico. Each time of year has its own magnificent beauty, whether on a peaceful desert hike on a dazzling summer morning or cuddling up in front of a sweet piñon fire after a winter afternoon walk through snowy Santa Fe. There's nothing better than an early November stroll through Taos, when the cottonwoods are still golden and the scent of autumn piñon smoke is in the air. Whatever season you choose for your visit, New Mexico has the power to touch and satisfy your soul. And these days, worthwhile bargains may be found during the quieter times of spring and fall.

In New Mexico, be prepared to be surprised. The sweep of a red earth vista, the sight of a 10-foot stark white Penitente cross on a hillside, the faded altar paintings of a centuries-old Spanish colonial church, the drumbeats and jangling shells of hundreds of dancers at a Pueblo corn dance, the unexpected connection with a local grower at the Santa Fe Area Farmers' Market, the sight of more stars than you've ever seen in the clear night sky—any of thousands of moments have the power to move you deeply and perhaps change your life in some way you could never have predicted.

In this eighth edition of *Explorer's Guide: Santa Fe & Taos, A Great Destination*, we've included new restaurants and lodgings, some of which replace enterprises that have moved or gone out of business. This book is written to inform you of a wide range of the best values, opportunities, and experiences in lodging and cuisine. All the restaurants in these pages have been taste tested and evaluated for price, service, and atmosphere. New Mexican cuisine is one of the great adventures available here, so enjoy the native foods unique to this place.

Once you visit, you may find, like so many, that a single vacation isn't enough. And no matter how much time you've spent here, it's still possible to make new discoveries. As I travel the state, I continue to find new discoveries and adventures, and so I

Altar screen at El Rancho de Las Golindrinas

invite you, too, to return to this unique place to learn more, see more, and continue the delightful adventure.

The Way This Book Works

THIS BOOK IS DIVIDED INTO EIGHT CHAPTERS, each with its own introduction. If you are especially interested in one chapter or another, you can turn to it directly and begin reading without losing a sense of continuity. You can also take the book with you on your travels and skip around, reading about the places you visit as you go. Or you can read the entire book through from start to finish.

If you're interested in finding a place to eat or sleep, we suggest you first look over the "Lodging Index" and "Restaurant Index" near the end of this book (organized by area and price); then turn to the pages listed and read the specific entries for the places you're most interested in.

Entries within most of the chapters are arranged alphabetically under four different headings: "Santa Fe," "Taos," "Near Santa Fe," and "Near Taos." The first two headings refer to the area within the city or town limits. "Near Santa Fe" and "Near Taos" mean within a 30-mile radius of these two centers. (Look at the map facing the table of contents; all points within the two circles are less than an hour—and frequently not more than a few minutes—from Santa Fe or Taos.) And for those "don't miss" places in parts beyond, we've included another category called "Outside the Area."

It's Java Junction for a coffee break in Madrid while touring the Turquoise Trail.

Some entries, most notably those in chapter 3, *Lodging*, and chapter 6, *Restaurants*, include specific information organized for easy reference in blocks at the head of each entry. "All details given in the information blocks—as well as all phone numbers and addresses in other parts of the book—were checked as close to publication as possible. Even so, such details do change. When in doubt, call ahead.

For the same reason, we've usually avoided listing specific prices, preferring instead to indicate a range. Lodging price codes are based on a per-room rate, double occupancy, during high season (summer and ski months). Low-season rates are likely to be 20–40 percent less. Once again, it's always best to call ahead for specific rates and reservations.

Restaurant prices indicate the cost of an individual meal including appetizer, entrée, dessert, tax, and tip but not including alcoholic beverages.

PRICE CODES

	Lodging	Dining
Inexpensive	Up to $90	Up to $30
Moderate	$90–150	$30–50
Expensive	$150–250	$50–75
Very expensive	Over $250	Over $75

There are two telephone area codes for New Mexico: 505 and 575. Santa Fe is 505; Taos is 575. For areas in between, if one does not work, try the other.

The best sources for year-round tourist information are the **Santa Fe Convention and Visitors Bureau** (505-955-6200; 800-777-2489; www.santafe.org; scenter@santafenm.gov) 201 W. Marcy St., Santa Fe, NM 87501 and the **Taos Visitor Center** (575-758-3873; 800-348-0696; information@taosvisitor.com) 1139 Paseo del Pueblo Sur, Taos, NM 87571. For specific information on activities near Taos, contact the **Angel Fire Visitor Center** (575-377-6555; 866-668-7787; www .angelfirefun.com) 3365 Mountain View Blvd., #7, Angel Fire, NM 87710; the **Eagle Nest Chamber of Commerce** (575-377-2420; 800-494-9117) 60 W. Therma Dr., Eagle Nest, NM 87718; or the **Red River Visitor Information Center** (575-754-3030; 877-754-1708; www.redriver.org) 100 E. Main, Red River, NM 87558.

TOWNS IN THE SANTA FE–TAOS AREA

Though we focus primarily on Santa Fe and Taos, many other towns in the area are worth a visit. Within the circle to the south of Santa Fe, for example, you'll find Golden and Madrid on the road known as the Turquoise Trail and Galisteo and Lamy, all old towns that retain some of their Wild West and old New Mexico flavor. A few minutes to the north of Santa Fe lies the picturesque village of Tesuque, a favored suburb of Santa Fe with the Shidoni Gallery and the gathering spot of the Tesuque Village Market. To the west is Los Alamos, home of the Los Alamos National Laboratory and the birthplace of the atomic bomb.

Scattered up and down the Rio Grande are 11 Indian pueblos—not towns but separate nations—each unique in its own way, from ceremonies and dances to crafts and cooking. On the way to Taos via the Rio Grande on NM 68, you'll pass through the little farming and orchard villages of Velarde and Embudo, with the artists' community of Dixon and its La Chirapada Winery a quick side trip east. And if you take the High Road to Taos via NM 76 and NM 518, you'll cruise through more than half a dozen old villages where time virtually stands still— Chimayó, with its famous Santuario known for its healing "holy dirt," Truchas, Peñasco, Vadito, and others—that offer everything from wonderful crafts and galleries to venerable Spanish colonial churches and looks at quieter times.

North of Taos are the old mining towns of Questa, Red River, and Angel Fire,

Vintage quilts displayed at Dixon can tell the story of New Mexico pioneer women.

today all hubs of outdoor sports and backwoods places with wild and rustic flavors. West of Taos is Ojo Caliente, site of the famed mineral springs spa. And if you go as far west as Abiquiu, you'll find the home of artist Georgia O'Keeffe. One look at the landscape with its pink and red cliffs is enough to explain why she was so entranced with northern New Mexico and why her work seems so inspired. Another journey outside the area, this time 60 miles to the southeast via I-25, will take you to the busy metropolis of Albuquerque with its numerous historical and cultural attractions, including the botanic gardens, aquarium, and zoo that compose the Biopark; the University of New Mexico with its famous basketball stadium The Pit, which makes national TV during "March Madness," bustling Nob Hill with its shops and cafés; and the Albuquerque Isotopes baseball team.

History

THE DINOSAURS TO THE PRESENT

This was a land of vast spaces and long silences, a desert land of red bluffs and brilliant flowering cactus. The hot sun poured down. This land belonged to the very old Gods. They came on summer evenings, unseen, to rest their eyes and their hearts on the milky opal and smoky blue of the desert. For this was a land of enchantment, where Gods walked in the cool of the evening.

—From *Land of Enchantment: Memoirs of Marian Russell Along the Old Santa Fe Trail*

THE HISTORY OF NORTHERN NEW MEXICO is one of turbulent change. From hot, crushing forces that originally shaped the land to the often violent social movements that molded its present-day mix of cultures, the area has been embroiled in flux since prehistoric times. The story of the Santa Fe–Taos area is one of an enchanting land and its varied peoples: of ancient hunter-gatherers and modern Pueblo Indians; of Spanish conquistadores and colonists; of American mountain men, French trappers, German merchants, and adventurers of various origins; and more recently of artists, tourists, skiers, and spiritual seekers. The 2012 marked its centennial.

New Mexico is a land that, through the centuries, has continually been "discovered"—first by wandering bands of indigenous people, then, five centuries ago, by the Spanish, and successively by 19th- and 20th-century pioneers determined to build a better life than the one they left behind. Each new group of discoverers attempted a new wave of colonization, claiming New Mexico's resources for itself. The area's remoteness from major population centers, times of extreme weather conditions, scarce water, and challenging terrain have proven both blessing and curse. Isolation protected and strengthened Native cultures while simultaneously cutting off New Mexico from innovation and economic growth.

LEFT: Santa Fe's Scottish Rite Cathedral is as old as the state itself.

Many are surprised to learn that the myth of the "tricultural" state—Spanish, Indian, and Anglo—is one that was coined early in the 20th century by Santa Fe town fathers seeking to encourage tourism and is a big simplification. This myth has been questioned as greater understanding of the complex cultural mix of northern New Mexico's residents has been gained.

NATURAL HISTORY

If we could compress 2 billion years into a few minutes, we would see the New Mexico landscape being shaped and reshaped. The invasion and retreat of inland seas, the rise and fall of great mountain ranges, the shifting of subterranean plates, the cracking of mantle and crust, the explosions of volcanoes, the seeping of magma, the shifting of sands, and the continual erosion by wind and water—each of these forces has left its mark on the modern landscape.

More than 100 million years ago great dinosaurs roamed the land, as evidenced by skeletons now on display at the Ghost Ranch Conference Center. At the same time, colorful sands and silts from the ancestral Rockies formed pink and red cliffs, and volcanoes spewed ash over the landscape. As the modern Rockies rose to the north, the dinosaurs mysteriously disappeared, giving way to the mammals.

To the east of Santa Fe and Taos, the Sangre de Cristo Mountains began to rise near the end of the Mesozoic. Later, about 30 million years ago, an upwelling in the earth's mantle created a pair of massive fault lines, and the land between them caved in, resulting in the Rio Grande Rift, a trench up to 5 miles deep. It filled with debris, and water from the mountains created a long chain of basins. Finally, about 2.5 million years ago, the Rio Grande became a continuous river flowing 1,800 miles to the Gulf of Mexico. Thereafter, volcanic activity on the west side of the Rio Grande created basaltic mesas and broad volcanic tablelands, including the present-day Taos Plateau.

The Jemez (HAY-mess) Mountains west of Santa Fe are the remains of a composite volcano that geologists believe was once almost as high as Mount Everest. About a million years ago, the volcano blew its top and caved in. The explosion, 600 times more powerful than the 1980 eruption of Mount St. Helens, left a crater 15 miles wide and buried much of the land with ash up to 1,000 feet thick. Later, some of that volcanic tuff became home to the Anasazi Indians, whose cave dwellings still pepper the bases of canyon walls at Bandelier National Monument. This area, the Valles Caldera National Preserve, is open to the public on a limited basis.

During the recent ice ages, lava seeped in the foothills and glaciers scoured the mountains. Heavy snows and rains formed lakes and created wide, sloping foothills. As the weather warmed, these areas sprouted new vegetation, from scrub brush and small pines in the lowlands to lush aspens and evergreens in the mountains.

Such was the landscape discovered by the first human inhabitants of the Santa Fe–Taos area some 12,000 years ago. Today, it is essentially the same: the wide, fertile Rio Grande Valley flanked by spectacular sets of mountains. To the east lies the Sangre de Cristo range, a modern ski paradise that stretches north to the Colorado Rockies, while to the west lie the volcanic Jemez.

From north of Taos, the Rio Grande rushes through a 50-mile stretch of basalt, the gorge providing excellent year-round fishing and summer thrills and chills for whitewater enthusiasts. Likewise, the Chama River, flowing north of the

The aspens really do shimmer gold in autumn along the Enchanted Circle.

Jemez into the Rio Grande, offers some of the most spectacular wild and scenic excursions in the state. Flowing south through the fertile farms and orchards of Velarde, the Rio Grande eventually meanders through the ancient Pueblo lands north of Santa Fe and the hills and valleys to the west.

Elevations in the area range from under 6,000 feet in the valley to 13,161 feet at the top of Wheeler Peak, the highest point in the state. The air is clear and dry, with sunny skies 300 days of the year. A 14-inch average annual rainfall leaves a desertlike setting in the lowlands, while winter storms dump up to 320 inches of snow a year on lush mountain areas such as the popular Taos Ski Valley.

These factors make for a diversity of life zones and an especially rich flora and fauna. Santa Fe and Taos have wonderful shade trees, the most prominent being the giant willows and cottonwoods that grace municipal plazas and downtowns. Juniper and piñon pines dominate the dry lower elevations, giving way to scrub oak and thicker forests of ponderosa pine, and finally to high-alpine forests with a spectacular mix of fir, aspen, and spruce. Spring and summer wildflowers, especially in the mountains, make a colorful spectrum, from Indian paintbrush and woodland pinedrops to buttercups and alpine daisies.

Northern New Mexico is a haven for animals large and small. The *arroyos* (dry gullies or washes) and foothills are dominated by mice, prairie dogs, jackrabbits, and cottontails and by the coyotes and bobcats that feed on them. Muskrat and beaver thrive in some rivers and streams, and signs of river otter can be found on secluded parts of the Rio Grande. Some sure-footed and shy bighorn sheep still roam parts of the Sangre de Cristo, while pronghorn antelope are common on the plains. The mountains are home not only to snowshoe hares and various species of squirrels, but also to herds of mule deer and elk and a fair number of black bears.

The Chama River outside Abiquiu is a stream of silver serenity.

And mountain lions are sighted with increasing frequency in these parts. Recovery from the severe forest fires of the past decade in Los Alamos and above Taos is transforming the ecology from ponderosa pine dominated to open green meadows and young aspen stands inhabited by an increasing diversity of birds and wildflowers.

Birds fill every available avian niche, from seed-eating finches and bug-eating swallows to breathtakingly beautiful bluebirds and a variety of large, winged predators. Eagles and hawks soar above canyons, while quail, doves, and roadrunners (the state bird) skitter through the brush below. Lowland wet and marshy areas play host to myriad ducks, geese, and shorebirds, while the mountains are home to a wide range of species.

SOCIAL HISTORY

Early Human Inhabitants

The first human inhabitants of the Santa Fe–Taos area were Stone Age hunters who followed herds of giant bison and mammoth more than 12,000 years ago. As the centuries passed, they became less nomadic, gathering fruits, nuts, and greens in the lowlands, hunting deer and elk in the mountains, and trapping small game. By around 5500 B.C., these hunter-gatherers were living seasonally in what is today the Santa Fe–Taos area, mostly in caves and other natural shelters. Soon afterward, they began to plant corn and other crops and to make baskets. Eventually, they constructed circular pit houses, which centuries later gave way to aboveground dwellings of stone and adobe. Around 200 B.C. they began making pottery.

From A.D. 900–1300, great Anasazi complexes (*Anasazi* is a Navajo word meaning "ancient strangers") flourished at Chaco Canyon and Mesa Verde to the west and north. These centers were marked by extensive roadways and huge, multitiered complexes of stone. The people performed sophisticated ceremonies, irrigated extensive farmlands, and accurately predicted the movements of the sun and moon. Another group of Anasazi developed a similar complex in Frijoles (free-HOLE-ace) Canyon about 30 miles northwest of Santa Fe in what is now Bandelier National Monument. However, by A.D. 1300, most of these great centers had been abandoned. It is widely believed that the "ancient ones" were some of the ancestors of present-day Pueblo people.

Sometime during the era of the Anasazi, a number of stone and adobe villages sprang up in the Santa Fe area. The largest of these, called Ogapoge or Kuapoge (meaning "dancing ground of the sun"), once occupied part of Santa Fe. Scores of other small settlements, including the beginnings of present-day Taos Pueblo and other pueblos north of Santa Fe, were built along the Rio Grande.

Ogapoge and other settlements around Santa Fe were abandoned around 1425, during the worst drought in 1,000 years. Others remained and continued to flourish, including Pecos Pueblo to the southeast and the present-day pueblos of Tesuque, Pojoaque, Nambe, San Ildefonso, Santa Clara, San Juan, Jemez, Picuris, and Taos to the north. When the first Spaniards arrived in New Mexico, the Pueblo Indians (*pueblo* is Spanish for "village") were well established in some 150 adobe villages, large and small, scattered along the Rio Grande and its tributaries. In New Mexico today, 19 Indian pueblos carry on their ancestral customs.

Before the arrival of the Spaniards, the Pueblos lived a life of ceremony in accordance with the seasonal cycles of hunting and planting. They cultivated corn, beans, and squash and gathered greens, berries, fruits, and seeds. They hunted wild game, from prairie dogs, rabbits, and turkeys to deer, elk, and antelope. They made clay pottery; wove baskets and mats from corn, cattail, and yucca leaves; and fashioned blankets from feathers and animal hides. Although they traveled exclusively on foot, they not only maintained close ties with each other but also had trade links with the Plains Indians, the Pacific Coast Indians, and tribes in Mexico.

The ancient Pueblos, like their modern counterparts, spoke a number of different languages. They continually honored the Great Spirit and the forces of nature. Underground, they built circular chambers called kivas, adaptations of their ancestral pit houses that served as centers for prayer and teaching. They also developed elaborate ceremonial dances that expressed their sense of oneness with nature. With the exception of raids from neighboring Plains tribes, their lives were generally tranquil until the arrival of the Spaniards from Mexico.

The Spanish Influence

One of the first Spaniards to come to New Mexico, then known as New Spain, was Fray Marcos de Niza, a Franciscan friar who arrived in 1539 after hearing fabulous accounts of the Seven Cities of Cibola, supposedly made of gold. De Niza never visited these cities himself, but he embellished the stories he heard. His own overblown reports of riches spurred a massive expedition in 1540, in which Francisco Vasquez de Coronado rode north from Mexico City with 300 soldiers. Cibola turned out to be nothing more than the little pueblo of Zuni, which Coronado and his men conquered and subjugated. Other pueblos to the north were similarly invaded, yet neither Coronado nor those who followed him could find any gold. Thereafter Spain turned its focus toward colonization.

The first official colonizer of the area was Juan de Oñate. In 1598, with 129 soldier-colonists and their families, 10 Franciscan friars, and thousands of cattle, sheep, horses, and mules, he set out to establish the first permanent Spanish settlement in New Mexico. Many of the horses escaped, eventually providing the Plains Indians and the rest of North America with a new form of transportation.

Oñate chose a spot across the Rio Grande from Okay Owenge Pueblo, about 25 miles north of present-day Santa Fe, near present-day Espanola. The settlement, called San Gabriel, was beset with problems from the beginning. Some settlers were apparently still under the illusion that they would find easy riches. Others balked at the hard labor and difficult living conditions, still others at the difficulty of converting the Indians to Catholicism. By 1600, almost half the settlers had given up and gone back to Mexico. A few years later, referring to the stories of fantastic riches and abundance in the area, the viceroy of New Spain wrote to the king from Mexico City, "I cannot help but inform your majesty that this conquest is becoming a fairy tale. . . . If those who write the reports imagine that they are believed by those who read them, they are greatly mistaken. Less substance is being revealed every day."

Many Spaniards thought the most reasonable alternative was to leave New Mexico altogether. However, after long debate, they decided to stay, partly to maintain their claim to the huge territory west of the Mississippi but primarily because the friars were so reluctant to abandon the Indians to paganism. A new governor, Pedro de Peralta, was appointed and sent to New Mexico to found a permanent settlement. He chose a spot south of San Gabriel that offered more water and better protection. The result was La Villa de Santa Fe—the City of Holy Faith. (In 1823, St. Francis became its patron saint, hence its current name: the Royal City of the Holy Faith of St. Francis of Assisi.) In 1610, a decade before the arrival of the Pilgrims at Plymouth Rock, the Spanish settlers laid out their new plaza and began building the Palace of the Governors, today the oldest continuously occupied public building in the United States. That same year, supplies began moving northward to Santa Fe along the newly opened Camino Real (meaning "royal road") from Chihuahua, Mexico. A caravan might take three years to make the journey, stopping at *posadas* (inns) along the way to trade.

Over the years, the settler-soldiers built adobe houses and dug a network of *acequias*, or irrigation ditches, to divert water from the Santa Fe River. They cultivated fields of beans, squash, corn, and wheat with handheld plows and wooden hoes. Accompanied by Franciscan friars, they ranged far and wide, subjugating the Pueblos, building churches, and trying to convert the Indians to Catholicism. By 1625, the Spaniards had built some 50 churches in the Rio Grande Valley with forced Indian labor, and more than half of the original pueblos had disappeared.

One that continued to thrive was Taos Pueblo, about 70 miles north of Santa Fe. (*Taos* is the Spanish version of a Tewa phrase meaning "place of the red willows.") The first Spanish settlers moved there with Fray Pedro de Miranda in 1617. They settled near Taos Pueblo, even moving within its walls during the 1760s for protection against the Comanches. Taos Pueblo, a World Heritage Site, has existed for approximately 1,000 years in the same location.

The Indians objected to Spanish encroachment. All through the Rio Grande

Taos Pueblo is a World Heritage Site.

Valley, Pueblo spiritual and political leaders were routinely treated harshly, while others were forced to build churches, work in the fields, and weave garments for export to Mexico. Conflicts between Spanish civil and religious authorities fueled the discontent. Over a 75-year period, the Indians attempted a number of revolts, most of them stemming from attempts to outlaw their religious ceremonies. None was successful. Rebellions at Taos and Jemez Pueblos in the 1630s resulted in the deaths of several priests and were met with even more repression from the Spaniards. While some governors allowed the Indians to continue their dances, most supported the Franciscans in their attempts to stamp out all remnants of Pueblo ceremony.

One of the most brutal of these attempts came in 1675, when Governor Juan Francisco de Trevino charged 47 Pueblo religious leaders with sorcery and witchcraft and sentenced them to death or slavery. A San Juan leader named Popé, who was frequently flogged because of his religious influence, secretly vowed revenge. For several years, he hid at Taos Pueblo, quietly plotting and sending out runners to orchestrate a revolt of all the pueblos.

The revolt took place on August 10, 1680. At the break of day, Indians in pueblos from Taos in the north to Acoma in the south, and Hopi in the west suddenly turned on the Spaniards, killing men, women, children, and priests and setting the mission churches ablaze. In Santa Fe, about 1,000 settlers holed up in the Palace of the Governors. When Governor Otermín learned of the widespread devastation, he and the others loaded their belongings onto mules and wagons and abandoned Santa Fe on August 21.

The refugees eventually made their way to El Paso del Norte, near the site of present-day Juarez, Mexico, where they lived in exile for the next 12 years. Meanwhile, the Indians took over the Palace of the Governors at Santa Fe. Despite several Spanish attempts at reconquest, they lived there largely unhindered until 1692.

Even so, the Spaniards had left deep and indelible marks on Pueblo society—and even on the rebels themselves. After 70 years, Catholicism was almost as alive as Pueblo ceremonialism, and most of the Indians spoke Spanish as well as their own native languages. Moreover, like their Spanish predecessors, Popé and other Indian leaders now ruled with an iron hand, demanding tributes and trying to stamp out forcibly all remnants of Spanish influence. Crop failures and attacks by the Apaches and Navajos eroded the Pueblo resolve, and by the time the new territorial governor returned in September 1692, the Indians seemed ready to submit once more.

That governor was Don Diego de Vargas, a man as bold and fearless as he was vain and arrogant. With only 40 soldiers, he confronted the fortified pueblo that had once been the Palace of the Governors. To allay the Indians' fears, he entered the palace completely unarmed. Reassured that they would be pardoned and protected from marauding Plains Indians, the Pueblos agreed to Spanish rule.

Dressed as Comanches, Taoseños commemorate their Plains Indian heritage every New Year's Day.

Unfortunately, Vargas's reconquest was only briefly bloodless. When he returned the following December with more soldiers and colonists, he was met with defiance and hostility. After many days of suffering in the cold and snow, the Spaniards stormed the palace, killing 81 Indians in the process. In subsequent years, Vargas met similar resistance; once, his soldiers even rode north to raid Taos Pueblo after its leaders refused to supply the starving settlers with grain. Only in 1696—after a number of bloody battles, another Taos revolt, and the deaths of many Pueblo leaders—did the new governor finally succeed in establishing a new Spanish reign.

With the exception of repeated Comanche raids on Taos, the 1700s were relatively peaceful, a time of festivity, drama, and art. In the fall of 1712, the colonists celebrated the first annual Fiesta de Santa Fe, a holiday commemorating Vargas's "bloodless" reconquest of New Mexico and his return of La Conquistadora, the small statue of the Virgin Mary that the colonists believed protected them when they fled Santa Fe for Mexico. Frequent dances, musicals, and comedies celebrated the Spanish heritage. Silversmithing, goldsmithing, woodworking, and weaving flourished among the Spaniards, while the Pueblos supplied the colonists with cookware and crockery of all kinds.

Meanwhile, as the *acequias* (ditches) irrigated the land, farms, and orchards around Santa Fe, and Taos sprouted fields of wheat, corn, beans, and a variety of fruits and vegetables. Gambling and smoking were popular among men and women alike, and cockfights were frequently held on the plazas in the afternoon. By the time of the American Revolution (which some wealthy Santa Feans helped finance), more than 100 colonial families were living in the Santa Fe area. Horses, cattle, and sheep, first brought into the New World by the Spaniards, had proliferated, and annual fairs at Pecos and Taos provided major trade opportunities among the Spanish, the Pueblos, and the Plains Indians.

After the reconquest, the Indians were no longer treated as slaves, and church and kiva coexisted side by side. By midcentury, Franciscan friars, frustrated over their failure to stamp out Native ceremonies after eight generations, were replaced by secular priests. The new priests seemed satisfied as long as the Indians professed to be Catholic. Some of the Indians still worked as indentured servants, and many were abused.

On the other hand, fundamental changes took place after the reconquest that contributed to lasting respect and cooperation between Hispanics and Pueblos. One, they often banded together to fight their common enemies, usually the raiding Plains tribes. (On one occasion, the Villasur Expedition of 1720, Spaniards and Pueblos fought side by side against French and Pawnees who were encroaching on their eastern territory.) Two, the Pueblos incorporated Catholicism and certain Hispanic ceremonies (the Matachines dances, for example) into their own Native traditions. More fundamental still, they intermarried; today, the great majority of Pueblo people are of mixed blood, and many have Hispanic surnames.

Arrival of the Anglos

Though the Spanish government forbade foreigners inside New Mexico, a few mountain men and explorers sneaked into the Santa Fe–Taos area in the early 1800s. One of these was Zebulon Pike, who was arrested by the Spaniards in 1807 while on a mission to explore the area west of the Louisiana Purchase. As Pike was escorted into Santa Fe under armed guard, he made the following observations of the capital city (from *The Journals of Zebulon Montgomery Pike, with Letters and Related Documents* [Norman: University of Oklahoma Press, 1966]):

> *Its appearance from a distance struck my mind with the same effect as a fleet of the flat-bottomed boats which are seen in the spring and fall seasons descending the Ohio River. There are two churches, the magnificience [sic] of whose steeples form a striking contrast to the miserable appearance of the houses.*

After his release from prison in Chihuahua, Pike published his journals, which attracted more American adventurers to the area.

Gradually, especially during the Napoleonic Wars, Spain loosened its grip on its colonies, and Mexico drifted further from the king. In 1821, Mexican independence was celebrated in Santa Fe with "universal carousing and revelry," according to American observer Thomas James. The great event brought many more Anglos, as mountain men filtered in from the Rockies to hunt and trap around Taos, and New Mexico was finally opened up to foreign trade.

That same year, trader William Becknell drove a heavily laden wagon over Raton Pass, making Santa Fe the western terminus of the Santa Fe Trail from Independence, Missouri, some 800 miles to the east. Now an unstoppable stream of Americans began rushing into and through the area. Stretching across the prairies like great billowing armadas, covered wagons initially took almost a month to get to Santa Fe. They carted tremendous amounts of merchandise—including textiles, tools, shoes, flour, whiskey, hardware, medicines, musical instruments, ammunition, and even heavy machinery. Some merchants sold their goods in Santa Fe or Taos; others pushed on to Mexico over the Camino Real.

One of the most famous of those who stayed was Indian fighter and federal agent Kit Carson, who once observed, "No man who has seen the women, heard the bells or smelled the piñon smoke of Taos will ever be able to leave." True to his word, Carson lived in Taos for 42 years, and many merchants, traders, and mountain men followed suit.

During the 1820s the increasing number of Americans in New Mexico and Texas became a major threat to the Mexican government. Mexico itself was struggling with severe instability at this time, and it both neglected and overtaxed its northern colony. Colonial anger over these policies came to a head in 1837 when a group of northern New Mexicans formed a mob, decapitating Governor Albino Perez and killing 17 of his officers. The rebellion was put down by former governor Manuel Armijo, who was returned to office.

Haunting 1820s Pecos Ruins embody the history of New Mexico's Spanish and indigenous ancestry and is sacred to both people.

Armijo served New Mexico well, often bending the law to meet the real needs of the people. However, it soon became obvious that the U.S. was eyeing the area for westward expansion. In 1846, President James K. Polk declared war on Mexico and sent a contingent of 1,600 soldiers along with General Stephen Watts Kearny to take over Santa Fe and all of New Mexico. The takeover was bloodless. The few Spanish who resisted were put in jail, and Taos merchant Charles Bent was appointed the new governor.

Bent's tenure was short. In January of the following year, a large group of irate Taoseños, including enraged Hispanics and Indians fearful of losing their land, broke into Bent's house, killed and scalped him, and then went looking for other Anglos. As the revolt spread, a contingent of U.S. troops under Colonel Sterling Price rode from Santa Fe to Taos, where the rebels had taken cover in the mission church at the west end of the pueblo. The soldiers destroyed the church with cannonballs, and the rebels were hanged after a brief trial. Today Bent's house is a museum (see chapter 4, *Culture*), and the remains of the mission church in Taos Pueblo—surrounded by graves—still stand as a grim reminder of the violence that undergirds today's multicultural New Mexico.

Mexico reluctantly signed the Treaty of Guadalupe Hidalgo with the U.S. in 1848, giving up its claim to New Mexico, Texas, Arizona, and California. Two years later, New Mexico officially became a U.S. territory, inspiring an even bigger rush of soldiers, traders, and pioneers from the East. Women first came to New Mexico with their soldier and trader husbands or as missionaries and also as health seekers and seekers of personal and artistic freedom not available to them in the East.

From the outset, the Americans had troubles with raiding Apaches and Navajos. A group of powerful citizens known as the Santa Fe Ring was instrumental in the takeover of New Mexicans' property during the late 19th and early 20th centuries. The American government reneged on its promise to give the Pueblos full citizenship; instead, through the removal of Indian children from their homes and their forced education in government-run Indian schools, it greatly suppressed Pueblo religion and culture. Though New Mexico became the nation's 47th state in 1912, Indians were not recognized as U.S. citizens until 1924 and were not allowed to vote until 1948. Newly arrived Santa Fe and Taos artists and writers, such as Mabel Dodge Luhan and Mary Austin, who made northern New Mexico their adopted home, were instrumental in winning Indian rights and in cultural preservation.

One of the men who fought vigorously for the rights of poor Hispanics was Father Antonio José Martinez, head of the parish at Taos from the 1830s through the 1850s. Martinez not only openly opposed the mandatory church tithe but also fought Anglo land takeovers and championed Hispanic folk traditions. In these and other activities, Martinez defied the authority of Bishop Jean Baptiste Lamy (the subject of Willa Cather's classic novel *Death Comes for the Archbishop*). Though Martinez was excommunicated in 1857, he continued to lead his people spiritually and politically until his death 10 years later. Lamy, though no champion of the poor, made major contributions to education and architecture, overseeing the construction of such lasting landmarks as Santa Fe's Romanesque Cathedral of St. Francis, reminiscent of the churches of his childhood France, and the nearby Gothic-style Loretto Chapel.

During the Civil War, Santa Fe fell briefly into the hands of Confederate troops when General Henry H. Sibley marched into New Mexico from Texas on March 10, 1862. Two weeks later, Sibley was defeated at the Battle of Glorieta Pass, about 20 miles east of Santa Fe. After the Civil War, railroads took the place of the Santa Fe Trail, reaching Santa Fe and Taos around 1880. Over the next several decades, the iron horse brought hordes of farmers, gold diggers, outlaws, businessmen, health seekers, and tourists to the Land of Enchantment.

Between 1880 and the turn of the 20th century, the Anglo population of New Mexico quadrupled, from fewer than 10,000 to almost 40,000. One of the first Anglos to popularize the area's attractions was Governor Lew Wallace, who in 1878 finished his famous novel *Ben Hur* while occupying the Palace of the Governors. "What perfection of air and sunlight!" Wallace wrote to his wife, Susan, after arriving in Santa Fe. "And what a landscape I discovered to show you when you come—a picture to make the fame of an artist, could he only paint it on canvas as it is."

The Artists' Era

The man usually given credit for igniting the art boom was Joseph Henry Sharp, who in 1883 spent the summer painting in Taos. He was followed by Bert Phillips, Ernest Blumenschein, and Irving Couse, and a few years later these four founded the Taos Society of Artists. By the 1890s artists were displaying their works first at the Palace of the Governors and then in the Museum of Fine Arts, the architectural model of what was to become known as Santa Fe style.

The crystal light of northern New Mexico calls to artists.

Other artists and writers quickly filtered into the Santa Fe–Taos area. During the 1920s, the Santa Fe Art Colony was founded by Will Shuster and four others, who became known to some as Los Cinco Pintores (the five painters) and to others as "the five nuts in adobe huts." Soon the area also boasted the likes of Mabel Dodge Luhan, Georgia O'Keeffe, Willa Cather, Mary Austin, and D. H. Lawrence. Lawrence spent only a few seasons in Taos but was deeply moved, especially by Pueblo life. Among his posthumous papers is the following passage:

You can feel it, the atmosphere of it, around the pueblos. Not, of course, when the place is crowded with sightseers and motor-cars. But go to Taos Pueblo on some brilliant snowy morning and see the white figure on the roof; or come riding through at dusk on some windy evening, when the black skirts of the silent women

The carousel known as Tio Vivo was hand-painted by members of the Taos Society of Artists.

blow around the wide boots, and you will feel the old, old root of human consciousness still reaching down to depths we know nothing of.

Other events during the 1920s and 1930s contributed to Santa Fe's reputation as a center for the arts. Dr. Edgar Lee Hewett, director of the Museum of New Mexico, and other recent arrivals organized the first Indian Market in 1922, which continues to be held annually on the third weekend of August. Three years later, Mary Austin and others founded the Spanish Colonial Arts Society to encourage a revival of Hispanic folk art. The annual Spanish Market is held on the last weekend of July. In 1926, Will Shuster created Zozobra, an effigy of "Old Man Gloom" that each year since has been set ablaze to touch off the annual Fiesta de Santa Fe. At the same time, Indian potters such as Maria Martinez of San Ildefonso began to achieve popularity. The Santa Fe Concert Series was founded in 1936, followed by the opening of the Wheelwright Museum of the American Indian, founded by Bostonian Mary Cabot Wheelwright and Navajo medicine man Hosteen Klah. It was also during the 1930s that the dedicated Dorothy Dunn began nurturing a new generation of artistic talent at the Santa Fe Indian School.

World War II brought more changes. One of the most profound was the 1943 purchase of the Los Alamos Ranch School for Boys and its conversion into Los Alamos National Laboratory, birthplace of the atomic bomb. Since the war, the lab has been a focal point for defense research, from hydrogen bombs to Star Wars technology.

The venerable pickup truck is a New Mexico icon.

A lesser-known fact is that during the war there was a Japanese detention camp in Santa Fe. Surrounded by barbed wire and located in the Casa Solana area, the camp imprisoned more than 4,500 Japanese American men from the East and West coasts who, by virtue of their origins, were considered "dangerous enemy aliens."

After the war, Santa Fe and Taos were again "discovered." As artists and tourists continued to arrive, the first galleries began to sprout in Santa Fe and Taos. During the latter half of the 1950s, the newly opened Taos Ski Valley spurred tourism in the area, as did the Santa Fe Opera and the Museum of International Folk Art.

At the same time, Santa Fe and Taos became known as a spiritual power center, attracting individuals and groups that have promoted everything from Asian philosophies and healing to American Indian and New Age thought. The Santa Fe Institute brings Nobel Laureates and other top thinkers together, and intriguing public presentations are a result. During the 1960s and 1970s, Indians and Hispanic farmers accommodated thousands of hippies and experimenters in alternative living. Today, both Santa Fe and Taos have large alternative healing communities offering everything from massage and acupuncture to herbology, ayurveda, and past-life regression. In recent years, the area has also attracted the film industry, and numerous well-known movie stars have taken up at least part-time residence here. Star spotting has become a popular spectator sport around Santa Fe and Taos. Whatever the future holds for the Santa Fe–Taos area, it will be shaped by a combination of factors, including the national economy, the availability of water, and the will of the people. If trends are any indication, it will continue not only as a fascinating tourist destination but also as an ongoing stage for the interactions of the many diverse cultures that have shared in the area's rich and turbulent past.

2

Transportation

GETTING HERE, GETTING AROUND

SANTA FE AND TAOS are beautiful auto destinations—which is a good thing, because neither is directly accessible by train or by major commercial airlines. The nearest train station is in the hamlet of Lamy, 18 miles southeast of Santa Fe. A shuttle service coordinates its runs with the arrival of trains, so this is one relatively easy way to reach Santa Fe without a car. Shuttles run frequently from the Albuquerque Sunport and between Taos and Santa Fe. The majority of visitors, however, simply drive straight from their homes or fly into Albuquerque and rent a car.

By whatever means you arrive, once you're here you need a car, because towns in New Mexico tend to be far apart. Also, driving northern New Mexico's back roads through centuries-old Hispanic villages, Indian pueblos, and magnificent desert and mountain scenery is an experience you won't forget. You'll be happiest if you pace your own tour through this part of the world.

For your convenience, a host of details about Santa Fe–Taos transportation follows.

GETTING TO SANTA FE AND TAOS

By Car

From Albuquerque

The quickest route to Santa Fe is I-25 north (65 miles). A more scenic route is I-40 east to Cedar Crest, then north along NM 14, known as the Turquoise Trail, which meanders through several old mining villages: Golden, the site of the first gold rush west of the Mississippi; Madrid, a coal town turned arts-and-crafts center; and Cerrillos, a once bustling mining camp and subsequent film setting that is now a photogenic, sleepy town with plenty of Old West character. Whichever way you go, you'll be struck by the crystal-clear air and expansive views.

LEFT: All aboard the Rail Runner Express from downtown Santa Fe all the way to Albuquerque.

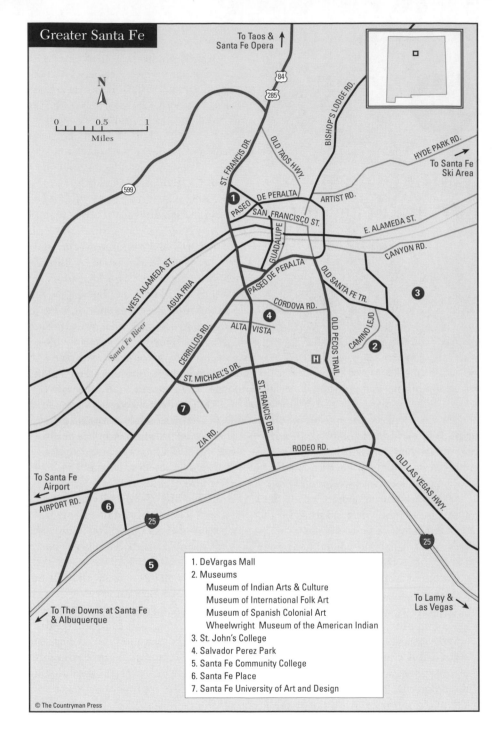

Greater Santa Fe

To Taos &
Santa Fe Opera

N

0   0.5   1
Miles

To Santa Fe
Ski Area

84
285

ST. FRANCIS DR.
OLD TAOS HWY.
BISHOP'S LODGE RD.
HYDE PARK RD.

599

PASEO DE PERALTA
1
ARTIST RD.
SAN FRANCISCO ST.
GUADALUPE
E. ALAMEDA ST.
CANYON RD.

WEST ALAMEDA ST.
AGUA FRIA
Santa Fe River
PASEO DE PERALTA
OLD SANTA FE TR.
3

CERRILLOS RD.
ALTA VISTA
CORDOVA RD.
4
CAMINO LEJO
2

ST. MICHAEL'S DR.
OLD PECOS TRAIL
H

7
ST. FRANCIS DR.

ZIA RD.
RODEO RD.
OLD LAS VEGAS HWY.

To Santa Fe
Airport
AIRPORT RD.
6
25
25

5

To The Downs at Santa Fe
& Albuquerque

To Lamy &
Las Vegas

1. DeVargas Mall
2. Museums
   Museum of Indian Arts & Culture
   Museum of International Folk Art
   Museum of Spanish Colonial Art
   Wheelwright Museum of the American Indian
3. St. John's College
4. Salvador Perez Park
5. Santa Fe Community College
6. Santa Fe Place
7. Santa Fe University of Art and Design

© The Countryman Press

The most direct way to get to Taos from Santa Fe is to take US 84/285 north to Española, then NM 68 up the Rio Grande, a 47-mile drive. This is scenic all the way, but the last part, through the Rio Grande Gorge and up onto the expansive Taos Plateau, is particularly magnificent. Two of the greatest views in the world are available on this route: the sweep of piñon-studded desert as you crest Opera Hill north of Santa Fe and the unforgettable unfolding of the Taos Plateau as you approach Taos while driving out of the gorge. Also a beautiful drive, but at least an hour longer, is the High Road to Taos, which winds its way along the Sangre de Cristo range, passing through 17th-century Hispanic villages, including Truchas, the setting for Robert Redford's film *The Milagro Beanfield War*. Don't miss the church in Las Trampas, a masterpiece of Spanish Colonial architecture built in 1763.

Classical Gas Museum on the road to Taos is a true roadside attraction.

To absorb the true flavor of old northern New Mexico, a tour of the High Road is a must. To follow this route, take NM 76 east out of Española 11 miles to Chimayo, go another 17 miles to Truchas, then go east for a few miles on NM 75 to Penasco, then north on NM 518. This highway eventually hooks up with NM 68, the main route to Taos. Taos is 70 miles from Santa Fe and 135 miles from Albuquerque. The best way to go would be to take the gorge road one way and the High Road the other.

From Dallas
Another long haul. Take I-20 west through Fort Worth, then go northwest on US 84 through Lubbock, Clovis, and Fort Sumner to Santa Rosa, where you'll take I-40 to Clines Corners. Then go north on US 285 to I-25 and south on I-25 to Santa Fe. Distance: 718 miles.

From Denver
A beautiful drive along Colorado's rugged Front Range. It's simple, too: Just go south on I-25; after 386 miles you'll be in Santa Fe.

From Las Vegas
Take US 95 to Hoover Dam, US 93 to I-40, then proceed according to I-40 travel directions to Albuquerque and I-25 north to Santa Fe. Distance: 625 miles.

From Los Angeles
This is a 2-day drive at minimum. Flagstaff is a good halfway point. The quickest and easiest route is to take I-15 northeast to Barstow, then I-40 east all the way to Albuquerque, where you'll take I-25 north to Santa Fe. Distance to Santa Fe: 850 miles.

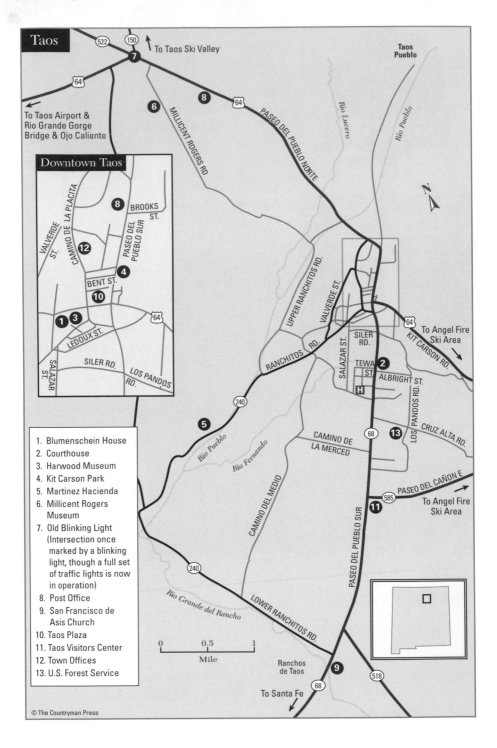

Taos

522 150 ↑ To Taos Ski Valley

Taos
Pueblo

7

64

8

64 PASEO DEL PUEBLO NORTE

6

MILLICENT ROGERS RD.

Rio Lucero

Rio Pueblo

To Taos Airport &
Rio Grande Gorge
Bridge & Ojo Caliente

Downtown Taos

8 BROOKS ST.

VALVERDE ST.

CAMINO DE LA PLACITA

12

PASEO DEL PUEBLO SUR

4

BENT ST.

10

1 3

64

LEDOUX ST.

SALAZAR ST.

SILER RD.

LOS PANDOS RD.

UPPER RANCHITOS RD.

VALVERDE ST.

64 To Angel Fire
Ski Area

SILER RD.

KIT CARSON RD.

RANCHITOS RD.

SALAZAR ST.

TEWA ST. 2

H ALBRIGHT ST.

240

5

Rio Pueblo

Rio Fernando

CAMINO DE
LA MERCED

68 13

LOS PANDOS RD.

CRUZ ALTA RD.

PASEO DEL CAÑON E →

To Angel Fire
Ski Area

585

11

1. Blumenschein House
2. Courthouse
3. Harwood Museum
4. Kit Carson Park
5. Martinez Hacienda
6. Millicent Rogers
   Museum
7. Old Blinking Light
   (Intersection once
   marked by a blinking
   light, though a full set
   of traffic lights is now
   in operation)
8. Post Office
9. San Francisco de
   Asis Church
10. Taos Plaza
11. Taos Visitors Center
12. Town Offices
13. U.S. Forest Service

CAMINO DEL MEDIO

PASEO DEL PUEBLO SUR

240

Rio Grande del Rancho

LOWER RANCHITOS RD.

0   0.5   1
        Mile

Ranchos
de Taos

9

518

68

To Santa Fe ↙

© The Countryman Press

From Phoenix
Take I-17 to Flagstaff, then proceed as in directions for I-40 travel to Albuquerque. Distance: 525 miles.

From Salt Lake City
There is no direct route from Salt Lake to Santa Fe. One option is to take I-15 south to I-70, then I-70 east through the heart of the Rockies to Denver, then I-25 south to Santa Fe for a journey of 879 miles. A shorter and more scenic route, albeit more complicated, is to cut through the southeastern corner of Utah (magnificent canyons) and the southwestern edge of Colorado (equally magnificent mountains) before entering northern New Mexico. Or drive a little farther south into northeastern Arizona and see the Navajo and Hopi Indian reservations. There are any number of interesting ways to go; consult a map to help you choose.

From Tucson
Take I-10 east to Las Cruces, then I-25 north up the Rio Grande Valley to Santa Fe. Distance: 636 miles.

By Bus
Greyhound Lines (505-243-7922; 505-243-4435; 800-231-2222; www.greyhound .com/en/contactus.aspx; 320 First St. SW, Albuquerque). Serves Albuquerque from outside the state.

From Dallas (19 hours)
Two buses depart daily to Albuquerque from the Greyhound station at 205 S. Lamar St. (214-849-6831). The 2012 one-way fare was $120; round-trip, $232.

From Denver (9 hours)
Two buses run daily to Albuquerque from the station at 1055 19th St. (303-293-6555). One-way ticket prices in 2012 were $53; round-trip, $100.

From El Paso (8 hours)
Greyhound has three buses leaving for Albuquerque every day from its station at 200 W. San Antonio (915-532-5095). A one-way ticket in 2012 cost $30; round-trip, $58.

From Las Vegas (16 hours)
Two buses run daily to Albuquerque from the Greyhound station at 200 S. Main St. (702-383-9792). In 2012, one-way tickets cost $108; round-trip, $214.

From Los Angeles (20 hours)
Three buses depart daily to Albuquerque from the downtown station at 1716 E. Seventh Street (213-629-8401). The 2012 one-way fare was $116; round-trip, $224.

From Phoenix (12 hours)
Buses leave three times a day for Albuquerque from the station at 2115 E. Buckeye Rd. (602-389-4200). The 2012 one-way fare was $79; round-trip, $158.

From Salt Lake City (20 hours)
Two buses run daily to Albuquerque from the station at 600 West 300 South Temple (801-355-9579). One-way tickets in 2012 cost $157; round-trip, $300.

From Tucson (13 hours)
Seven buses depart daily to Albuquerque from the Greyhound station at 471 West Congress St. (520-792-3475). The 2012 one-way fare was $125; round-trip, $242.

Shuttle Service
The following shuttle service companies provide transportation between Santa Fe and Albuquerque and Santa Fe and Taos.

ABQ Ride (505-768-2000; www.cabq.gov/abqride). To get from the Rail Runner train to the Sunport, take ABQ Ride Route 350, the Sunport Express. Fare is $1, and there are senior discounts.

New Mexico Rail Runner Express (866-795-RAIL (7245); www.nmrailrunner .com). Provides train service from downtown Albuquerque, at the Alvarado Multi-Modal Transportation Center at Central Avenue and First Street NW, to Santa Fe. Tickets are approximately $7 one way.

Sandia Shuttle Express (505-474-5696; 888-775-5696; www.sandiashuttle.com; reservations required). Provides 15 round-trip runs daily between the Albuquerque airport and downtown Santa Fe. It also drops off and picks up guests at all hotels, motels, and B&Bs in Santa Fe. The 2012 one-way fare was $27; round-trip $47.

Santa Fe Shuttle (888-833-2300; 24-hour advance reservation required). Provides van service 30 times a day from the Albuquerque airport to Santa Fe. The 2012 one-way fare was $27; round-trip $47.

Taos Express (575-751-4459 daily; 575-770-1097 after hours and weekends; reservations required). Provides nonstop weekend shuttle service between Santa Fe and Taos.

Twin Hearts Express & Transportation (575-751-1201). Provides four buses from 11:30 AM to 5:30 PM each day to the major hotels in Taos from the Albuquerque airport. The cost of a round-trip ticket in 2012 was $90.

By Train
Getting to Santa Fe and Taos by train can be fun and relaxing. The nearest train station is in the little village of Lamy, 18 miles southeast of Santa Fe. The **Lamy Shuttle** (505-982-8829) runs once a day. The 2012 cost was $20 one way. It's a good idea to call the shuttle service a day ahead of time to reserve a spot, because the van holds just 15 people. Another way to get into town is to call a cab. **Capital City Cab Co.** (505-438-0000) is the only taxi service in Santa Fe. The 2012 fare from Lamy to the Plaza was approximately $45.

Santa Fe cannot be reached by passenger train from either Dallas or Denver, but you can take the Amtrak (800-872-7245) train from Chicago, Los Angeles, or New York:

From Chicago
Amtrak also runs a daily train from Chicago. It takes approximately 22 hours. The 2012 fares started at $252-496 in coach, round-trip. Sleepers are priced at $233-1129, plus $126 rail fare per person each way.

From Los Angeles
Amtrak has a train leaving downtown LA each evening and arriving in Lamy the following afternoon. Round-trip rates in 2012 ranged from $140–274 for coach. Sleepers, depending on time of year, go from $175–831 round-trip, plus $70 rail fare per person each way.

From New York
The train ride from New York takes two days. Fares in 2012 go from $416–814 (coach) and $432–2063 (sleepers) round-trip, plus $208 per person rail fare each way.

By Plane

If you're like most people, you'll get to Santa Fe and Taos by flying into the Sunport, as the Albuquerque airport is known. As you disembark and head for the baggage-claim area, take note of the southwestern décor, the pastel colors, the outstanding regional artwork on the walls, and the huge cast-metal sculpture of a soaring Indian clutching an eagle. The airport commissioned works by 93 major New Mexico artists, including 30 Native Americans. If you have doubts about New Mexico's reputation as a land apart, they'll begin to evaporate in the Sunport.

The **Santa Fe Municipal Airport (SAF)** is open to private aircraft and **American Eagle Airlines** (800-433-7300), which offers two nonstop daily flights between Dallas and Santa Fe and one nonstop daily flight between Los Angeles and Santa Fe.

Shuttle service is available from the Albuquerque airport, the Santa Fe airport, and the train station in Lamy about 20 miles from Santa Fe.

GETTING AROUND SANTA FE AND TAOS

Given the relatively long distances between towns in the Santa Fe–Taos region, the best way to see the area is by car. However, there are other options.

Santa Fe Trails (505-955-2001) is Santa Fe's first and only widespread public transportation system. Operations began in 1993, and the attractive tan buses provide service along 11 different routes covering most parts of the city, including Rail Runner stops. Descriptions of routes and schedules can be picked up at city hall (200 Lincoln Ave., two blocks north of the Plaza), the public library (145 Washington Ave., one block north of the Plaza), and most supermarkets. The buses run 6 AM–10 PM on weekdays, and 8 AM–8 PM on Saturday. There is 8:30 AM–6:30 PM service on Sunday. Fares are $1 for adults and 50 cents for seniors and kids under 18.

Faust's Transportation (575-758-3410) operates one bus daily from Santa Fe to Taos at 2:30 PM and one each day from Taos to Santa Fe at 8 AM. They'll pick you up or drop you off at almost any motel or hotel in Taos. The pickup and drop-off spot in Santa Fe is the Santa Fe Hilton, 100 Sandoval St. The 2012 rates were $35 one way, $70 round-trip.

The Taos bus service is known as the **Chile Line** (575-751-4459) and offers transportation seven days a week for exact change—50 cents. You can take the Chile Line to Taos Ski Valley and to Santa Fe as well as around town; ADA van service is available.

By Taxi

Maybe you just need a good old-fashioned taxi to get you from point A to point B as quickly as possible.

Santa Fe
Capital City Cab Co.: 505-438-0000

Taos
Faust's Transportation Service: 575-758-3410

By Rented Car

Perhaps the simplest thing to do if you arrive by air is to rent a car at the Albuquerque airport. Virtually all the major car rental agencies are based there:

Advantage: 800-777-5524	**Enterprise:** 800-261-7311
Avis: 800-831-1212	**Hertz:** 800-654-3131
Budget: 800-404-8033	**National:** 800-227-7368
Dollar: 800-800-3665	**Thrifty:** 800-847-4389

Once you're in Santa Fe and Taos, you can also rent a car from one of the following companies:

Santa Fe
Avis: 505-471-5892; 121 Aviation Dr.
Budget: 505-984-1596; 1946 Cerrillos Rd.

Enterprise: 505-986-1114; 1611 St. Michaels Dr.
Hertz: 505-438-4650; 2010 Cerillos Rd.

Taos
Enterprise: (575) 758-5553

Most rental cars come equipped with air-conditioning for summer weather and all-terrain tires for winter conditions. Virtually all the agencies listed above also rent a limited number of four-wheel-drive trucks or jeeps for bumpy dirt roads. Ski racks can also be requested, usually at a small additional cost.

By Bicycle

Northern New Mexico, with its abundant open space and miles of dirt roads, is prime mountain biking territory. In 2012,a mountain bike rental in Santa Fe runs $60 a day. For further information, see "Bicycling" in chapter 7, *Recreation*.

On Foot

Perhaps the best way to see Santa Fe and Taos is on foot. Good walking maps can be found at the **Santa Fe Convention and Visitors Bureau** (505-955-6200; 800-777-2489; santafe.org 201 W. Marcy St., in the Sweeney Center). Also try the **Santa Fe County Chamber of Commerce** (505-988-3279; 8380 Cerrillos Rd., Ste. 302). In Taos, the **Taos Convention and Visitors Bureau** (575-758-3873; 800-348-0696; taos.org; 1139 Paseo del Pueblo Sur) is most helpful. There are also hundreds of miles of superb hiking trails in the Santa Fe and Carson National Forests outside Taos. For further information on walking, see "Hiking and Climbing" in chapter 7, *Recreation*; "Guided Tours" in chapter 9, *Information*; or Elaine Pinkerton's book *Santa Fe on Foot*.

Near Santa Fe and Taos are 10 Indian pueblos (see "Pueblos" in chapter 4, *Culture*); three ancient Indian ruin sites; and at least a score of old Hispanic villages, all in a marvelous desert-mountain setting that offers endless recreational opportunities. Listed below are some of the things to do and places to see within the area.

Near Santa Fe

Santa Fe is flanked by two mountain ranges, the Sangre de Cristo to the east and the Jemez to the west. Both offer hiking, cross-country skiing, downhill skiing, fishing, car camping, and backcountry camping—all within less than an hour's drive. There are a number of Indian pueblos to visit, as well as three major Indian ruins: **Pecos National Historical Park** (28 miles east of Santa Fe), **Bandelier National Monument** (45 miles west of Santa Fe), and **Puye Cliffs** (45 miles northwest of Santa Fe). For a taste of the rich cultural traditions of rural Hispanic New Mexico, you can do no better than to visit the old village of **Chimayó** (25 miles north of Santa Fe on the High Road to Taos), known for its historic church and its tradition of fine Spanish weaving. If you have a hankering for the Old West, check out the old mining towns of **Cerrillos** and **Madrid** (20 to 25 miles southwest of Santa Fe).

Near Taos

Taos is surrounded by natural and human-made marvels. **Ojo Caliente Hot Springs**, a curative bathing spot for ancient Indians—and today a delightful spa offering mud baths, salt glows, and massage, in addition to four kinds of mineral waters—lies some 70 miles to the west. About 30 miles south of Taos is **Las Trampas Church**, which dates from the early 1800s, and **Picuris Pueblo**, the only pueblo in the mountains (the rest are in the Rio Grande Valley or on the Taos Plateau). Less than an hour's drive north from Taos you'll find the Taos and Red River ski areas. Deep in the Sangre de Cristo Mountains, 60 miles to the northeast, shimmers **Eagle Nest Lake**, a prime fishing and boating spot, and Angel Fire Ski Resort, along the "Enchanted Circle." To the west of Taos, the Rio Grande cuts a dramatic gash in the Taos Plateau known as the Rio Grande Gorge, a playground for boating and fishing enthusiasts.

Outside the Area

A little outside the area to the west on US 84 sits the Hispanic village of **Abiquiu**, where artist Georgia O'Keeffe lived. You'll see why when you get a look at the landscape with its spectacularly colored cliffs and mesas. A few miles up the road, you'll come to spacious Abiquiu Lake and the **Ghost Ranch Living Museum**. The nearby Chama River, a federal Wild and Scenic River, flows through some of the most gorgeous desert scenery on the planet. Farther north, you can take a trip on the Cumbres and Toltec scenic railroad, an old-fashioned, steam-powered narrow-gauge that runs between Chama and Antonito in southern Colorado. Snaking back and forth along the border through the San Juan Mountains, it's a wonderful way to see spectacular mountain scenery from the comfort of a railroad car. Beyond the Sangre de Cristo to the east, at the edge of the Great Plains, stands historic Cimarron, one of the major way stations along the Santa Fe Trail. A few hours' drive outside the area to the west and north will take you to Chaco Canyon and Mesa Verde, two of the most spectacular Ancestral Pueblo sites.

3

Lodging
THE KEYS TO YOUR ROOM

THERE WAS A TIME when the only roadside lodge in all northern New Mexico was located at the end of the Santa Fe Trail, on the site now occupied by La Fonda Hotel. In the late 19th century, the railroad brought more visitors, and the number of lodging establishments increased accordingly. But the lodging boom didn't really get going until the motorcar appeared on the scene in the 1920s and 1930s. Many of Santa Fe's and Taos's oldest hotels date from that era. The Taos Inn, dating from 1936, was and still is a gathering place for visitors and Taoseños. Santa Fe's De Vargas Hotel, built in 1924 and now known as the Hotel St. Francis, was a popular hangout for state and local politicians.

The 1980s brought an explosion of bed & breakfast inns, many of them restored adobe and Victorian residences 100 to 200 years old and in some cases even older. The Madeleine, on Santa Fe's east side, dates from 1886 and is possibly the only Queen Anne Victorian in the world with a Spanish tin roof. Nearby is La Posada, a hotel-and-casita complex that includes the Staab House, a 19th-century Victorian reputed to have a ghost roaming its corridors. And up in Taos is the luxurious Casa Europa, which occupies a restored adobe farmhouse so old no one is sure when it was first built, complete with "the oldest door" in Taos.

In addition to the B&Bs and old-time hotels, there are a large number of roadside motels built in the 1940s and 1950s. The bulk of them do not offer luxurious accommodations, but they do provide nostalgia, often with reasonable rates. Finally, there are the newer hotels, built at the height of Santa Fe's popularity, such as the Eldorado and the Inn of the Anasazi—offering over-the-top luxury— and the fashionable Hotel Santa Fe, partly owned by the Picuris Pueblo of northern New Mexico. If you prefer a chain motel, you have an abundance of choices in both Taos and Santa Fe. Both cities offer accommodations to suit every taste and pocketbook.

LEFT: El Pueblo Lodge is a favorite with skiers.

In this chapter we describe and review dozens of lodgings in Santa Fe, Taos, and surrounding communities. This list covers the spectrum, from low- to high-budget options. In evaluating them, we've considered numerous factors, including history, architecture, friendliness, convenience, service, and atmosphere.

RATES

Traveling through northern New Mexico, you may encounter a somewhat confusing and inconsistent array of off-season and in-season definitions. In Santa Fe, many lodging establishments have summer and winter rates, summer being more expensive because it's the high season. Taos gets a bigger ski crowd than Santa Fe, and its high season is less well defined; consequently, many Taos lodges have one set of rates that applies throughout the year, but sometimes summer brings lower rates. Rates tend to rise at Christmas and New Year's. If you are planning a holiday visit, or are arriving for Indian Market in August and want your choice of accommodations, it is best to make reservations a year in advance. Off-season rates in both Santa Fe and Taos may range from 10 to 30 percent lower. If you are planning a stay of at least a week or more, or if you are traveling during a quiet time, such as Oct.–Nov. or March–May, it pays to ask about off-season rates, even if the establishment has no declared policy. In addition, it never hurts to ask if a place is offering the best possible rate. Surprising deals may be had, even at the best establishments in Santa Fe, particularly during the week. It's a buyers' market, so don't be afraid to bargain. Hotels are after "heads in beds." Also, if you book online, you may get a better deal than over the phone. Price codes in this chapter are based on a per-room rate, double occupancy, during the high season.

Lodging Price Codes

Inexpensive	Up to $125
Moderate	$125–175
Expensive	$175–300
Very Expensive	Over $300

These rates do not include required room taxes, parking fees, Wi-Fi use, or service charges that may be added to your bill.

MINIMUM STAY

Many higher-priced lodgings in Santa Fe and Taos, including the B&Bs, require a minimum stay of two or three nights on high-season weekends and busy holidays. During such times, your best bet for a single night's stay is a motel.

DEPOSIT/CANCELLATION

To reserve a room in Santa Fe or Taos, you generally must make a deposit to cover the first night, although more is sometimes required—particularly if you're going to be staying for several nights. If you have to cancel a reservation, you'll usually get your deposit back provided you cancel 10 days to two weeks before your arrival. Be sure to check the particular cancellation policy of your lodging, though, because these regulations vary widely. Some establishments refund the deposit minus a 10 to 15 percent service fee, a few will refund only if your room gets rented, and many don't give refunds at all for cancellations at peak times (such as Indian Market weekend and during the Christmas holiday). If you cancel only a few days before your expected arrival, you're most likely to lose your deposit, although sometimes it may be applied to a future stay. During the high season, the demand for lodging often exceeds the supply, so plan well in advance—at least three to six months ahead for the most popular lodgings—so you will not be disappointed.

OTHER OPTIONS

For information on all kinds of camping, from tents to RVs, see "Camping" in chapter 7, *Recreation*. If you plan on camping with an RV, be sure to make reservations well in advance of your visit. If you plan on tent camping, most of the public campgrounds in the national forests and state parks are available on a first-come, first-served basis, although a few can be reserved.

INFORMATION

For last-minute or emergency lodging arrangements in the Santa Fe and Taos area, here are some numbers to phone.

Canyon Road Casitas: 505-989-9930

Kokopelli Real Estate & Property Management: 505-982-2823

Santa Fe Central Reservations: 505-983-8200

Santa Fe Detours: 505-986-0038

Taos Ski Central: 888-971-6881

Taos Travel Ltd.: 575-758-4246

CONDOMINIUMS AND SHORT-TERM RENTALS

Tired of the tourist scene? Want to live in Santa Fe and Taos like a native, in a real home or apartment or at least a condominium compound? You've got plenty to choose from. They're usually rented on a weekly or monthly basis, although some rent for single nights. In the case of condominiums, you have the option to buy your own home-away-from-home in the Land of Enchantment. Rental prices vary widely. Weekly rates can run from several hundred to a few thousand dollars. Maid service is often, but not always, provided. Here is a partial list of condominium complexes and other short-term rental possibilities, as well as some property-management firms that can mail you current listings in the Santa Fe and Taos areas. (Under the Taos listings, TSV stands for Taos Ski Valley.)

Santa Fe

Fort Marcy Compound Condominiums: 505-988-2800

Manzano House: 505-983-2054

Zona Rosa: 505-982-9884

Kandahar Condominiums (TSV):
505-776-2226; 800-756-2226

Sierra del Sol Condominiums (TSV):
575-776-2981

Sonterra Condominiums (TSV):
575-758-7989

Taos Lodging Vacation Properties:
575-751-1771

Pick Your Spot
Best places to stay in Santa Fe

Adobe Abode (505-983-3133; fax
505-983-3132; www.adobeabode.com;
202 Chapelle, Santa Fe, NM 87501,
4 blocks west of the Plaza; moderate;
1 full handicapped access). Tucked
away in a turn-of-the-20th-century
neighborhood, this small, unpretentious B&B is a wonderful jumble of
architectural styles, works of art, and
knickknacks. There are 10 units. The
rooms combine New Mexican, Victorian, and art deco furnishings. Some
rooms are quite spacious, with 12-foot
ceilings, vigas, brick floors, patios, and
fireplaces. This inn specializes in hearty
breakfasts. It's located in a quiet residential area a short, lovely walk from
downtown and has received raves from
many national publications. It is especially convenient to the Convention
Center and the Georgia O'Keeffe
Museum.

Alexander's Inn (505-986-1431;
alexandinn@aol.com; www.alexanders
-inn.com; 529 E. Palace Ave., Santa Fe,
NM 87501, 5 blocks east of the Plaza;
moderate–expensive; no handicapped
access). Alexander's Inn is actually one
of three neighborhood sister inns that
can accommodate just about any size
group, plus a luxury spa. Located in a
wooded residential area, this lovely
Victorian B&B is within easy walking

distance of the Plaza and Canyon
Road. Originally built in 1903, windows
and skylights have been added to make
it sunnier, but it retains a delightful
charm of its own. If you like antiques,
four-poster beds, stained glass, and the
scents of lilac and lavender, you'll love
this place. The ample continental
breakfast includes homemade muffins,
granola, and fresh fruit. In winter,
breakfast is served in the cozy kitchen
warmed by a roaring woodstove. An
all-day tea service (also included in the
room rate) offers cheese and freshly
baked cookies, which you may want
to enjoy on the front-porch swing.
The outdoor hot tub is available for
guests, as are mountain bikes and guest
privileges at a nearby spa. Luxurious
bedding, meticulous attention, and
a romantic Santa Fe feel make this a
good bet.

Casa de la Cuma (505-216-7516;
info@casacuma.com; www.casacuma
.com; 105 Paseo de la Cuma, Santa Fe,
NM 87501, 4 blocks north of the Plaza;
moderate; no handicapped access).
Informal and unpretentious, this B&B
features three attractive southwestern-
style rooms, an outdoor hot tub, and a
common patio. Continental breakfasts
feature strong coffee, fresh fruit, and
homemade breads. If you walk up the
road, you'll find a hill leading to a large
cross, a Santa Fe landmark known as
the Cross of the Martyrs. The climb
will give you a superlative view of
Santa Fe. Cozy with warm, attentive
hospitality. Breakfast is served al fresco

in the warmer months and is a memorable, delightful experience.

Dancing Ground of the Sun (505-986-9797; 800 745-9910; dgsfrontdesk@santafehotels.com; www.dancingground.com; 711 Paseo de Peralta, Santa Fe, NM 87501, 3 blocks east of the Plaza; expensive; 1 full handicapped access). From the outside, this B&B, named for the original Indian pueblo that stood in Santa Fe, looks like a tiny apartment or condominium complex. But walk into any of the five 1930s-era bungalows, now spacious casitas, each with an evocative name such as Buffalo Dancer or Spirit Dancer, and you'll enter a delightfully different world. They're all distinctive and offer a great sense of privacy. Authenticity prevails in the décor. *Nichos*, vigas, Indian drums, locally made furniture, hand-painted tiling, alcoves, and archways abound. Most units have a fireplace, a couple have their own washer and dryer, and all have their own kitchen. There is a delightful courtyard with a fountain. This place sings of being lovingly cared for, as is evident from the surroundings and the exceptional welcoming friendliness of the innkeeper.

Dunshee's (505-982-0988; sdunshee@gmail.com; www.dunshees.com; 986 Acequia Madre, Santa Fe, NM 87501, 10 blocks southeast of the Plaza; moderate; no handicapped access). Tucked into Santa Fe's historic and picturesque east side, this romantic B&B is located on the town's most beautiful, winding old street. It features two units: one, a spacious suite done up tastefully with all the usual New Mexico touches: kiva fireplace, viga ceilings, folk art, Mexican tile bath; the other, a two-bedroom adobe casita. In warm weather, there's a sheltered, flower-filled patio for relaxing.

Best of all, perhaps, is the hostess, a gracious artist who can clue you in on the local arts scene and serve as your personal concierge. This B&B is only a short hop away from the gallery district of Canyon Road and Camino del Monte Sol. Be sure to get specific directions before you arrive, because this place is really tucked away! You get a scrumptious gourmet breakfast if you stay in the suite; the casita is furnished with fresh fruit and granola.

Eldorado Hotel & Spa (505-988-4455; 800-955-4455; rez@eldoradohotel.com; www.eldoradohotel.com; 309 W. San Francisco St., Santa Fe, NM 87501, 3 blocks west of the Plaza; very expensive; 4 with full handicapped access). If any hotel in Santa Fe has an air of big-city luxury, it's the Eldorado. Spacious and imposing, this AAA Four Diamond winner has its own underground parking lot, valet service, two restaurants, several retail shops, live music every night in the Agave Lounge, butler service, and the largest banquet halls in the city. This is a place intended for grown-ups and those accustomed to sophisticated travel. Built in the 1980s, the five-story, 291-room hotel has a monolithic appearance that initially seemed out of scale for Santa Fe; yet, it is actually about the same height as the much older La Fonda Hotel. The Eldorado also has a couple of oddities for a hotel its size: a tiny swimming pool and no lobby. Reports are that it is now possible to make a deal on pricing here. Guests rave about the service, which sets the Eldorado apart from many other lodgings; the Nidah Spa is a ticket to relaxation. The views from the top floor are magnificent; they will run you $350–400 a night. Shopping, ski, romance, and "bargain" packages are available.

El Farolito (505-988-1631; 888-634-8782; innkeeper@farolito.com; www.farolito.com; 514 Galisteo St., Santa Fe, NM 87501, 5 blocks south of the Plaza; expensive; no handicapped access). This B&B offers seven renovated adobe casitas, some with private courtyard, each with a fireplace, plus one suite. The establishment has a few unusual touches such as cedar ceilings and varnished plaster walls for an antique, rough-hewn look. The rooms also include some of the more typical features of southwestern style: flagstone floors, Mexican hide chairs, trasteros, Spanish-style beds, exposed vigas, and skylights. Nice but pricey.

El Paradero (505-988-1177; info@elparadero.com; www.elparadero.com; 220 W. Manhattan Ave., Santa Fe, NM 87501, 5 blocks south of the Plaza; moderate; limited handicapped access). This family-owned and -operated B&B, one of the oldest in town, has an informal air to it. The front part of the building was a Spanish farmhouse in the early 1800s. Later additions, both Territorial and Victorian, give the inn a rambling character. It's full of nooks, crannies, private alcoves, and hideaways to curl up in with a book, talk, or unwind. The 15 rooms are charming, sunlit, and accented with handwoven textiles and folk art. The mood here is delightfully unpretentious, and it is apparent the owners take pride in the hospitality they offer. The location, just off the Guadalupe Street shopping area and 10 minutes walking distance from the Plaza, is most convenient. A major plus is the substantial delicious breakfast prepared daily that will set you up for a day of sightseeing. A good buy for the dollar.

El Rey Inn (606-982-1931; www.elreyinnsantafe.com; 1862 Cerrillos Rd., Santa Fe, NM 87505; moderate; 4 with full handicapped access). Built in 1935, El Rey is a classic roadside motel, offering both nostalgia and updated comfort. Many of the 87

El Rey Inn offers visitors a bargain without sacrificing amenities.

rooms have flagstone floors, exposed vigas, Indian rugs, carved furniture, and ornate tinwork. Nine have wood-burning fireplaces; 11 others have gas log fireplaces in operation year-round. A large central courtyard is graced with a fountain and several large cotton-woods, creating a special world reminiscent of Mexico. Beautiful tile paintings both inside and out give the motel a Spanish flavor. A unit of passive-solar rooms overlooks a heated pool, and indoor and outdoor hot tubs await. This is one of the most in-demand lodgings in Santa Fe, so book early. A word of caution: I once spent a night here and the in-room antique gas heater was so noisy I could not sleep. Please check the heating system in your room before you accept it; in summer, this should not be an issue. Stay five nights and get the sixth free.

Four Kachinas Inn & Bed & Breakfast (505-982-2550; 888-397-2564; info@fourkachinas.com; www .fourkachinas.com; 512 Webber St., Santa Fe, NM 87501, 5 blocks south of the Plaza; expensive; 1 partial handi-capped access). Located in a quiet residential area, this B&B features four lower-level guest rooms with private garden patios and an upstairs room with a spectacular view of the Sangre de Cristo Mountains. All are layered in Santa Fe style. An adobe casita with a wood-burning stove serves as a common area. One additional guest room has been added in the historic brick cottage, originally built by one of the stonemasons Archbishop Lamy brought from Italy to build St. Francis Cathedral. Expect to pay around $200 per night.

Garrett's Desert Inn (505-982-1851; 800-888-2145; info@garretts desertinn.com; www.garrettsdesertinn .com; 311 Old Santa Fe Trail, Santa Fe, NM 87501, 1.5 blocks south of the Plaza; moderate; no handicapped access). Nothing fancy here. Just a standard, well-maintained, light, very conveniently located and reasonably priced motel, which is probably why the 83 rooms are perennial favorites with those who do business in Santa Fe. If you want to be less than two blocks from the Plaza and avoid the hassle of driving and parking, this is as good a bargain as it gets. And how much time do you spend in your room, anyway? There is a French restaurant on the premises. Cerrillos Road motels provide similar accommodations at more reasonable rates, but it's nice to be downtown. *Note:* There's an $8-per-day parking fee.

Hotel Santa Fe (505-982-1200; 855-825-1876; 1501 Paseo de Peralta, Santa Fe, NM 87501, 6 blocks south of the Plaza; very expensive; 4 with full handicapped access). This is the most pet-friendly lobby in town, and this aspect of the hotel gives a homey feel to a luxury stay. In fact, Pampered Pooch packages are offered with every luxury for the beloved companion. This three-story hotel at the southern entrance to Santa Fe's downtown area is the result of a partnership between the Picuris Pueblo and a group of Santa Fe developers. Its terraced, Pueblo-style architecture gives the facade a pleasingly varied appearance. Its 163 rooms are attractively furnished in contemporary southwestern style, and guests will find a hot tub and heated pool. The Hacienda holds 35 luxury rooms, all with fireplace, including 10 suites plus 2 very spacious suites. The lobby, a matrix of wooden beams and columns, serves as a dining room during the daily breakfast buffet and as a lounge in the afternoon and evening. Free shuttle service to the Plaza (10 minutes away on foot) is available. Emphasizing its Native American aspect, the hotel offers Native

American flute music of an evening in the lounge as well as storytelling and lectures. Private tepee dining is also available.

Hotel St. Francis (505-983-5700; 800-529-5700; www.hotelstfrancis.com; 210 Don Gaspar Ave., Santa Fe, NM 87501, 1.5 blocks south of the Plaza; moderate–expensive; 1 full handicapped access). Between the world wars, the De Vargas Hotel was one of Santa Fe's grand hotels and a popular gathering place. Its glory had all but vanished by the early 1980s when a group of local investors decided to restore its old romantic grace. A $6 million renovation job and a new name have not destroyed the hotel's Roaring Twenties charm. The atmosphere evokes a faraway time and place and is a favorite with European travelers. Art deco lamps, potted plants, original works by the Cinco Pintores (founding members of Santa Fe's art colony), and high-backed chairs adorn the most attractive hotel lobby in Santa Fe. The 81 rooms feature high ceilings, casement windows, brass and iron beds, porcelain pedestal sinks, and period pieces of cherrywood and marble. High style and pet-friendly, too. A shuttle tour of the city is available daily. You'll enjoy hanging out at the Secreto wine bar.

Inn and Spa at Loretto (505-988-5531; 800-727-5531; reservations@innatloretto.com; www.innatloretto.com; 211 Old Santa Fe Trail, Santa Fe, NM 87501, 2 blocks south of the Plaza; very expensive; 2 with full handicapped access). Built in 1975 on the site of Loretto Academy, a reputedly haunted girls' school founded in the 19th century, this inn's terraced architecture is modeled after Taos Pueblo. The building, with 135 guest rooms, is an impressive sight, especially at Christmastime when it's decked out with

The Loretto Chapel's Miraculous Staircase contains no nails.

hundreds of electric *farolitos*. Rooms start at $229 a night and go up from there. It includes a swimming pool, a bar with live entertainment, a restaurant, and a number of retail businesses. The Loretto Chapel with its Miraculous Staircase is next door. The hallways are adorned with Indian-style murals, and the rooms, while of standard design, are attractive. Some of the southwestern furnishings are made by local craftspeople. There is an insanely deluxe spa on the premises. Billing itself as a "luxury boutique" hotel, the inn is a member of the Destination Hotel & Resort group. This is the only New Mexico hotel to hold a Condé Nast Gold designation. If you stay in touch, it is possible to get a deal here.

Rosewood Inn of the Anasazi
(505-988-3030; 800-688-8100; reservations@innoftheanasazi.com; www.innoftheanasazi.com; 113 Washington Ave., Santa Fe, NM 87501, 0.5 block north of the Plaza; very expensive; 1 full handicapped access). An impeccable address. A place to impress and be impressed. How else to say it? A class act. This striking and surprisingly intimate 57-room hotel is about as close to the Plaza as you can get without being on it. It is done in classic Pueblo Revival style, with viga-and-*latilla* ceilings throughout, stone floors and walls, and a beautiful flagstone waterfall on the second floor. The local artwork reflects New Mexico's three major ethnic groups, as does the cuisine in the hotel's restaurant, which, in all honesty, has been up and down. The austerely elegant hotel also maintains a small library. An underground wine cellar with a capacity of 12 guests is available for dinner. Offering the best sense of peace and privacy money can buy, this small luxury hotel reigns among Santa Fe's most chic address for visitors. Convenient on-site services are available for business travelers. In the off-season, it's possible to stay two nights and get the third free.

Inn of the Five Graces (505-992-0957; 866-992-0957; info@fivegraces .com; www.fivegraces.com, 4 blocks south of the Plaza; very expensive; partial handicapped access). Secluded in the city's oldest neighborhoods, a five-minute stroll to the Plaza, this ultra-luxurious inn offers 26 suites in a complex of six restored historic buildings, two interior courtyards, and elegant touches of antiques, tapestries, hand-carved furnishings, richly colored carpets, and featherbed mattresses. The style is "Oriental meets Old West." Most suites have wood-burning fireplace. A full buffet breakfast is served,

and the inn provides parking. Suites start at $500 per night, but it is possible to get three nights for the price of two at certain times. The inn distinguishes itself by its high level of personal service to guests. "Well-trained and quiet" pets are welcome, but expect to put up a hefty security deposit, refundable provided your pet is quiet and causes no damage, plus significant extra pet charges. This lodging receives top ratings on TripAdvisor despite the price tag.

Inn of the Governors (505-982-4333; 800-234-4534; gm@innofthe governors.com; www.innofthegovernors .com; 234 Don Gaspar Ave., Santa Fe, NM 87501, 2 blocks south of the Plaza; expensive; 1 full handicapped access). Enclosed patios, carved vigas, and deep red doors set this inn apart from

Inn of the Five Graces is the essence of luxury.

standard motels. Many of the 100 rooms, located in three buildings, have a wood-burning kiva fireplace, most have a stocked minirefrigerator, and there's complimentary coffee, newspapers, and a restaurant on the premises. There's also a year-round heated outdoor pool in this efficiently run lodging. The rooms facing south on Alameda Street, a popular cruising drag for teenagers, used to be a tad noisy on weekend nights, but more stringent police controls have quieted the kids down. This site is considered one of the best examples of Territorial architecture in downtown Santa Fe. You are invited to ask about discounts. This is the home of Del Charro, one of the liveliest bars and most reasonable eating places in downtown.

Inn on the Alameda (505-984-2121; 888-335-3410; info@inn-alameda .com; www.innonthealameda.com; 303 E. Alameda, Santa Fe, NM 87501, 3 blocks east of the Plaza; very expensive; 1 with full and 3 with partial handicapped access). I admit to being partial to this inn. Maybe it's the slightly out-of-the hustle-and-bustle location; maybe it's the divine breakfast buffet with vegan and gluten-free selections included; maybe it's the complimentary afternoon wine and cheese by the fire. Within easy walking distance of the Plaza and Canyon Road, this 72-room inn across the street from the Santa Fe River has two hot tubs, an exercise room, a full-service bar, a comfortable sitting room, and a conference room. The décor is a tasteful mix of southwestern style and modern convenience. With private patios and a daily breakfast feast, this inn makes a good choice for the guest who prefers the casual elegance and custom service of a smaller inn. And pets are welcome!

Inn on the Paseo (505-984-8200; 888-598-6270; stay@innonthepaseo .com; www.innonthepaseo.com; 630 Paseo de Peralta, Santa Fe, NM 87501, 3 blocks northeast of the Plaza; moderate; 1 full handicapped access). A sister property of the Hotel Santa fe, you'll find here that part of this inn is a three-story A-frame, a rarity in this land of low-lying adobe. On either side of this structure are two recently renovated brick homes. One of the more luxurious rooms (there are 18 light-filled rooms in all) is the honeymoon suite, which has a floor all to itself and its own hot tub. Another has a wonderful brick fireplace and a classic French armoire. Guests may enjoy afternoon snacks on the large sunporch or before a fire in the reading room. The inn faces a busy street, so it's not as quiet as it could be.

Santa Fe Sage Inn (505-982-5952; www.santafesageinn.com; 725 Cerrillos Rd., Santa Fe, NM 87501, 6 blocks south of the Plaza, across the street from The Railyard; inexpensive). Surprisingly quiet for a location tucked away on a busy intersection of Cerrillos Road. Also serene, due to what feels like solid construction, and decorated in tasteful southwest style. Walking distance to many attractions, including the Plaza. A great value.

La Fonda Hotel (505-982-5511; 800-523-5002; stay@lafondasantafe .com; www.lafondasantafe.com; 100 E. San Francisco St., Santa Fe, NM 87501, on the Plaza; very expensive; 2 with full handicapped access). For almost all of Santa Fe's nearly 400-year history, there has been an inn of some sort on the southeast corner of the Plaza. Throughout much of the 19th century, the U.S. Hotel stood there, and its location at the end of the Santa Fe Trail made it a major destination for trappers, traders, merchants, soldiers, gamblers, politicians, and others. Kit Carson and a brigade of Confederate

At La Fonda Hotel bar, have a shot of history with your beverage.

soldiers stayed here, and Billy the Kid did a stint as a dishwasher. By the 1920s, the old hotel, which had become a boardinghouse, was torn down. Within a few years, a new hotel, La Fonda (*fonda* means "inn") rose in its place.

Today, this grand dame hotel remains locally owned, and the days when it was the hotel in Santa Fe are long gone. But it is still the only hotel on the Plaza, and no other can match its storied past. The La Fonda still embodies the essence of Santa Fe romance. The lobby, though a bit dark, still has the feel of a crossroads, and the rooms exude old Spanish charm. Even if you don't stay here, pay a visit to the rooftop lounge for a marvelous view of the city or sip a margarita in the historic bar, its dark wood and tile redolent with Santa Fe of yesteryear, and enjoy live music nightly. The rooms are small; however, the bedding is the best. There's also a restaurant

(see "La Plazuela" in chapter 6, *Restaurants and Food Purveyors*), plus the delightful French Pastry Shop, a swimming pool, hot tubs, and a spa. La Fonda features 14 totally nontoxic deluxe suites for environmentally sensitive guests at the privately accessed, concierge-level Terrace, and *bizcochitos* (cookies) and milk for kids at night. A word to the wise: as of this writing, La Fonda is scheduled for total renovation. It is possible to bargain for better rates—which are remarkably reasonable, starting at $129 per night—off-season or during the week.

La Posada Resort and Spa (505-986-0000; 866-331-7625; www.laposada desantafe.com; 330 E. Palace Ave., Santa Fe, NM 87501, 5 blocks east of the Plaza; very expensive; 7 with full handicapped access). La Posada is the place for a pampering, with its full-service spa with eight treatment rooms. It has changed ownership frequently and is currently a Rock Resort with a

AAA Four Diamond rating. A 19th-century mansion, a complex of Pueblo-style casitas, and six acres covered with huge cottonwoods and fruit trees are just some of the hallmarks of this unusual inn. The central building is known as the Staab House, for 19th-century German immigrant Abraham Staab. The three-story brick residence was a classic of its time, and the original interior remains intact. On its main level is a restaurant and lounge that offers live music. Upstairs are four turn-of-the-20th-century rooms, including Room 100, where the ghost of Julia Staab is alleged to reside. The majority of guests stay in the casitas, where the décor is classic New Mexican: adobe fireplaces, flagstone floors, archways, hand-painted tiles, stained-glass windows, Indian rugs, exposed vigas, and skylights. La Posada has a good-sized swimming pool and a lovely courtyard for drinking and dining in nice weather.

The Madeleine (505-982-3465; 888-321-5123; madeleineinn@aol.com; www.madeleineinn.com; 106 Faithway St., Santa Fe, NM 87501, 5 blocks east of the Plaza; expensive; partial handicapped access). The Madeleine may be the only Queen Anne Victorian in the world with a Spanish tin roof. Eight of the 15 rooms are located in the main house, built in 1886. Stained glass, heavy furniture, brass beds, frilly curtains, high ceilings, and ornate woodwork abound. There are two lovely cottages in the backyard. A decanter of sherry and a bowl of fresh fruit await every occupant. Guests' every need is beautifully catered to. Another plus is the quiet location on a cul-de-sac five minutes from the Plaza. A sister inn to the Alexander.

Pecos Trail Inn (505-982-1943; www.thepecostrailinn.com; 2239 Old Pecos Trail, Santa Fe, NM 87505; moderate; 1 full handicapped access). This is the first motel you run across if you're coming into Santa Fe from the east, located at the convergence of two Old West trails—Old Santa Fe Trail and Old Pecos Trail. The modern lodging has 23 rooms, a good-sized swimming pool, a hot tub, and a family-friendly restaurant. It has a pleasant, family-welcoming attitude, with a park, walking trails, and a children's playground. Add easy access to town (only a few minutes' drive), and this becomes an even more attractive place to stay. Modern comfort, airiness, and cleanliness supersede "old Santa Fe charm" here. Kitchenettes are available. All in all, a good value. Only seven minutes to town. And for three seasons out of four, you can stay for under $100.

Pueblo Bonito Bed and Breakfast Inn (505-984-8001; 800-461-4599; pueblo@pueblobonitoinn.com; www.pueblobonitoinn.com; 138 W. Manhattan Ave., Santa Fe, NM 87501, 3 blocks south of the Plaza; moderate; 1 full handicapped access). Of all the B&Bs that popped up in Santa Fe in the 1980s, this one has some of the most charming and distinctive guest rooms, each of the 18 named for an area Indian tribe. The look is rustic and colorful southwestern, with wood floors, three-foot-thick adobe walls, small corner fireplaces, Indian rugs, Mexican pottery, and Spanish carvings of saints, called *bultos*. The grounds are graced by private courtyards, narrow brick paths, adobe archways, and huge shade trees. Although near a busy street, this inn is secluded while still convenient to shopping, restaurants, and cultural activities. The owners pride themselves on providing a good value.

Santa Fe International Hostel and Budget Bed & Breakfast (505-

988-1153; www.hostels.com; 1412 Cerrillos Rd., Santa Fe, NM 87505; inexpensive; partial handicapped access; no credit cards). For the most affordable—but not the most private—lodging in Santa Fe (from $18 a night for a dorm room to $25 a night for a shared bath; $35 for a private room), you can't beat this place. In typical hostel style, men and women stay in separate, dorm-style rooms, and the kitchen is available for $1 a day. It's pretty spartan, and there aren't many extras (no TV, no pinball, just a radio), but for little more than a song, you've got a safe, warm place to stay and a great, convenient base of operation. Like most hostels on the worldwide circuit, this is an excellent place for networking and information gathering. This is a "chore hostel," so each guest is required to do a 10- to 15-minute chore per day, such as sweeping the front porch. Reservations must be made well in advance by check or money order. Neither personal checks nor credit card are accepted, so arrive with your travelers' checks in hand.

Santa Fe Motel & Inn (505-204-7805; 800-930-5002; info@santafe motel.com; www.santafemotel.com; 510 Cerrillos Rd., Santa Fe, NM

87501, 5 blocks south of the Plaza; inexpensive–moderate; no handicapped access). If you're looking for an attractive, affordable motel in a downtown location, this is the place. It's set just far enough off a busy road to have an air of seclusion. In addition to typical motel rooms, it includes 10 adobe casitas with refrigerator, microwave, and patio entrance. Across the street, kitchenettes (only $99) are available. Many will find this an excellent value and a reasonable way to stay in comfort without breaking the bank. Complimentary full breakfast is included.

Silver Saddle Motel (505-471-7663; silversaddle@earthlink.net; www.motelsantafe.com; 2810 Cerrillos Rd., Santa Fe, NM 87507; inexpensive; 2 with full handicapped access). Clean and affordable, this budget motel has 25 rooms, 10 with kitchenettes. Despite the nostalgia pitch, you can't get much more basic than this place. Jackalope, a southwestern furniture and import outlet, is located next door. Noise from Cerrillos Road may be offset by the convenience to the shopping experience of Jackalope, which now operates the motel. It is possible to have an affordable Santa Fe vacation when you stay here.

Pick Your Spot

Best places to stay near **Santa Fe**

The Bishop's Lodge Ranch Resort & Spa (505-629-4822; 800-768-3586; atiberi@bishopslodge.com; www.bishopslodge.com; 1297 Bishop's Lodge Rd., Santa Fe, NM 87504, 3 miles north of Santa Fe; very expensive; 6 with full handicapped access). Bishop Jean Baptiste Lamy chose this spot in the foothills of the Sangre de Cristo range for his retirement and getaway home and garden some 100 years ago. Back then, the old adobe was a small ranch that had been planted with fruit trees by Franciscan fathers in the early 17th century. After Lamy died, the property was briefly owned by publisher Joseph Pulitzer, who constructed two summer homes. In 1918, James Thorpe, a Denver mining magnate, bought the property and turned it into a resort. His family owns it to this day.

The lodge's four-season activities

The Bishop's Lodge, once the sanctuary of Archbishop Lamy, is the place to find serenity.

Escondida, or "hidden house." Built in the Spanish colonial adobe style typical of this region and situated on six beautiful acres, this is the perfect place to rest deeply, to go for long, undisturbed country walks, and to enjoy the pleasures of the brilliant light, the scent of a piñon fire, and the profound sense of history and the sacredness of the land that characterize northern New Mexico. Lovingly decorated with antiques and rustic southwestern-style furnishings, this inn wraps you in its sense of tradition. A scrumptious hot breakfast is served in a light-filled room with French doors, and a large hot tub is tucked into a stand of trees. Pets and children are welcome. If you want to be away from the crowd yet not too far away from the attractions, this could be your spot.

Hacienda Rancho de Chimayó (505-984-2100; Box 11, 300 County Rd. 98, Chimayó, NM 87522, 25 miles north of Santa Fe; inexpensive–moderate; 1 partial handicapped access). This charming place is located in the heart of the ancient village of Chimayó, known for its historic church and its tradition of fine Spanish weaving. The inn was converted from a 19th-century rural hacienda in 1984. The plasterless, straw-streaked adobe walls are adorned with red chile *ristras*, and the enclosed courtyard is bursting with fruit trees. Seven guest rooms, predominantly Spanish in appearance but with an air of the Victorian, feature dark massive vigas and heavy, handwoven curtains, the work of a local artisan. Antiques, wallpaper, and high ceilings give the rooms an almost American colonial touch. Some have a private balcony, and all have fireplaces. The hacienda is directly across the street from the acclaimed Rancho de Chimayó Restaurant (see chapter 6, *Restaurants and Food Purveyors*), also

are family oriented: Horseback riding, tennis, swimming, trap- and skeet shooting, and fishing are all available in-season on its more than 450 acres. The rooms have plenty of New Mexican flavor, and the Fuentes restaurant offers a very good Sunday brunch and more than acceptable cuisine generally. Best of all, there's still an air of serenity here, and Lamy's private chapel stands untouched. The addition of the Shana Spa makes this a vacation locale you won't want to leave. And you can get bargain rates for as low as $149 per night if the time is right. The serenity here is an elixir for the soul.

Casa Escondida (505-351-4805; 800-643-7201; info@casaescondida .com; www.casaescondida.com; P.O. Box 142, Chimayó, NM 87522; 28 miles north of Santa Fe; moderate; 3 with partial handicapped access). The beautiful simplicity of northern New Mexico awaits the visitor at the secluded and serene eight-room Casa owned by Florence Jaramillo and her family.

Rancho Arriba (505-689-2374; rancho@ranchoarriba.com; www .ranchoarriba.com; P.O. Box 338, Truchas, NM 87578, 40 miles north of Santa Fe; inexpensive–moderate; no handicapped access; no credit cards). You won't find a setting much more spectacular than this. Located on the Truchas Plateau above 8,000 feet, this hacienda-style adobe B&B sits at the foot of the southern Rockies with amazing views of the Sangre de Cristos. A mile to the west is the centuries-old Hispanic village of Truchas, one of the more picturesque of northern New Mexico's mountain communities.

The four guest rooms are fairly small; one has a private bathroom, but all are authentically decorated in Spanish colonial style. The inn, also a small working farm and ranch, is organized around a central courtyard big enough to qualify as a plaza. Family-style breakfasts, cooked up on a woodstove, are served in a cozy common area with a fireplace and viga-and-*latilla* ceilings. Frank knows the mountains well and can recommend hikes. A winter or spring visit should not be attempted without a four-wheel-drive vehicle or tire chains. Here's a place to unwind for those with a bit of a sense of adventure.

Rancho Manzana (505-351-2227; 888-505-2227; manzana@newmexico .com; www.ranchomanzana.com; 26 Camino del Canon, Chimayó, NM 87522, 24 miles northeast of Santa Fe; inexpensive; no handicapped access). Set on four lush acres, this ecofriendly establishment is a working farm; highlights include an adobe with 29-inch-thick walls from the 1700s reclaimed from the ancient Plaza del Cerro, fruit orchards, fields of New Mexico chile, lavender that blooms in June and September, and an age-old *acequia*. The full organic breakfasts can be enjoyed under a grape arbor in warm weather. An outdoor fire pit made of river rock and flagstone inlaid with mosaic is a splendid place for a barbecue, and a bubbling hot tub offers a relaxing spot to contemplate Chimayó's starry sky. There are two guest rooms downstairs in the ancient adobe. It's possible for one party with as many as six people to rent the entire lower level. A garden cottage with a two-room guest suite overlooking the lavender fields is available. Not only is there a hot tub, but a pond (for dipping) graces the grounds as well. Rancho Manzana is known as a spot for many special events, and cooking classes are offered. Don't even try to resist.

Pick Your Spot
Best places to stay in Taos

Alma del Monte-Spirit of the Mountain (575-770-8993; 800-273-7203; info@almaspirit.com; www.alma spirit.com; 372 State Rd., B143, Taos, NM 87571; expensive; partial handicapped access). If Martha Stewart came to Taos, she'd very likely choose to stay in this meticulously appointed and run inn. Custom built as a green luxury inn, this exquisite hacienda with five guest rooms is surrounded by spectacular panoramic views. Guests can relax in the antiques-filled living room, luxuriate in a private whirlpool, snuggle into European down comforters and pillows, or swing in courtyard hammocks. Rooms are furnished in a stunning combination of antique and

Southwest style, each with its own kiva fireplace. Located on Hondo Seco Road, midway between the Plaza and Taos Ski Valley, this place has the feeling of a true getaway. If you have an ability to appreciate the hosts' consideration for every detail, including dietary preferences, lavish three-course breakfasts, and snacks, this could be the place for you. Horse boarding is available. Specializing in weddings.

American Artists Gallery House B&B (575-758-4446; 800-532-2041; aagh@newmex.com; www.taosbedand breakfast.com; 132 Frontier Lane, P.O. Box 584, Taos, NM 87571, 1 mile south of the Plaza; moderate; 1 partial handicapped access). As the name implies, artists and their art are celebrated at this peaceful B&B on a secluded Taos lane. The inn displays more than 300 works of art, and artists are sometimes invited to discuss their work. Kiva fireplaces and knockout views of Taos Mountain contribute to your developing love of place. With 10 rooms and 3 very private, luxurious Jacuzzi suites in the southwestern-style complex, this B&B offers an ideal opportunity to relax and catch up on some genuine R&R.

Best Western Kachina Lodge, Resort Hotel & Meeting Center (575-758-2275; 800-522-4462; P.O. Box NN, 413 Paseo del Pueblo Norte, Taos, NM 87571, 4 blocks north of the Plaza; inexpensive; 7 with partial handicapped access). Learn to time travel in Taos. Just north of the city center, this Best Western is a classic roadside motel straight out of the 1950s. Don't miss the circular Kiva Coffee Shop, dominated by a bizarre hand-carved totem pole. A delicious, cooked-to-order hot breakfast there is included. All 118 guest rooms look out onto a spacious courtyard with a broad lawn, tall pine trees, and a large outdoor heated swimming pool. The grounds have a country club feel. The Indian décor is laid on a bit thick, and there are even Indian dances on summer nights, but that's how they did things 40 years ago. What makes this place is that it evokes nostalgia without really trying, right down to the Naugahyde chairs in the Kachina Cabaret. Close to town, homey, and the price is right.

Casa Benavides (575-758-1772; 800-552-1772; casabena@newmex.com; www.taos-casabenavides.com; 137 Kit Carson Rd., Taos, NM 87571; 1 block east of the Plaza; moderate–expensive; 1 full handicapped access). Airy, light, and colorful, this sprawling B&B boasts 38 guest rooms in six different buildings on five downtown acres. Five of the buildings are traditional southwestern adobe, and one is a western Victorian home. The rooms are spacious and modern with all the usual southwestern accents: Navajo rugs, flagstone floors, ceiling fans, skylights, Indian pottery, and kiva fireplaces. There are even a few surprises, including deerskin drums and an authentic Indian tomahawk. Owners Tom and Barbara McCarthy are native Taoseños who've headed a number of different retail businesses in town. Return for afternoon tea to the aroma of freshly baked cookies. The big breakfasts include homemade tortillas and waffles, Mexican eggs, and homemade muffins. A short walk to the Plaza. Guests are inevitably pleased.

Casa de las Chimeneas (575-758-4777; 877-758-4777; info@VisitTaos .com; www.visittaos.com; Box 5303, 405 Cordoba St., Taos, NM 87571, 1 block east of NM 68, 2 blocks from the Plaza; very expensive; 1 partial handicapped access). Screened from the surrounding residential neighborhood by a high adobe wall and shaded by giant cottonwoods and willows, this hacienda-like inn offers eight guest rooms, each with a fireplace, that look out onto a spacious lawn and brilliantly colored flower garden. Five newer rooms feature vaulted ceilings, skylights, and jetted tubs. Potted plants, hand-carved wooden columns, dark brown vigas, skylights, flagstone floors, and regional works of art make it an example of New Mexico style at its most refined. Breakfast, which has been featured in *Bon Appétit* and *Gourmet*, is different every day and may include a fruit frappé, blue corn pancakes, or strata. A complimentary buffet supper, with homemade stews and soups, is also served. Not to worry! The fitness/workout room is truly state of the art. Guest laundry facilities, sauna and hot tub, plus on-site masseuse make this a total luxury getaway for those who expect the best of the best.

Casa Europa Bed & Breakfast Inn & Gallery (575-758-9798; 888-758-9798; casa-europa@travelbase .com; www.casaeuropanm.com; HC 68, Box 3F, 840 Upper Ranchitos Rd., Taos, NM 87571, 1.7 miles west of NM 68, 1.3 miles from the Plaza; moderate; no handicapped access). It's hard to say what's better at Casa Europa: the inn itself (a 200-year-old restored adobe ranch house) located amid huge cottonwood trees, the superb breakfasts, or an afternoon tea that includes fresh-baked treats of peach cobbler, banana coconut cream cake, and chocolate-caramel pecan squares.

There are seven guest rooms. One of the loveliest, the French Room, has a marvelous 1860s French brass bed, 100-year-old hand-hewn wood floors, a marble bath, and a triangular blue mirror. This inn has everything—even "the oldest door" in Taos. The Spa Room has its own full-sized hot tub, while the Taos Mountain Room has a picture-perfect view of Taos Mountain. Outside, the hot tub bubbles invitingly in an enclosed courtyard; there's also a sauna on the premises. The site possesses an air of country spaciousness. Two-night minimum stay required. Perfect for your romantic getaway.

Cottonwood Inn (575-776-5826; 800-324-7120; www.taos-cottonwood .com; cottonoodinn@gmail.com; HCR 74, Box 246092, State Rd. 230, El Prado–Taos, NM 87529; moderate–expensive; 1 full handicapped access). Located just off the route to Taos Ski Valley, Cottonwood Inn is the brainchild of two delightful and charming California refugees who are very much in love with their renovated classic Pueblo estate, formerly the residence of flamboyant local artist Wolfgang Pogzeba. With kiva fireplaces, balconies, viga ceilings, Jacuzzis, wet bars, and skylights in most rooms, all guests need to do is kick back and enjoy the spectacular views and fabulous breakfasts. Winters bring the warmth of a roaring fire, while summer is the time to enjoy the lovely gardens. You'll enjoy the organic, locally sourced breakfasts (including herbs grown right here) that emphasize quality ingredients. Special dietary needs are accommodated. You may feel as though a magic carpet has landed you in a bygone era of gracious living and casual elegance "before the invention of the wristwatch."

Dreamcatcher Bed and Breakfast (575-758-0613; 888-758-0613; dream @dreambb.com; www.dreambb.com; P.O. Box 2069, 416 La Lomita, Taos, NM 87571, about 1 mile southwest of the Plaza moderate; 2 with full handicapped access). Done up in true southwestern style, the seven cozy rooms, each with fireplace, have some unusual touches, like an aqua-colored tile floor (with radiant heat, most appreciated in winter). Big country breakfasts are served. Within walking distance of the Plaza, this casual B&B with hot tub tucked away in a countrylike setting, makes for a most comfortable stay. The emphasis here is on green; much of the produce is garden fresh, grown in the garden on the premises. And there is no more delightful hostess than Prudie. She and husband John left the corporate world for Taos, and they are now "living the dream."

El Monte Sagrado Living Resort & Spa (575-758-3502; 888-213-4419; info@elmontesagrado.com; www.el montesagrado.com; 317 Kit Carson Rd., Taos, NM 87571; very expensive; 3 with full handicapped access). The phrase *green grandeur* might best describe the ecofriendly opulence of this resort. Some might find it a bit over the top. It feels like a tropical jungle transplanted to the high desert, and it is known for its claims of environmental purity and innovative recycling. The 84 lodgings include 5 casitas, each with its own private courtyard, and 8 Global Suites, each with a wet bar, private courtyard, and gas-burning fireplace. The themes run from Native American to Kama Sutra. You may stroll the exquisitely landscaped grounds studded with cascading waterfalls and crystal ponds. In addition to the Living Spa, with exotic body treatments you've never even heard of, this oasis offers a fabulous Aqua Center with pools, hot tub, and fitness center. The restaurant, De la Tierra, strives for elegance, while the light-filled Gardens serves a more casual breakfast and lunch. The Anaconda Bar is famous as a hangout for movie stars. If money truly is no object, this is the place to check in; they put the "up" in this upscale Marriott property.

Hacienda Del Sol (505-758-0287; 866-333-4459; fax 505-758-5895; stay @taoshaciendadelsol.com; www.taos haciendadelsol.com; P.O. Box 177, 109 Mabel Dodge Lane, Taos, NM 87571; moderate–expensive; 1 full handicapped access). Shaded by giant trees, this B&B was chosen by *USA Today Weekend* as one of America's 10 most romantic inns. Two of the 11 guest rooms are located in the main house, a beautiful 180-year-old adobe; 5 are in a casita, with an additional room found in a separate casita; and 3 are attached to the main house. Brick floors, Saltillo tiles, and hardwood floors are found in the main building, as are Pueblo-style archways, viga-and-*latilla* ceilings, *bancos*, *nichos*, and stained-glass windows. Four rooms have their own steam bath, while the honeymoon suite has a double-sized black Jacuzzi with a skylight for stargazing. The level of comfort provided by the hosts, who have experience as an executive chef and cruise director, is superlative. Cooking classes are a highlight of the experience. You could easily wake up here from a restful night on the most comfortable bed in the world, look out at Taos Mountain and weep for joy, have a vision, and decide to move to Taos! Another place to put at the top of your list when shopping for accommodations.

Hotel La Fonda de Taos (575-758-2211; 800-833-2211; info@la fondataos.com; www.hotellafonda.com; 108 S. Plaza, Taos, NM 87571, on the Plaza; moderate–expensive; 1 full handicapped access). If you want to be in the thick of the action, here's the place for you, directly on the Plaza. The historic 1937 La Fonda, the grande dame known for years as the gallery of D. H. Lawrence's paintings, underwent a complete renovation a while back. The art-embellished lobby is still sheltered by giant vigas, and the mezzanine, where continental breakfast is served, retains a mood of old-fashioned comfort. Many of the 24 beautifully redecorated rooms now have kiva fireplaces and a view of the Plaza below. To stay here is to travel back in time (without sacrificing any contemporary amenities) and experience the nostalgia of Taos's heyday, when such movie stars and celebrities as Gary Cooper, Judy Garland, and Tennessee Williams visited here.

Inn on the Rio (575-758-7199; 800-737-7199; info@innontherio.com; www.innontherio.com; 910 Kit Carson Rd., Taos, NM 87571, 1.5 miles east of the Plaza; inexpensive–moderate; 4 with partial handicapped access). Brilliant flower gardens and brightly painted flowers adorn this charmingly renovated 1950s-style motor court inn with heated outdoor swimming pool and hot tub, all beautifully tended by Robert and Julie Cahalane, who will do whatever it takes to make your stay perfect. Julie is a master baker who provides fresh-baked quiche, lemon poppy-seed cake, and blueberry blue corn muffins each morning to accompany a full, hot, hearty breakfast. This vintage inn, with baths whimsically hand decorated by Taos artists, is a superb place to really kick back and relax—and a great family spot as well. Featured as a choice destination in numerous national magazines with a AAA Three Diamond rating. As if you couldn't tell, I just love this place!

La Doña Luz Inn (575-758-9000; 800-758-9187; info@stayintaos.com; www.stayintaos.com; 114 Kit Carson Rd., Taos, NM 87571, 0.5 block east of the Plaza; inexpensive–expensive; 1 full handicapped access). If you want to be surrounded by colorful folk art and have the Plaza right out your front door, this 200-year-old inn is the place for you. These walls contain enough history and stories to keep you intrigued during your entire visit. The five guest rooms in this centrally located inn are all dazzlingly different—decorated with a collection of angels from around the world or filled with authentic Indian artifacts nestled in *nichos* or displaying a Franklin stove, claw-foot tub, blacksmith's tools, or Winchester rifle. One room features hand-carved teak woodwork, Afghani rugs, a Kuwaiti chest, and a Balinese fertility goddess suspended over the queen-sized bed. Much of this amazing array comes from a trading post on the property. Rooms are located in three different buildings (including an adobe compound with its own courtyard). Four rooms have their own hot tub, and seven have whirlpools. Personally, I find this place wonderful but a tad dark.

La Posada de Taos (575-758-8164; 800-645-4803; laposada@laposadade taos.com; www.laposadadetaos.com; 309 Juanita Lane, Taos, NM 87571, 2.5 blocks west of the Plaza; moderate–expensive; limited handicapped access). Opened in 1982 with the claim to being Taos's "first B&B," this inn has an air of romantic seclusion, perhaps because it's located at the end of a quiet dirt road that may take a bit of patience to find. Or maybe it's the honeymoon suite with a skylight directly over the bed. Whatever it is, this is an especially wonderful place to stay. The house, built by a founding member of the Taos Society of Artists, is replete with kiva fireplaces and private patios. The owners have installed their personal antique collection from England, making the six-room inn a distinctive blend of Southwest style and English country. The two styles make an amazingly harmonious blend. You won't find a better mix of relaxation, romance, convenience, and congeniality. The owners pride themselves on the stimulating conversations held around the breakfast table among guests.

San Geronimo Lodge (575-751-3776; 800-894-4119; sgl@newmex .com; www.sangeronimolodge.com; 1101 Witt Rd., Taos NM 87571-6449, 1.4 mi. from the Plaza east off Kit Carson Rd./US 64; moderate–expensive; 2 wheelchair-accessible rooms). To immerse in the essence of Taos, and to float in Taos's only chile-shaped swimming pool, book a stay in this 1925 inn, the town's first resort. If you have the heart of a time traveler, if you yearn for old New Mexico as it was in the heyday of the Taos Society of Artists, this 18-room lodge is your place. Thick adobe walls and viga ceilings envelop the visitor in a sense of the past as authentic as the imagination fancies. Authentic period art and New Mexican wooden furniture contribute to the well-worn elegance; kiva fireplaces create a glow at day's end. It's off the beaten path yet, once you know the way, it's close to town, on its northern end, toward Taos Ski Valley. Situated beside an acequia, with a clear view of Taos Mountain, amidst ancient cottonwoods and lush apricot and pear trees, San Geronimo is a place to escape to, relax, and wrap up in the romance of the distinctive locale that is Taos. A labyrinth and prayer path trail, open to guests and to the public, enhance meditative moments. Dog-friendly rooms may be shared with your beloved pooch, and dietary needs are graciously honored—advance notice requested. A luscious hot breakfast, included in the price of a stay, is highlighted by fresh fruit and house-made jams, salsas, and chutneys. Specialties like blue corn–blueberry pancakes, apricot scones, and green chile strata make breakfast an event every day. No wonder guests are known to break into song when the host plays the piano!

Mabel Dodge Luhan House (575-751-9686; 800-846-2235; mabel @MabelDodegeLuhancom; www .mabeldodgeluhan.com; 240 Morada Lane, Taos, NM 87571, 1 mile north of US 64; moderate; partial handicapped access). Set on five acres at the edge of a vast open tract of Taos Pueblo land, this rambling three-story, 22-room adobe hacienda *is* Taos history. This is primarily because of Mabel Dodge Luhan, famous patroness of the arts who arrived in New Mexico in 1918, and let's face it, if people are still telling stories about you 50 years after you're gone, you've lived quite a life. She came at the urging of her husband at the time, artist Maurice Sterne, who was in Taos to paint Indians. Sterne eventually left, but Mabel stayed, married Taos Pueblo Indian Tony Luhan, and bought and renovated this 200-year-old structure. It quickly came to be known as the Big House, where she lived, wrote such classics as *Winter in Taos*, and entertained.

From the 1920s through the 1940s, the Big House was visited by artistic and literary figures, including D. H. Lawrence, Georgia O'Keeffe, Carl Jung, Aldous Huxley, and Willa Cather. After Mabel died in 1962, the property was bought by actor-producer Dennis Hopper, who lived there during the filming of *Easy Rider*. In 1977, it was bought by a group of academics as a center for seminars and study groups. It became a B&B in the early 1980s, although workshops are still held here.

The house is filled with viga-and-*latilla* ceilings, arched Pueblo-style doorways, fireplaces, and dark hardwood floors. Just to curl up in the living room is to inhale the essence of what makes Taos Taos. Mabel's Bedroom Suite still contains her original bed; Tony's Bedroom opens out onto a sleeping porch; and the Solarium, accessible only by a steep, narrow staircase, is literally a room of glass (Mabel sunbathed in the nude here). There are nine rooms in the main house, a cottage for two, and a guesthouse containing eight southwestern-style rooms. Breakfast, included in the room rates, is served in the spacious dining room. If you want to immerse in Taos history, sleep here.

Old Taos Guesthouse (575-758-5448; 800-758-5448; oldtaos@newmex .com; www.oldtaos.com; 1028 Witt Rd., Taos, NM 87571, 1.8 miles east of the Plaza; moderate; no handicapped access). You can't argue with success. Owners Tim and Leslie Reeves are entering their third decade as innkeepers here. Nestled amid a stately grove of trees in a rural area just east of Taos, this 150-year-old adobe hacienda has plenty of rural Spanish charm—not to mention wonderful views of the nearby Sangre de Cristo range and Taos Plateau, a nature trail of its own, and a traditional *acequia* (ditch). Its nine guest rooms, with handmade aspen furniture and all sorts of thoughtful little touches, look out onto a lovely courtyard, and the century-old central living area is classically southwestern in design and décor with a red oak floor. Hosts Tim and Leslie are exceptionally gifted in their ability to make you feel at home and are outdoor enthusiasts who can discuss in detail what the Taos area has to offer, from downhill skiing to hot-springs bathing. They profess to "cater to a blue jeans crowd" and delight in helping you find the hike perfectly suited to you.

Adobe & Pines Bed & Breakfast (575-751-0947; www.adobepines.com; 4107 Road 68, Taos, NM 87557; moderate). A highly acclaimed 1830s adobe where rooms have a kiva fireplace and soaking tub. Lovely gardens surround the flagstone courtyard, and there is a labyrinth to walk and meditate in that is also open to the public. Full gourmet breakfast included. Although just off the highway south of Ranchos de Taos, the place retains a serene, secluded feel. A top choice.

Adobe & Pines B&B offers a labyrinth right outside your door.

El Pueblo Lodge (575-758-8700; www.elpueblolodge.com; 412 Paseo del Pueblo Norte, Taos, NM, 87571, 0.5 mile north of the Plaza; inexpensive–moderate). My family, which includes an English springer spaniel and an Airedale terrier, loves staying in this convenient, unpretentious 1940s-style motel with hot tub and pool. A simple breakfast is included in the warm breakfast room. Popular with skiers.

Sagebrush Inn and Conference Center (575-758-2254; 800-428-3626; fax 505-758-5077; sagebrush@newmex .com; www.sagebrushinn.com; P.O. Box 557, 1508 Paseo del Pueblo Sur, Taos, NM 87571, NM 68, 2 miles south of the Plaza; inexpensive-moderate; 2 with partial handicapped access). How does this sound: a Taos getaway special for $115 for two that includes deluxe lodging, dinner, and breakfast for two and a bottle of New Mexico wine? I say, sign me up! The posh Sagebrush has some amazing deals for you, with early bird specials as low as $69. Opened in 1929 to cater to the trade between New York and Arizona, the Sagebrush Inn is one of Taos's oldest hotels. It's also one of the town's hottest nightspots, with live music and dancing, where you'll be treated to some of the best local bands every evening. Built in Pueblo Revival style, the inn is a sprawling structure with 97 rooms, two restaurants, a famously friendly bar, a swimming pool, and two indoor hot tubs. The décor, both Indian and Spanish, includes a fabulous collection of paintings by southwestern masters, along with Navajo rugs. You may want to stay in the third-floor room where Georgia O'Keeffe painted. The separate Executive Suites offer alternative family lodging, including spacious suites (sleeping up to six people each) with fireplaces. A complimentary breakfast is included in the rate. Ski packages with reduced rates are also available. The inn is pet-friendly.

Sun God Lodge (575-758-3162; 800-821-2437; sungod@taosnet.com; www.sungodlodge.com; 919 Paseo del Pueblo Sur, Taos, NM 87571, NM 68, 1 mile south of the Plaza; inexpensive; 1 full handicapped access). This roadside motel done in Pueblo style has been at this location since 1958. The 53 rooms are quiet, attractive, and with handmade Taos-style furniture. Most are organized around a parking lot and a grassy area with trees, and all are of standard motel design. Some have kitchenettes. There is a shuttle to the ski mountain. This place is not as well kept-up as it could be, and it used to be a bigger bargain. While I would not rule it out, you may want to check out your room before you check in. You may find a better deal.

Taos Inn (575-758-2233; 888-519-8267; taosinn@newmex.com; www.taos inn.com; 125 Paseo del Pueblo Norte, Taos, NM 87571, 0.25 block north of the Plaza; all price ranges; 1 full handicapped access). If immersion in the colorful atmosphere of New Mexican arts, crafts, history, and legend is your cup of tea—or tequila—you can do no better than to stay at the 1936 Taos Inn. You would join a guest register that includes the likes of Greta Garbo, Thornton Wilder, and D. H. Lawrence. It has National Landmark status and was thoroughly restored and modernized in the early 1980s. The lobby is both an art gallery and a people-watcher's paradise, and the Adobe Bar is fondly known as "Taos's living room," with events from Dia de los Muertos community altars to open mike and live music every night. Doc Martin's Restaurant, winner of the 2011 Wine Spectator Award of Excellence, is popular and atmospheric, but to be honest, the menu is not one of my favorites.

Do check the menu before committing to dining here.

Each of the 44 guest rooms in four separate buildings at the inn is graced with a distinct personality. Most have pueblo fireplaces, Taos-style antique furniture, bathrooms with Mexican tile, handwoven Indian bedspreads, and even cable TV. Several rooms open onto a balcony overlooking the lobby, while several more open onto a quiet courtyard in the rear. You may have to choose between the character of the main inn and the updated amenities of the back properties. Rooms run from $75 to $225 per night. The inn offers specials, such as weekday nights lodging for $100 or stay two nights with the third free. A swimming pool is available in warm weather, and for weary skiers, a Jacuzzi bubbles invitingly in the plant-filled greenhouse.

Touchstone Inn Spa & Gallery (575-779-1174; 800-758-0192; Info @TouchstoneInn.com; www.touch stoneinn.com; 110 Mabel Dodge Lane, Taos, NM 87571, 1 mile north of the Plaza; moderate-expensive; no handicapped access). Located on the edge of Taos Pueblo lands, bordered by tall trees, with splendid views of Taos Mountain from the two-acre grounds, Touchstone Inn is a lovingly restored historic adobe that fulfills every fantasy of Taos. Added to artist-owner Bren Price's gourmet vegetarian breakfasts, in-room Jacuzzi tubs, outdoor hot tub, lovely gardens, and historic associations with salon diva Mabel Dodge Luhan, the spa treatments more than complete an already perfect experience. Most of the nine rooms, named for artists, have fireplaces. Exquisite attention has been paid to every detail, and the very same is lavished on each guest. Spa packages available.

Pick Your Spot
Best places to stay near Taos

The Abominable Snowmansion (575-776-8298; fax 505-776-2107; www.snow mansion.com; snowmansion@newmex .com; 476 NM 150, Arroyo Seco, NM 87571, off NM 150, halfway to Taos Ski Valley in Arroyo Seco; inexpensive; partial handicapped access). Located in the old Hispanic village of Arroyo Seco, the Abominable Snowmansion wins, hands down, the contest for the best-named ski lodge in the Taos area. It's also tops when it comes to informality, fun, and affordability. The Snowmansion is a youth hostel and campground in summer; in winter, a hostel and budget B&B, with a wide selection of tepees, private rooms with private baths, and dorm rooms. You can prepare your own meals here if you like. You can rent a bunk for $150 a week or a cabin for $42. The bedding is surprisingly high quality. Though it attracts mainly young people, old-timers are more than welcome. Most of the quarters are dormitory style with bunk beds, and the sexes are segregated. There are four private rooms for couples. The lodge offers a continental breakfast in winter. The common area is a social hub. This clean, well-run lodging makes a vacation totally affordable.

Alpine Lodge & Hotel (575-754-2952; 800-252-2333; info@alpinelodge redriver.com; 417 W. Main St., Red River, NM 87558, at the ski area; inexpensive-moderate; 3 with full handicapped access). On the banks of the Red River at the base of the main ski lift, Alpine Lodge was run by native German Ilse Woerndle and her family for more than 30 years. The current owners have spruced up some of the 46 rooms, located in cabins, condos, or the hotel, and are keeping the lodge open year-round. Full kitchens are available. The lodge is very clean and comfortable, with two hot tubs—an excellent choice for a ski-in, ski-out vacation. reservations@angelfireresort .com; www.angelfireresort.com

Angel Fire Resort (575-377-6401; 800-633-PINE; 10 Miller Lane, Angel Fire, NM 87710, at the ski area; expensive; 2 with full handicapped access). Steps away from the Chile Express chairlift, with 157 rooms, each with two queen beds, Angel Fire Resort is by far the biggest lodging establishment in Angel Fire. The décor is contemporary southwestern, and the ski area is right outside the window. Legends Restaurant has seven flat-screen TVs, a lounge, an indoor pool, and a hot tub and serves burgers, pizza, chicken-fried steak, and microbrews on tap. Pet-friendly rooms available, as well as a business center and fitness room.

Arrowhead Lodge (575-754-2255; 800-299-6547; arrowhead@newmex .com; www.arrowheadlodge.com; 405 Pioneer Rd., Red River, NM 87558; inexpensive; no handicapped access). This quiet, no-frills lodge is located on a side street off Red River's main drag, within easy reach of the ski area. There are 19 units, most with kitchens, plus a few larger accommodations; some have fireplaces. In warm weather, a sundeck, barbecue pit, and several picnic tables are available for your use. The lodge prides itself on being family-oriented and offering good value.

Austing Haus Hotel (505-776-2649; 800-748-2932; austing@newmex .com; www.theaustinghaus.com; 1282 NM 150, Taos Ski Valley, NM 87525: 1.5 miles west of Taos Ski Valley; moderate; 2 with full handicapped access).

Austing Haus Hotel is minutes from Taos Ski Valley lifts.

More than 70,000 board feet of timber with 3,000 interlocking joints were used in the construction of this hotel, making it the tallest timber-frame building in the United States. An impressive feat, but this Alpine-style lodge is missing that intangible thing called character. A large continental breakfast is included. Pets are allowed, and ski packages are available. The hotel caters to groups and families. Offers a shuttle to the slopes.

The Bavarian (575-776-8020; www.thebavarian.net; bavarian@the bavarian.net; 100 Kachina Rd., Taos Ski Valley, NM 87525; very expensive; no handicapped access). Completed in 1996, this is the last word in ski lodging, conceived, as the genial young German owner says, "as a private high Alpine retreat for a few precious guests." The midmountain log mansion is perched at 10,200 feet in the Wheeler Wilderness Area, surrounded by mountain peaks. Modeled on high-Alpine guesthouses of Austria and Bavaria, the Bavarian invites you to ski to its exquisite restaurant. Or you may be driven up from the lower Ski Valley. The luxurious guest suites feature marble-tiled bathrooms, Bavarian antiques, and hand-carved and -painted appointments. The slope-side restaurant, with a real European feel, is definitely the place to be during the day or après ski.

Hotel St. Bernard (575-776-2251; stbhotel@newmex.com; www.stbernard taos.com; 112 Sutton Pl., Taos Ski Valley, NM 87525; moderate [weekly ski packages only]; no handicapped access; no credit cards). Closed outside ski season. Jean Mayer, owner of Hotel St. Bernard (named for the patron saint of skiers), is also technical director of the Taos Ski Valley Ski School. All guests accepted at the hotel are those on the ski school's six-day plan. The package includes three meals a day, including seven-course gourmet dinners prepared

Hotel St. Bernard in Taos Ski Valley is famous for fine food and drink.

by French chefs, as well as lift tickets and lessons. The hotel's 28 rooms are located in three buildings and include attractive A-frame units with sundecks at the bottom of the slopes. The ski season is often booked by July, so planning ahead to avoid disappointment is essential. The hotel's staff is exceptionally professional and helpful, and the Rathskeller Bar is a well-known après-ski spot. A top choice for anyone serious about skiing and having a good time. Spa and fitness center on the premises.

The Little Tree B&B (575-776-8467; www.littletreebandb.com; P.O. Box 509, 226 County Rd. B143, Arroyo Hondo, NM 87513, 10 miles northeast of Taos; moderate; partial handicapped access). Located about halfway between Taos and Taos Ski Valley, this charming Pueblo-style adobe B&B looks as if it's been part of the landscape for decades. In fact, it was built in the early 1990s. The owners have added private courtyards as well as a two-person air-massage Jacuzzi. They offer a two-course breakfast served on china and crystal. Four guest rooms, arranged around a courtyard bursting with flowers in springtime, are named for four species of small trees native to the Taos region: piñon, juniper, aspen, and spruce. Each room has its own private entrance, two have kiva-style wood-burning fireplaces, two have glazed adobe mud floors, and one has an outdoor private hot tub. You'll find one cat and three rare Belgian sheepdogs in residence; however, an allergen-free environment is maintained. In summer, the place is alive with hundreds of hummingbirds. The owners' favorite season is fall, but this facility is also a favorite of cross-country skiers.

Ojo Caliente Mineral Springs (505-583-9131; 800-222-9162; inn ojo@ojocaliente.com; www.ojospa.com;

11 NM 414, Ojo Caliente, NM 87549, US 285, 35 miles southwest of Taos; inexpensive-moderate; 1 full handicapped access). In the 1500s, Spanish explorer Cabeza de Vaca chanced upon these desert hot springs, a favorite bathing spot of local Indians, and described them as "wonderful waters bursting out of a mountain." (See "Spas and Hot Springs" in chapter 7, *Recreation.*) Locals have come to "take the waters" for half a century. Today, the springs are the focus of this no-frills, 36-room resort, and the place still retains the air of a dusty, old-fashioned sanatorium. The resort offers special rates for overnight stays with a soak. You may stay in the somewhat drafty old lodge or rent a private cottage. Campsites are available, and a restaurant featuring healthful offerings is located in the lodge. There's a little wine bar now, too. Lately, lots of updating has taken place here: Ojo Caliente has increasingly been catering to the more affluent tourist trade, while locals bemoan the higher rates and modernization.

Snakedance Condominium Hotel (575-776-2277; 800-322-9815; info @snakedancecondos.com; www.snake dancecondos.com; 110 Sutton Place, Taos Ski Valley 87525; expensive–very expensive). The Ski-Better-Week package at $867 per person, two-person minimum, with seven nights lodging, six days lift tickets, and morning lessons, is by far the best deal in this posh, comfortable resort.

Taos Mountain Lodge (575-776-2229; 866-320-8267; 1346 NM 150, Taos Ski Valley, NM 87525; moderate; partial handicapped access). Get an entire condo for the price of a room. Located on a south-facing mountainside, Taos Mountain Lodge has 10 condominiums, which are split-level A-frame suites that can hold from four

Santa Fe–Taos Access

The chart below will tell you about how long a drive it is from the following cities to Santa Fe. Times do not include stops and are calculated to the nearest hour at the posted speed limit. Allow more time for bad weather.

City	Time	Miles
Albuquerque	1 hr.	59
Amarillo	7 hrs.	348
Cheyenne	9 hrs.	481
Dallas	13 hrs.	718
Denver	7 hrs.	385
El Paso	6 hrs.	330
Flagstaff	7 hrs.	375
Houston	17 hrs.	959
Las Vegas, NV	12 hrs.	625
Los Angeles	15 hrs.	850
Oklahoma City	10 hrs.	607
Phoenix	10 hrs.	525
Reno	21 hrs.	1,078
Salt Lake City	14 hrs.	680
San Antonio	16 hrs.	952
Wichita	13 hrs.	754

Taos is 70 miles north of Santa Fe, about a 1.5-hour drive in good weather. The two circles on this map indicate points within a 30-mile radius of Santa Fe and Taos. These circles delineate the areas referred to in the text as "Near Santa Fe" and "Near Taos." All points within the circles are less than an hour's drive from either center.

to six people. This is a great deal for friends or family. Eight have fireplaces, and wood is supplied free of charge. The suites are equipped with satellite television and outfitted kitchens. All the rooms are done in tasteful, if typical, southwestern décor. Indoor and outdoor whirlpools can relieve your aches, and there is a steam room. Outdoor gas grills are available. Com-

pletely surrounded by national forest. You can have serenity plus a seven-minute trip to the lift! Summer rates are a great bargain.

Three Suggested Strolls

SANTA FE

For a 30- to 45-minute walking tour of Santa Fe, we suggest starting on the Plaza, perhaps right at the monument that stands in the middle of the old square. Take time to look at the blend of the old and new, the Spanish and Territorial architecture that coexists with gleaming art galleries and boutiques. Then head east for a block, stopping in at Sena Plaza on Palace Avenue, a hidden courtyard filled with shops. Turn south onto Cathedral Place past tree-filled Cathedral Park, and pay a visit to the magnificent St. Francis Cathedral. Then go west on San Francisco Street back toward the Plaza and peek in at the historic La Fonda Hotel, located at the end of the Old Santa Fe Trail. Stroll south along this famous commerce route, and you'll soon come to lovely Loretto Chapel with its marvelous spiral staircase. Continue south across the Santa Fe River until you come to San Miguel Mission, the oldest church in America, dating from the early 1600s. Another block south is the state capitol, also known as the Roundhouse (see "Architecture" in chapter 4, *Culture*). A major renovation was completed in 1992.

For another Santa Fe stroll, walk over to Guadalupe Street, then take a left, and continue past Sanbusco Center to The Railyard, home of the Santa Fe Farmers Market and a bustling new center of historic preservation and adaptive reuse with restaurants, nightlife, cafés, boutiques, and galleries. Directly adjacent to The Railyard is the Baca Street neighborhood, which has its own funky Soho-like character and more galleries.

TAOS

For a similarly pleasant tour of Taos, start at the Kit Carson Home and Museum go half a block north of the Plaza. Then walk toward the Plaza. Just before you get there, turn north onto NM 68, Taos's main street. A short stroll away is the historic Taos Inn, a popular gathering place for Taoseños and visitors. After you've poked your head in or sat for a bit, cross Paseo del Pueblo Norte and amble down Bent Street. It's filled with art galleries and alluring boutiques, bookstores and kitchenware shops. Then make your way to the Plaza and the recently renovated Hotel La Fonda. From the Plaza, go west one short block and turn south onto Placitas Road. Follow Placitas until you come to Ledoux Street, then turn west again. Here is the former home of Ernest Blumenschein, one of the founding members of the Taos Society of Artists. A beautiful example of southwestern architecture, it, too, has been recently renovated, and the famous artist's private collection—including paintings by his wife, Mary, and daughter, Helen, accomplished artists in their own right—is open for public viewing.

4

Culture
WHAT TO SEE, WHAT TO DO

THE RENOWNED ENCHANTMENT of the Santa Fe–Taos area has simple origins: The place is powerfully unlike any other in the world. With the exception of nature itself, nothing is more enchanting here than the interweaving of the area's three primary cultures: Indian, Spanish, and Anglo. Native Americans were building complex communities across the Southwest when Europe was in the Dark Ages, and Santa Fe was founded more than a decade before the Pilgrims set foot on Plymouth Rock.

Partly because of its ancient roots, many visitors are drawn to the art of the area's Indian and Hispanic peoples art that grew out of what Taos photographer Bill Davis calls "the mixture of the divine and the human in the landscape." Dances are offered as prayers for the well-being of the people. Likewise, the creation of objects such as pottery, jewelry, and baskets is an act guided by spirit.

Many Indian artists acknowledge spirit as the source of their talents. "Clay is very special," says Santa Clara potter Ray Tafoya. "It's giving us life. We can't use it with disrespect." Prayers are said when beginning to work with the clay.

The art of Hispanic people springs from an everyday life permeated with Catholic faith. The statue of San Ysidro carried to the fields each spring to ensure a good planting and the *retablos* (paintings on wood boards) of Our Lady of Guadalupe touched each morning with a whispered prayer are artworks that are both loved and used. Likewise, the murals of the Virgin that grace many adobe homes, the pageantry of fiestas, the village parades on saints' days—even the meticulously accessorized "low-rider" automobiles—are forms of art found in everyday life.

The Santa Fe–Taos area provides fertile ground for art rooted in Europe. In the early part of the 20th century, Santa Fe and Taos were home to eastern artists who established the southwestern "Sohos" of their day. Their paintings hang in

LEFT: Santa Fe's International Folk Arts Festival draws hundreds of juried artists from all over the world.

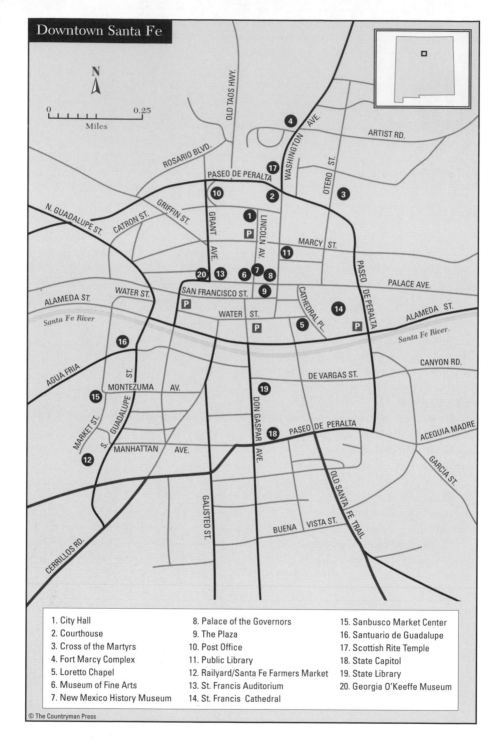

Downtown Santa Fe

N

0   0.25
Miles

OLD TAOS HWY.

ARTIST RD.

ROSARIO BLVD.

PASEO DE PERALTA

WASHINGTON AVE.

OTERO ST.

N. GUADALUPE ST.

CATRON ST.

GRIFFIN ST.

GRANT AVE.

LINCOLN AV.

MARCY ST.

PASEO DE PERALTA

PALACE AVE.

ALAMEDA ST.

WATER ST.

SAN FRANCISCO ST.

WATER ST.

CATHEDRAL PL.

ALAMEDA ST.

Santa Fe River

Santa Fe River

CANYON RD.

AGUA FRIA

MONTEZUMA AV.

ST.

DE VARGAS ST.

ACEQUIA MADRE

MARKET ST.

S. GUADALUPE

MANHATTAN AV.

DON GASPAR AVE.

PASEO DE PERALTA

GARCIA ST.

GALISTEO ST.

OLD SANTA FE TRAIL

BUENA VISTA ST.

CERRILLOS RD.

1. City Hall
2. Courthouse
3. Cross of the Martyrs
4. Fort Marcy Complex
5. Loretto Chapel
6. Museum of Fine Arts
7. New Mexico History Museum

8. Palace of the Governors
9. The Plaza
10. Post Office
11. Public Library
12. Railyard/Santa Fe Farmers Market
13. St. Francis Auditorium
14. St. Francis Cathedral

15. Sanbusco Market Center
16. Santuario de Guadalupe
17. Scottish Rite Temple
18. State Capitol
19. State Library
20. Georgia O'Keeffe Museum

© The Countryman Press

area galleries and museums (see "Traditional Art" under "Galleries" in chapter 8, *Shopping*). These painters—men like Jozef Bakos, Nicolai Fechin, Ernest Blumenschein, and Randall Davey—inspired generations of successors who continue to explore the landscape and the unusual clarity of light. And the work of Georgia O'Keeffe—recognized in Santa Fe in a museum of her own—conveys in color and light the magic of a place that continues to inspire visitors to come find it for themselves. Europe has also provided Santa Fe and Taos with magnificent opera and chamber music, both of which thrive in the clear desert air.

To Do

Check out these great attractions
and activities . . .

ARCHITECTURE

Adobe architecture, as much as the landscape, gives New Mexico a distinctive identity. In a nation where many places look the same, the Santa Fe–Taos area still displays its identity.

For a look at the old adobe architecture, stroll around the Santa Fe Plaza, along East De Vargas Street and up Canyon Road. Or explore Taos Plaza and its intriguing side streets. The soft, rounded adobe structures appear to have grown right out of the earth.

As centuries passed, people adapted their techniques and materials. For example, mud walls were built up a handful at a time, a technique called puddling. Or they were laid with "bricks" of mud cut from streambanks. Ruins such as those at Chaco Canyon and Bandelier National Monument reveal sophisticated use of natural sandstone and other rock for the construction of four- and five-story apartment-type buildings. The stone walls were mortared with mud.

When Spanish settlers arrived in the early 1600s, the Pueblo Indians quickly adopted the newcomers' adobe-brick-making techniques. The Spaniards' knowledge of adobe construction can be traced back to the Middle East and Mesopotamia, as can their use of the *horno* (OR-no), a beehive-shaped outdoor oven originally acquired from the Moors.

Twentieth-century architects Isaac

Find exactly the turquoise bracelet you're looking for at Jackies Trading Post in Taos Plaza.

Outdoor adobe beehive ovens called *hornos* are still used throughout New Mexico to bake delicious breads and pies.

Hamilton Rapp and John Gaw Meem embraced the Spanish-Pueblo Revival style that was originally inspired by Laguna and Acoma Pueblos. The style found early expression in sites such as La Fonda Hotel and the Museum of Fine Arts.

To get a feel for the city's early adobe residences, visit the oldest house in the U.S. at 215 East De Vargas Street in Santa Fe. The cavelike interior features a corner fireplace of Spanish origin. The oldest parts of the walls are of puddled adobe. Contrast this humble home with the modern, five-story Eldorado Hotel at 309 West San Francisco Street to see how flexible the idea of mud construction can be. The Eldorado is a recent expression of the Santa Fe style, or Spanish–Pueblo Revival style, which has been in vogue since the 1920s. Like most newer buildings in Santa Fe, however, the Eldorado is not real adobe; it simply wears an adobe-style stucco veneer.

Santa Feans were especially proud of their new state capitol. Dedicated in 1900, with a rotunda and an Ionic-columned portico, it was a fine example of the classical style then in vogue in the United States—and totally out of place in New Mexico. This structure was completely redesigned in the 1950s to make it consistent with Spanish–Pueblo Revival style.

A group of artists, archaeologists, and civic activists, alarmed by the loss of the city's architectural heritage, dedicated themselves to preserving older Spanish structures and to searching for a new regional building style. This group staged an exhibit in 1912 called "The New-Old Santa Fe Exhibition" to awaken interest in preserving the old Santa Fe and to promote Santa Fe as the "unrivaled tourist center of the Southwest." It was this second goal that eventually won over the city's business community. The city fathers realized that in order to attract tourists, Santa Fe must remain unique.

Success did not come overnight. One of the key battles took place over the Palace of the Governors, three years before the exhibition. Progressives wanted to demolish this symbol of New Mexico's Hispanic past and put up a proper "American" courthouse. But in 1909, the conservatives—Dr. Edgar Lee Hewett, director of the Museum of New Mexico, and his followers—persuaded the legislature to preserve the palace as a historical museum. In the restoration that followed, the building's Territorial-style portal and brick coping were replaced with a Spanish-Pueblo portal and vigas. These renovations were intended to evoke the building's early history, and they helped establish the emerging Santa Fe style.

The Museum of Fine Arts across from the palace, designed by Isaac Hamilton Rapp, was another milestone that helped establish the "new-old" style Hewett and others wanted to achieve. Building the structure of brick rather than adobe, Rapp nevertheless incorporated many elements of Hispanic Mission-style churches for the museum design. Though the museum was built in 1916 to 1917, its evocative design makes it appear far older.

Two commercial buildings designed by Rapp to boost the Santa Fe style can still be seen: the Gross, Kelly & Co. Almacen, a warehouse near the railroad tracks on Guadalupe Street, and La Fonda, off the southeast corner of the Plaza. The warehouse, though in poor condition, still clearly displays its Spanish-style towers, portals, vigas, and *canales*.

As a result of accolades for the museum and the palace, the city adopted the Santa Fe style (called Spanish–Pueblo Revival), carried on by enthusiasts like John Gaw Meem and writer Oliver La Farge. Meem, who like many in his day believed New Mexico's climate to be a cure for tuberculosis, stayed in Santa Fe to become the most eloquent architect of Santa Fe style. One of the most memorable of his dozens of buildings is the Cristo Rey Church. (See "Historic Buildings and Sites" in this chapter.) This massive structure, built in 1940 with 150,000 adobe bricks, bespeaks the architect's love for New Mexico's early mission churches.

The look of Santa Fe's downtown Plaza also owes much to Meem, who remodeled several Victorian and commercial buildings there, among them the former Woolworth building, the Franklin store, the Renehan building, and the old Masonic Lodge. In 1966, he also designed the portals that run along three sides of the Plaza.

In 1957, after six years of study, the city council adopted the Historic Zoning Ordinance and established Santa Fe's Historic District, which roughly encompasses the downtown area and Canyon Road. The ordinance gave an official stamp to two architectural styles: Spanish–Pueblo Revival and Territorial. The first, a modern version of the Santa Fe style, is characterized by massive walls, rounded parapets, and hand-hewn woodwork. Territorial style is recognized by brick coping atop adobe walls, milled woodwork, and decorative pediments on doors and windows. A number of fine Victorian buildings from New Mexico's Territorial days still survive in Santa Fe (for example, the First Ward School at 400 Canyon Road); however, that style was deemed politically incorrect in 1957 and remains so today.

Anglicization came somewhat later to Taos, which lost many of its original buildings to "progress" in the 1920s and 1930s. In 1984, the Taos Town Council approved a Historic Design Review Ordinance that included many elements borrowed from Santa Fe's ordinance. The Historic District includes the Plaza and several clusters of buildings within Taos's 3 square miles.

The blue gates of Santa Fe and Taos are endlessly fascinating.

Though Spanish–Pueblo Revival style borrows some important features from Pueblo architecture, such as rounded contours, large blank surfaces, and stepped-back levels, the philosophy and purposes of the two styles are quite different. To feel the difference, visit the older sections of some of the pueblos (see "Pueblos" in this chapter).

Santa Clara Pueblo native and architectural consultant Rina Swentzell writes: "Landscaping, or the beautification of outdoor spaces, was a foreign concept. The natural environment was primary, and the human structures were made to fit into the hills and around boulders or trees. In that setting, planting pretty flowers that need watering was ridiculous. Decoration for decoration's sake was unnecessary." In that Pueblo world, she concludes, "All of life, including walls, rocks and people, were part of an exquisite, flowing unity."

CINEMA

Santa Fe

Cinematheque (505-982-1338; www.ccasantafe.org; Center for Contemporary Arts, 1050 Old Pecos Trail, Santa Fe, NM 87505). Besides producing a full range of arts programs, the Center for Contemporary Arts offers foreign and American art films, including classics. Ethnographic and video presentations by independent artists are stimulating events.

The Screen (505-473-6494; http://thescreensf.com; 1600 St. Michael's Drive, Santa Fe, NM 87505). When you find The Screen by following the signs on campus, you will discover an intimate setting for independent film. Founded at the Santa Fe University of Art and Design, The Screen showcases the finest in World, Art, and independent cinema. Featuring a 16 speaker Dolby Digital 6.1 surround sound system, a high definition curved screen, and luxurious stadium seating, The Screen is a good place to catch actors' and directors' live presentations.

Commercial Movie Houses

Santa Fe

Santa Fe's commercial movie houses include **United Artists North** (505-471-3321; at Santa Fe Place Mall at Rodeo and Cerrillos Rds.); the **DeVargas Mall Cinema 6** (505-988-1110; 562 N. Guadalupe St.); and **Santa Fe Stadium 14** (505-424-0799; 3474 Zafarano Dr.).

Taos

The **Trans-Lux Storyteller** (505-758-9715) near the Holiday Inn on Paseo del Pueblo Sur screens commercial and offbeat films. **Taos Community Auditorium** (575-758-4677; http://tcataos.org/calendar), a block north of the Plaza on Paseo del Pueblo Norte, occasionally offers mostly independent and short-run films.

DANCE AND THEATER

Santa Fe

Aspen Santa Fe Ballet (505-983-5591; 550 Saint Michaels Dr., #B1, Santa Fe, NM 87505-7604). This professional dance school offers year-round classes for children and adults.

Maria Benitez Spanish Dance Company (505-467-3773; 750 N. St. Francis Dr., Santa Fe, NM 87501). Few who have seen New Mexican Maria Benitez flamenco diva perform this passionate dance can forget her powerful, concentrated energy. Her group takes the stage June–Sept. at the Maria Benitez Theatre in the Lodge at Santa Fe.

GALLERIES

Most galleries in the Santa Fe–Taos area are retail establishments (for listings, see chapter 8, *Shopping*).

Santa Fe

The **Center for Contemporary Arts** (505-982-1338; www.ccasantafe.org; 1050 Old Pecos Trail, Santa Fe, NM 87505) features progressive contemporary art by local and emerging artists.

The **State Capitol Rotunda Gallery** (505-827-3000; 986-4614; capitolarts@nm legis.gov; www.nmcapitolart.org/default.aspx; State Capitol Building, 490 Old Santa Fe Trail, Santa Fe, NM 87501) presents the best classic and contemporary New Mexico artists. The St. John's College Fine Arts Gallery (505-984-6199; www.st .johnscollege.edu; 1160 Camino Cruz Blanca, Santa Fe, NM 87501) presents student exhibitions.

Santa Fe Community College Visual Arts Gallery (428-1000; www.sfcc.edu; 6401 Richards Ave., Santa Fe, NM 87508) can be counted on for showing fresh, challenging student work.

Near Santa Fe

Fuller Lodge Art Center (505-662-1635; http://fullerlodgeartcenter.com; 2132 Central, Los Alamos, NM 87544) emphasizes the work of northern New Mexican artists and craftspeople. The center is located in the John Gaw Meem–designed building associated with the Manhattan Project. The center hosts seasonal and holiday arts and crafts events.

Taos

The Taos Center for the Arts (575-758-2052; www.tcataos.org; 133 Paseo del Pueblo Norte, Taos, NM 87571) is a principal exhibitor of contemporary art. The vibrant center offers a broad range of work by nationally and regionally recognized artists.

HISTORIC BUILDINGS AND SITES

Santa Fe

Canyon Road

One of Santa Fe's oldest and most colorful streets, Canyon Road was originally an Indian trail through the mountains to Pecos Pueblo (see "Pecos National Historical Site" in chapter 5, *Sacred Sites*). In the 1920s, it was adopted by artists from the

Canyon Road, winter twilight: one of America's great artwalks

windows, were brought from France and installed in 1884. The bronze doors of the cathedral, installed for its rededication in 1986, contain 16 panels depicting scenes in the history of the Catholic Church in Santa Fe. Also worth viewing is the *reredos* (altar screen) carved for the 100th anniversary celebration in 1986.

La Conquistadora Chapel, an adobe structure on the northeast side of the cathedral, was built in the 1600s to honor a statue of the Virgin Mary brought to Santa Fe in 1626. Originally called the *Lady of the Rosary*, the statue was renamed *Our Lady of the Conquest* in 1692, when the Spaniards reentered the city 12 years after the Pueblo Revolt. It is probably the oldest representation of the Virgin Mary in the United States.

Note: Visitors not attending Mass may slip into the cathedral quietly at other times, using the side doors and taking care not to disturb those at prayer.

Cristo Rey Church (505-983-8258; www.cristoreysantefe.parishesonline .com; 1120 Canyon Rd., Santa Fe, NM 87501, intersection of Canyon Rd. and Camino Cabra; open weekdays 8–5; call 1 month ahead to arrange tours; donations appreciated). An outstanding example of Spanish Colonial Mission architecture, Cristo Rey Church was designed by Santa Fe architect John Gaw Meem and built to commemorate the 400th anniversary of Coronado's arrival in the Southwest. This is one of the largest modern adobe structures in existence. The church is famous for the stone *reredos* (altar screen) carved by craftsmen from Mexico in 1760.

Cross of the Martyrs Walkway (on Paseo de Peralta between Otero St. and Hillside Ave; always open). Only a five-minute walk from the Plaza, this historic spot boasts the best view of downtown. A brick walkway winds up a small hill, and plaques posted along the way summarize highlights of Santa Fe's prehistory and history. The w cross at the summit is a memorial to 21 Franciscan monks killed in the Pueblo Revolt of 1680 (see chapter 1, *History*).

Loretto Chapel Museum (505-922-0092; www.lorettochapel.com; 207 Old Santa Fe Trail, Santa Fe, NM 87501; open summer Mon.–Sat. 9–6, Sun. 10:30–5; winter Mon.–Sat. 9–5, Sun. 10:30–5; closed Christmas; $2, under 7 free; gift shop). Loretto Chapel was built at the same time as St. Francis Cathedral (see below) for the Sisters of Loretto, the first nuns to come to New Mexico. The Chapel of Our Lady of Light, as it was called then, was begun in 1873 and intended to replicate Sainte-Chappelle in Paris, France. Stones for the chapel came from the same quarry as that for St. Francis Cathedral, and the same French architects and French and Italian stonemasons worked on the two structures.

The architects were a father and son named Mouly. The son was killed before the chapel was completed, and he left no plans for a stairway to the choir loft. Indeed, there wasn't enough space left for a conventional staircase. The story goes that the sisters prayed for help to St. Joseph, patron saint of carpenters. In due time an unknown carpenter arrived and proceeded to build an amazing circular staircase—a structure lacking both nails and visible means of support. He departed without leaving his name or asking for pay.

The Plaza (center of town; always open). Four hundred years of history speak from the Santa Fe Plaza. Originally the Plaza was a rectangle, laid out according to plans specified by Spain's King Philip II in 1610. For much of its history, it consisted mainly of packed earth. Though it has been dusty, it has

Archbishop Lamy made his mark on Territorial New Mexico with the Cathedral Basilica of St. Francis of Assisi, reminiscent of his childhood in France.

East Coast. The narrow, winding street has since become an internationally acclaimed art district.

A stroll along Canyon Road is a must for visitors. Enter off Paseo de Peralta, just south of East Alameda about six blocks southeast of the Plaza. Take time to view the old adobe buildings, constructed in typical Spanish colonial style with walls that begin at the edge of the street. A compound may surround a lovely patio or garden.

Take note of 18th-century El Zaguan (545 Canyon Rd.), now a private apartment complex and the site of Historic Santa Fe Foundation. The Victorian garden supports giant chestnut tree, so the story goes, planted by anthropologist Adolph Bandelier, who once lived here. You may enter the garden through the building and enjoy a picnic or quiet respite.

The Cathedral Basilica of St Francis of Assis (505-982-5619; www.cbsfa.org /home0.aspx; 131 Cathedral Place, Santa Fe, NM 87501, east end of San Francisco St.; open Mon.–Sat. 6–6, Sun. 7–7; donations accepted). This is one of Santa Fe's most spectacular structures—and also one of its most incongruous. Built in French-Romanesque style, it was the inspiration of Frenchman Jean Baptiste Lamy, Santa Fe's first archbishop. The cornerstone was laid in 1868, and construction proceeded with stone quarried in an area south of Santa Fe.

St. Francis Cathedral was dedicated in 1886 but was never fully completed. Its stained-glass windows, including the rose window in front and the lateral nave never been dull. Countless celebrations, both religious and secular, have been held here. This is also the spot where Hispanic residents used to conduct Saturday-night promenades complete with strolling musicians.

Today strollers and teenage plaza rats still keep the Plaza hopping on pleasant summer evenings. Hardly anyone would think of holding a demonstration or vigil anywhere but the Plaza, and it's still one of the best people-watching spots in the city.

Randall Davey Audubon Center and Sanctuary (505-983-4609; http://nm.audubon.org/center; P.O. Box 9314, 1800 Upper Canyon Rd., Santa Fe, NM 87504; trails open Tues.–Sun. 8–5; nature store/visitors center open Tues.–Sun. 10–4; $5 house tours, $2 trails, $1 children under 12; gift shop and bookstore). One of the few historic homes in Santa Fe open to the public, the Randall Davey Center is a state office, an environmental education center, and National Audubon Society wildlife refuge. Set on 135 acres at the mouth of the Santa Fe River Canyon, the home of musician and artist Randall Davey is listed in national, state, and city registers of historical and cultural buildings. What is now the house was the original mill; the *acequia* behind it served both as irrigation ditch and millrace. The house features massive beamed ceilings and 16-inch-thick stone walls covered by plaster.

Randall Davey moved to Santa Fe in 1920. His innovative works are exhibited throughout the house and his adjacent studio. The center is also a good introduction to local flora and fauna. Trails wind through natural vegetation of piñon, juniper, and ponderosa pine, and there is a large meadow. The area is rich in bird life and home to black bears, mountain lions, bobcats, coyotes, raccoons, and mule deer. The center offers an extensive schedule of bird walks, natural history workshops, home tours, a fine picnic area, and children's programs.

San Miguel Chapel (505-983-3974; www.santafe.org/Visiting_Santa_Fe; 401 Old Santa Fe Trail, Santa Fe, NM 87501; open summer 9–5:30, winter 9–5, all year Sun. 1:30–4, Sun. Mass 5 PM; $1, under 6 free; gift shop). The oldest church in the U.S., San Miguel was built around 1626. The original walls and adobe altar were likely built by Tlaxcalan Indians brought from Mexico by the Spaniards.

During the Pueblo Revolt of 1680 (see chapter 1, *History*), Indian attackers burned the chapel roof. The Spaniards returned in 1692 and put on a new roof so the chapel could be used until the

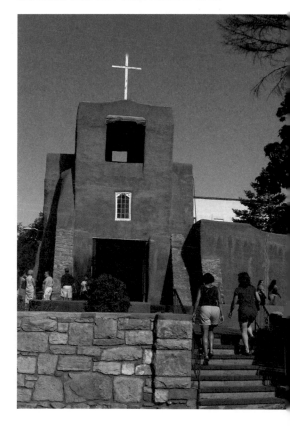

The Chapel of San Miguel in the Barrio Analco was originally constructed in 1626 and rebuilt after the Pueblo Revolt in 1710.

parish church was rebuilt. More renovations were made around 1710. Early in the 19th century the chapel was remodeled with an unconventional three-tiered tower that toppled in 1872. A new tower and stone buttresses supporting the front were added in 1887. In 1955 the interior was restored to its Spanish colonial appearance and the present tower constructed.

The chapel contains several magnificent oil paintings (restored in the 1950s) believed to date from around 1725. Colonial buffalo-hide paintings of the crucifixion and Good Shepherd hang on the walls. Displays show pottery shards and other archaeological findings dating from 1300 A.D.

Santuario de Guadalupe (505-988-2027; www.newmexico.org/nativeamerica /explore/sanctuario_guadalupe.php; 100 S. Guadalupe St., Santa Fe, NM 87501; open Mon.–Fri. 9–4, Sat. 10–4; closed Sun. in summer; donations accepted; gift shop). The Santuario is a longtime Santa Fe landmark and a performing arts center. It was built by Franciscan missionaries between 1776 and 1796 with adobe walls 3 to 5 feet thick. It is the oldest shrine in the United States dedicated to the Queen of the Americas, Our Lady of Guadalupe, who revealed herself in a vision to Indian convert Juan Diego in Mexico in 1531. Across the altar hangs a spellbinding painting of Our Lady of Guadalupe, the work of José de Alzibar, one of Mexico's finest colonial painters. A striking shrine in front of the building commemorates this site as the oldest shrine to Guadalupe in North America.

Our Lady of Guadalupe shrine in Santa Fe is the oldest such shrine in the United States.

Sena Plaza (125–137 E. Palace Ave., Santa Fe, NM 87501: enter on Palace Ave., just east of the Plaza; always open). A separate world that resonates with the flavor of colonial Santa Fe, Sena Plaza is reached by an adobe passage from busy Palace Avenue. In the 19th century, the most gracious homes were built as compounds with rooms surrounding a central placita (courtyard). In the 1860s, Major José D. Sena built just such a home a block from the downtown Plaza—and kept adding rooms as more children were born. Now Sena Plaza houses private shops and a restaurant, where you can enjoy a margarita in the patio garden.

San Jose de Gracia Church at Las Trampas is considered one of the most beautiful Mission churches of the High Road.

Near Santa Fe

San Jose de Gracia de Las Trampas (Las Trampas, NM 76, 40 miles northeast of Santa Fe; open daily in summer 8–5; donations accepted). This structure, built between 1760 and 1780, is frequently described as the most beautiful Spanish colonial church in New Mexico. The village of Las Trampas was established in 1751 by 12 Santa Fe families led by Juan de Arguello, who received a land grant from Governor Tomas Velez Capuchin. In summer, the church is usually open 8–5; in winter, you'll probably find it locked. Ask at one of the gift shops for the person who keeps the key.

In Taos

Ernest L. Blumenschein Home (575-758-0505; http://taosmuseums.org/view /blumenschein-home; P.O. Drawer CCC, 222 Ledoux St., Taos, NM 87571, just south of the Plaza; open summer Mon.–Sat. 10–5, Sun. 12-5, call for winter hours; $8 adults, $4 under 16; gift shop). Ernest and Mary Greene Blumenschein were among the founders of the famous Taos Society of Artists around 1915. Their home, a 1797 Spanish colonial adobe, is open for tours and exhibits of area artists' work. The house, recently restored, appears much as it did in the Blumenscheins' day: You'll find the original adobe plaster inside and out, with replication of the Blumenscheins' color scheme, as well as traditional Taos furniture, European antiques, and artwork from around the world.

Kit Carson Home and Museum (575-758-4945; www.kitcarsonhome .com; P.O. Drawer CCC, 113 E. Kit Carson Rd., Taos, NM 87571, 0.5 block east of the Plaza; open daily 11–5; closed Thanksgiving, Christmas, New Year's, and Easter; $5 adults, $4 seniors, $3 teens, $2 children, under 6 free; gift shop). Kit Carson was the consummate mountain man, scout, and soldier. He was also a family man. In 1843 he married Josefa Jaramillo, and the couple raised a large family in this 12-room adobe. Kit and Josefa both died in 1868, a month apart. Three rooms of the house are furnished as

Saver Cards are also available that admit one person to both THM museums—the Hacienda de los Martinez and the Blumenschein Home and Museum for $12. Ask about the **MAT Combination Ticket for $25, which** provides entrance to three other museums in the Taos area: the Harwood Museum of Art/University of New Mexico, the Millicent Rogers Museum, and the Taos Art Museum & Fechin House.

they might have been during the quarter century the Carsons lived there. Other rooms are filled with exhibits on Taos's colorful frontier history. Carson was an active Mason, and the Masons now operate this museum. Reenactors guide visitors through it.

Go next door to 117 Kit Carson Road (along the museum patio) to visit the Carson House Shop, an excellent showcase of Indian and folk art, jewelry, Christmas ornaments, and the work of noted Taos artist Valerie Graves.

Hacienda de los Martinez (575-758-1000; thm@taos historicmuseums.com; www.taosmuseums.org; P.O. Drawer CCC, 708 Hacienda Way, Taos, NM 87571, off Ranchitos Rd., 2 miles south of the Plaza on NM 240 or 4 miles west of Ranchos de Taos on NM 240; open Mon.–Fri. 10–4, Sun. noon–4; closed Christmas and New Year's Day; $8 adults, $ 4 ages 6–16; gift shop). This 19th-century hacienda features thick adobe walls and a windowless exterior, with 21 rooms enclosing two central *placitas*. This fortresslike building was designed to keep out Comanche and Apache raiders. Livestock were driven through the gates and into the *placitas* when raiders threatened.

This is perhaps the only hacienda in the Southwest that has been restored to its original condition. Rooms are furnished in Colonial style, reflecting a time when goods were either made by local artisans or hauled by oxcart from Mexico City. Exhibits tell the story of trade on the Camino Real and of the Spanish colonial culture of New Mexico. Demonstrations of contemporary and traditional crafts are presented on a regular basis. The Taos Trade Fair, held here each Sept., includes mountain men–style goods and historic reenactments.

Taos Art Museum and Fechin House (575-758-2690; museum@taosart museum.org; www.taosartmuseum.org; P.O. Box 1848, 227 Paseo del Pueblo Norte, Taos, NM 87571-1848, 2 blocks north of the Plaza; open summer Wed.–Sun. 10–5, winter Wed. 10–4, Sun. noon-10–4; $8 adults, $4 ages 6–16, under 6 free). This distinguished adobe home was designed in the Russian style by renowned artist Nicolai Fechin, a Russian emigrant. Built 1927 to 1933, the house features Fechin's hand-carved woodwork. Exhibitions feature Fechin's own paintings, his collections of Asian and Russian art, and many fine works by Taos founders.

San Francisco de Asis Church (575-758-2754; P.O. Box 72, Ranchos de Taos, NM 87557, about 4 miles south of Taos on NM 68; open Mon.–Sat. 9–4, Mass Sat. at 6 PM; Sun. at 7 AM [Spanish], 9 AM, 11:30 AM [English]; Mon., Tues., Wed., Fri. at 6:45 AM; Parish Hall open Mon.–Sat. 9–4; $3 to see video & Mystery Paintings in Parish Hall; gift shop next door). The most frequently painted and photographed church in the United States was built sometime between 1776 and 1813 and was in use by Franciscans in 1815. This iconic mission church symbolizes the purity and essence of New Mexico history and spirituality. Viewed from the west, its massive adobe walls change appearance hourly as the light changes, posing an irresistible challenge to artists. Visitors are also intrigued by artwork in the Parish Hall (found across the driveway to the right), including Henri Ault's *The Shadow of the Cross*.

Southern Methodist University (SMU) in Taos (575-758-8322; P.O. Box 314, Ranchos de Taos, NM 87557, about 8 miles southeast of Taos on NM 518; open June–Aug., varies with class). SMU is located in Fort Burgwin, an 1852 U.S. cavalry fort set in a small valley on a tributary of the Rio Grande. Now it's an archaeological research and training center for SMU based in Dallas, Texas. During summer, SMU in Taos offers cultural programs and a lecture series that emphasizes archaeology. Visit www.smu.edu/taos for current class listings.

LIBRARIES

If you want to delve a little more into southwestern lore, several libraries in Santa Fe and Taos can help you scratch the information itch.

The San Francisco de Asis Church in Ranchos de Taos is said to be the most painted and photographed church in the United States.

Santa Fe

The **Santa Fe Public Library** (505-955-6780; 145 Washington Ave.) is notable for its a Santa Fe–style architecture and southwestern furnishings. The Southwest Room contains a fine collection of Southwest literature

The Museum of New Mexico (www.museumofnewmexico.org) research libraries, open to researchers, are part of each of the four Santa Fe museums. (Be sure to call ahead.) The **Fray Angelico Chavez History Library** (505-576-5090) at the Palace of the Governors houses more than 12,000 volumes on regional history, as well as a vast repository of original documents and maps. Its photo archives section (505-476-5107) contains more than 340,000 historical images; prints are available for purchase or rental. The **Museum of Fine Arts Library** (505-476-5072) contains about 5,000 volumes emphasizing New Mexican and southwestern art. The **Museum of International Folk Art Library** (505-476-1200; www.moifa.org) has more than 10,000 volumes on folk art topics. The **Laboratory of Anthropology Library** (505-476-1264; www.miaclab.org), next to the Museum of Indian Arts and Culture, contains volumes on the Southwest, anthropology, and archaeology. The **State Records Center and Archives** at 1205 Camino Carlos Rey (505-476-7900; www.nmcpr.state.nm.us) is a rich collection of primary sources for genealogy and other researchers.

Taos

The **Taos Public Library** (575-758-3063; 402 Camino de la Placita) is housed in a beautiful new building. The 30,000-volume collection is strong in southwestern literature and history.

MUSEUMS

The state of New Mexico operates five museum facilities in Santa Fe under the aegis of the Museum of New Mexico. In 2012, a four-day pass to all five museums costs $20. The museums include the **Palace of the Governors** and the **Museum of Fine Arts**, the New Mexico History Museum, on the Plaza, and the **Museum of Indian Arts and Culture** and the **Museum of International Folk Art**, both on Camino Lejo, about a 15-minute drive southeast of downtown. Starting at 7:15 AM, at the Sheridan Street Station, seven days a week, is the M bus to Museum Hill. Fees: $1 each way, $2 all-day pass; seniors .50 each way, $1 all-day pass; under 17 free. For information about the individual museums, see below.

Santa Fe

New Mexico History Museum (505-476-5200; www.nmhistorymuseum.org; 113 Lincoln Ave.; open Tues.–Sun. 10–5, Fri. 10–8; closed Mon.; $9 nonresidents, $6 NM residents, free Sun. to NM residents, free Wed. to NM senior citizens, free Fri. evenings 5–8). The state's newest museum; the jewel in the crown. Next door, the previous history museum, the Palace of the Governors, offers permanent exhibits largely related to Spanish colonial history in the oldest continuously occupied government building (built in 1710) in the United States.

El Museo Cultural de Santa Fe (505-992-0591; www.elmuseocultural.org; 555 Camino De La Familia; open Mon.–Fri. 1–5; free to exhibits; variable for performances). This Hispanic museum showcases living contemporary and traditional artists of northern New Mexico. Exhibits of photography, weaving, tinwork, painting, and sculpture live alongside environmental and cultural issue-oriented exhibits. Check the Web site for live performances and classes.

Georgia O'Keeffe Museum (505-946-1000; fax 505-946-1091; www.okeeffe museum.org; 217 Johnson St., Santa Fe, NM 87501, 4 blocks west of the Plaza; open July–Oct. daily, Nov.–June Sat.–Mon., Thurs. 10–5, Fri. 10–8; closed Wed., Thanksgiving, Christmas, New Year's Day, Easter; $8 per day, $7 seniors, free Fri. 5–8 PM). Said to be the most visited museum in Santa Fe, this is the opportunity of a lifetime to view the iconic artist's work in a historic and artistic context. The discerning iconoclast O'Keeffe herself would probably have approved of this classically simple, adobe-colored, elegantly lit museum that houses her inspired work. Visitors can take in the span of the pioneering modernist's work—from early figurative watercolors, to her paintings of New York in the first decades of the 20th century, to her celebrations of New Mexico in enormous flowers, crosses, clouds, and studies of rocks, sky, and bone. To tour the O'Keeffe home in Abiquiu, call 505-685-4539 for information and reservations.

Museum of Contemporary Native Arts (505-983-8900; www.iaia.edu /museum; 108 Cathedral Place, Santa Fe, NM 87501, across from St. Francis Cathedral Basilica; open summer Mon.–Sat. 9–5, Sun. 10–5; winter Mon.–Sat. 10–5, Sun. noon–5; $10 adults, $5 seniors and students with ID; children under 16 free; Sun. free to NM residents; gift shop). The work of many of the best-known names in Indian art—Allan Houser, Fritz Scholder, T. C. Cannon are displayed here. The museum houses the nation's largest collection of contemporary Indian art. Don't miss the Performance Gallery and the Allan Houser Sculpture Park.

Museum of Fine Arts (505-476-5072 for 24-hour information; www.nmart museum.org; 107 W. Palace Ave., Santa Fe, NM 87501, on northwest corner of the Plaza; open Tues.–Sun. 10–5; closed Thanksgiving, Christmas, New Year's, Easter; $5 NM adults, $7 nonresidents, $20 for four-day pass to state museums, Fri. evening free, Sun. free to NM residents; gift shop). The Isaac Hamilton Rapp-designed 1917 Spanish Pueblo-Revival structure houses more than 8,000 works of art, including paintings, prints, drawings, photographs, and sculptures. The collection emphasizes 20th-century American art, particularly southwestern.

On permanent exhibition are works by early 20th-century New Mexico artists such as Jozef Bakos, Gustave Baumann, and William Penhallow Henderson. Also look for changing exhibitions of traditional and contemporary art assembled from the permanent collection or loaned by other institutions. The Alcove Show, which changes several times a year, features exciting contemporary work by area artists.

Art walking tours of Santa Fe are offered by the museum Apr.–Nov., Mon. at 10 AM. Tours are $10; children under 18 are free.

Museum of Indian Arts and Culture (505-476-1629; www.indianartsand culture.org; 710 Camino Lejo, Santa Fe, NM 87501; open Tues.–Sun. 10–5, Mon.–Sun. 10–5 Memorial Day–Labor Day; closed Thanksgiving, Christmas, New Year's, Easter; $6 NM adults, $9 nonresidents, $20 for four-day pass to state museums, under 17 free, Sun. free to NM residents, Wed. free to NM seniors with ID; gift shop). This state museum brings together the past and present of Southwest Indian culture. It houses an extraordinary collection of more than 50,000 Native American art and craft objects. Included in the collection are basketry, pottery,

Holiday highlight is the annual performance of Gustave Baumann's marionettes at St. Francis Auditorium.

textiles, jewelry, clothing, and other items. Artifacts are rotated on exhibit, emphasizing the Navajo, Apache, and Pueblo peoples.

The continuing exhibit "From This Earth: Pottery of the Southwest" covers archaeological, historic, and contemporary southwestern Indian pottery. Artist demonstrations, from pottery making to basket weaving, are offered in summer. The continuing exhibit "Natural Belongings: Classic Art Traditions from the Southwest" includes baskets, textiles, and jewelry.

Museum of International Folk Art (505-476-1200; 505-827-6463 for 24-hour information; fax 505-476-1300; www.internationalfolkart.org; 706 Camino Lejo, Santa Fe, NM 87501; open Tues.–Sun. 10–5, Mon.–Sun. 10–5 Memorial Day– Labor Day; closed Thanksgiving, Christmas, Easter, New Year's; $5 NM adults, $7 nonresidents, $15 for 4-day pass to state museums, under 17 free, Sun. free to NM residents, Wed. free to NM seniors with ID). You'll never see a collection like this unless you travel to six continents and 100 countries. Founded in 1953 by Florence Dibell Bartlett who believed that the art produced by craftspeople, not highbrow artists, would unite the different cultures of the world. Judge for yourself as you wander among traditional clothing and textiles, masks, folk toys, miniatures, and items of everyday use. The collection numbers more than 125,000 pieces, including 106,000 from the Girard Foundation Collection, which the museum received in 1976.

The Hispanic Heritage Wing, opened in 1989, must also be described in superlatives. With about 5,000 artifacts dating from the late 1600s to the present, it's the largest collection of Spanish colonial and Hispanic folk art in the United States. It emphasizes northern New Mexico but includes folk art from the Spanish colonial empire around the world—including religious folk art, textiles, tinwork, utilitarian implements, gold and silver jewelry, and furniture. Truly a must-see.

Museum of Spanish Colonial Art (505-982-2226; www.spanishcolonialblog .org; 750 Camino Lejo, Santa Fe, NM 87502; open Tues.–Sun. 10–5, daily 10-5 Memorial Day–Labor Day; $8 adults, $4 NM residents, under 16 free, $20 for four-day pass to state museums, Sun. free to NM residents; gift shop). Opened in 2002, the museum is housed in an intimate adobe structure designed by renowned architect John Gaw Meem in 1930. It was donated to the Spanish Colonial Arts Society in 1998.

The museum was created to house the Spanish Colonial Arts Society's 3,000-piece collection, which contains five centuries of art spanning four continents. Aside from the extensive art collection, the museum has a library with a 1,000-volume collection of books pertaining to Spanish colonial art and culture. A visit here makes a wonderful, yet not overwhelming, introduction to a more meaningful tour of Santa Fe. All exhibits are given a rich, clear historical context.

Santa Fe Children's Museum (505-989-8359; fax 505-989-7506; www.santafe childrensmuseum.org; 1050 Old Pecos Trail, Santa Fe, NM 87501; open year-round, Wed.–Sat. 10–5, Sun. noon–5; $6 NM residents; $9 nonresidents, Sun. $2 NM residents). This child-friendly museum is a place where youngsters are encouraged to touch, move, create, make noise, and play. It is filled with hands-on exhibits such as Make and Take, a wooden "house" where children can create collages with recyclable foam, spools, rubber, and the like. In other action exhibits, children can do experiments in the arts, humanities, science, and technology. The museum also sponsors ongoing family programs, workshops, demonstrations, and performances.

The Girard Wing at Santa Fe's Museum of International Folk Art, which holds the world's largest collection of folk art.

SITE Santa Fe (505-989-1199; fax 505-989-1188; www.sitesantafe.org; 1606 Paseo de Peralta, Santa Fe, NM 87501; open year-round, Thurs.–Sat. 10–5; Fri. 10–7; Sun. 12–5. Mon., Wed. closed; $10 general admission; $5 seniors, students). No Southwest style here. This is a seriously avant-garde, contemporary art space, with an International Biennial. Expect to see non-narrative video, huge images on bare walls, and plenty of art designed more to shake you up than to comfort you with beauty.

Wheelwright Museum of the American Indian (505-982-4636; 800-607-4636; www.wheelwright.org; P.O. Box 5153, 704 Camino Lejo, Santa Fe, NM 87502; open Mon.–Sat. 10–5, Sun. 1–5; closed Thanksgiving, Christmas, New Year's; donations welcome; gift shop). Mary Cabot Wheelwright, a wealthy New England heiress, scholar, and world traveler, went by horseback to the Navajo Reservation in 1921, at age 40. There she met Hosteen Klah, a powerful Navajo singer and healer. He spoke no English, and she spoke no Navajo, but somehow they developed a rapport. She wanted to know more about his religion, and he revealed that he was ready to pass on some of his knowledge to people who could write it down. Both feared that the traditional Navajo way of life was about to be lost.

The two spent years researching on the Navajo Reservation. In 1927 they founded the Museum of Navajo Ceremonial Art in Santa Fe to house all their sacred artifacts.

As it turned out, Navajo culture proved much more resilient than the two had predicted. Even today the Navajo ceremonial system remains very much alive. In acknowledgment of this fact, the museum returned much of the sacred material to the Navajo Nation in the 1970s, and its name was changed to the Wheelwright Museum of the American Indian to express the institution's interest in all Native American cultures.

The Wheelwright's collection is strong in Navajo weavings, including tapestries of sand-painting designs made by Hosteen Klah himself; southwestern jewelry, basketry, and pottery; cradleboards from throughout the United States; and contemporary Indian art.

Don't miss the **Case Trading Post**. Modeled after southwestern trading posts of the early 1900s, the Case is stuffed with top-quality Indian artwork in a range of prices, from Navajo weavings and Hopi baskets to old pawn jewelry and Pueblo pottery. You'll also find contemporary sculpture, books on Indians, and many tapes of Indian music.

Near Santa Fe

Bradbury Science Museum (505-667-4444; www.lanl.gov/museum; Mail Stop 330, 1350 Central Ave., Los Alamos, NM 87545, 35 miles northwest of Santa Fe via US 285 N and NM 502 W; open Tues.–Sat. 10–5, Sun.–Mon. 1–5; closed major national holidays; free). Photographs and documents give a glimpse of the unfolding of Project Y, the World War II code name for the laboratory that developed the first atomic bomb. But there's more: an impressive display of Los Alamos National Laboratory's weapons research program includes an actual rack for underground nuclear testing and presents an overview of the U.S. nuclear arsenal. You can also view a model of an accelerator and exhibits on the latest research in solar, geothermal, laser, and magnetic fusion energy. Hands-on exhibits allow you to peer through microscopes, align lasers, and talk to computers.

Films from the laboratory, screened in a small theater, include features on computer graphics, geothermal energy, and the history of the Manhattan Project, the creation of the first atomic bomb.

El Rancho de las Golondrinas (505-471-2261; www.golondrinas.org; 334 Los Pinos Rd., Santa Fe, MN 87507, exit 276 off I-25, 15 miles south of Santa Fe; guided group tours Apr.–Oct.; self-guided tours June–Sept., Wed.–Sun. 10–4; $6 adults, $4 seniors and teens, ages 5–12 free; festivals slightly more expensive, general admission; gift shop). El Rancho de las Golondrinas (the ranch of the swallows) has seen everything from settlers and traders to bishops and Indian raiders in its nearly 300-year history. Miguel Vega y Coca bought the ranch as a royal purchase in 1710, and it became the last stop before Santa Fe on the Camino Real from Mexico. Caravans of traders, soldiers, and settlers regularly made the six-month round-trip.

Visitors can see an 18th-century *placita* house, a defensive tower, a molasses mill, a threshing ground, water mills, a blacksmith shop, a wheelwright shop, a winery, weaving rooms, outdoor ovens, and more. The scene is complete with numerous farm animals.

Las Golondrinas celebrates spring and harvest festivals with costumed villagers portraying life in Spanish colonial New Mexico. San Ysidro, the patron saint of farmers, is honored in spring with a procession and Mass, and visitors may enjoy hot bread from the *hornos*. Music, dances, and plays are part of the celebrations. These two festivals are usually held the first weekends in June and October. The Santa Fe Wine Festival is held here the first weekend in July. Check also for the Renaissance Fair and other colorful special events. For information, contact www.nmwine.com.

Los Alamos Historical Museum (505-662-6272; 505 662-4493; www.los alamoshistory.org; P.O. Box 43, 1921 Juniper, Los Alamos, NM 87544, adjacent to Fuller Lodge; 35 miles northwest of Santa Fe via US 285 N and NM 502 W; open winter Mon.–Fri. 10–4, Sat. 11–4, Sun. 1–4; summer Mon.–Fri. 9:30–4:30, Sat. 11–4, Sun. 1–4; free; bookstore). This museum is housed in a log-and-stone building that was originally part of the Los Alamos Ranch School, the predecessor to the Manhattan Project. It covers a million years, beginning when the Jemez volcano exploded and created the Pajarito Plateau. Exhibits include artifacts of the first known residents, farmers and hunters who lived here about A.D. 1100. Another exhibit, Life in the Secret City, reveals the story of Los Alamos during World War II, when it was closed to outsiders as the best scientific minds in the nation rushed to make the bomb.

On the museum grounds are the remains of a Tewa Indian settlement of the 1300s. For a small fee, the museum provides a 12-page booklet for a self-guided walking tour of Los Alamos. Guided tours are available by prior arrangement.

Taos

Harwood Museum (575-758-9826; www.harwoodmuseum.org; 238 Ledoux St., Taos, NM 87571; open Tues.–Sat. 10–5, Sun. noon–5; closed major holidays; $8 adults, $4 ages 6–16, under 6 free; museum shop). The Harwood Museum, New Mexico's second oldest, is a treasury of Taos art. Founded in 1923, it contains paintings, drawings, prints, sculpture, and photographs by the artists who made Taos famous. Included are works by Victor Higgins, Ernest Blumenschein, Andrew Dasburg, Patrocinio Barela, Earl Stroh, Joe Waldrum, Larry Bell, and Fritz Scholder. There is also a collection of 19th-century *retablos*.

The museum is housed in a 19th-century adobe compound that was purchased by Burt and Elizabeth Harwood in 1916 and transformed into an outstanding example of Spanish-Pueblo architecture. Notable is the Agnes Martin Gallery, dedicated to the work of a leading American minimalist and Taos resident.

The Harwood Museum is an excellent place to see the work of the Taos Society of Artists.

Millicent Rogers Museum (575-758-2462; www.millicentrogers.org; 1504 Millicent Rogers Rd., Taos, NM 87571, 4 miles north of Taos Plaza; go left before the "old blinking light" to Millicent Rogers Rd.; open daily 10–5; closed Nov.–Mar. and major holidays; $8 adults, $4 ages 6–16, under 6 free; gift shop). This outstanding private museum was founded in 1953 by relatives of Millicent Rogers, a stunning blonde Vogue model, Standard Oil heiress, and style-setter who moved to Taos in 1947. Her study of regional architecture and Indian and Spanish colonial art resulted in an extensive collection of Native American jewelry, textiles, basketry, pottery, and paintings. Today it forms the core of a display that has been expanded to include religious and secular artwork of Hispanic New Mexico. The museum also holds one of the most important collections of pottery by famed San Ildefonso artist Maria Martinez and her family, as well as rare Penitente artifacts.

Outside the Area

Florence Hawley Ellis Museum of Anthropology (505-685-4312 ext. 4118; www .ghostranch.org/museums-and activities/anthropology; Ghost Ranch Conference Center, US 84, Abiquiu, NM 87510, 35 miles northwest of Española; open Mon–Sat. 9–5, Sun. 1–5; suggested donation: $2 adults, $1 children and seniors). Dr. Florence Hawley Ellis was a pioneer anthropologist who conducted excavations and research in Chaco Canyon and elsewhere. She initiated the archaeological digs at Ghost Ranch. The museum specializes in excavated materials from this Ghost Ranch Gallina digs. The little-studied Gallina culture of northern New Mexico comprised the people who left Mesa Verde, Chaco Canyon, and the Four Corners area during a long drought around A.D. 1200. Other exhibits feature the Spaniards of the area, Pueblo Indian clothing, and prehistoric pottery making.

The adjacent Ruth Hall Museum of Paleontology houses a copy of the *Coelo-*

physis dinosaur skeleton. The original was found near Ghost Ranch, one of the five best dinosaur quarries in the world. This sharp-toothed, birdlike carnivore, extinct for some 200 million years, is the official state fossil.

MUSIC

Several smaller groups lend variety and flavor to the musical scene year-round: Serenata of Santa Fe (505-989-7988) is a professional chamber group that performs at the historic Santuario de Guadalupe, (100 S. Guadalupe St.). The **Sangre de Cristo Chorale** (505-455-3707) is an ensemble that performs a repertory of classical, Baroque, Renaissance, and folk music. The **Santa Fe Women's Ensemble** (505-954-4922) is a group of semiprofessional singers who present a spring concert and four traditional Christmas concerts in Loretto Chapel. The **Thirsty Ear Festival** (918-289; www.thirstyearfestival.com), a heralded annual summer event is an exciting presentation of contemporary blues, roots, and folk music, as well as concerts throughout the year. The Southwest Traditional and Bluegrass Music Association (www.southwestpickers.org) keeps the tempo lively with their **Old Time Music Festival** in August.

Santa Fe
Lensic Performing Arts Center (505-988-1234; fax 505-988-4370; www.lensic .com; 211 W. San Francisco St., Santa Fe, NM 87501). The Lensic is Santa Fe's

Each year, the Millicent Rogers Museum hosts a Folk Arts Festival.

arts and music central. From Roseanne Cash to musical comedy to world beat, the Lensic is a venue for virtually every kind of sound. The stage is seldom dark. Tickets are available in all price ranges. Originally built as a motion picture palace, the 1930 Lensic is a fantastic creation of ornate sculpted plaster in a faux Moorish–Spanish Renaissance style. It boasts a silver chandelier from New York's Roxy in the lobby, along with the crests of Santa Fe's founding families and murals depicting the European settlement of the New World. State-of-the-art sound equipment makes this an ever-popular performance venue.

Santa Fe Chamber Music Festival (505-983-2075; www.sfcmf.org; P.O. Box 2227, 239 Johnson St., Santa Fe, NM 87504-2227; open July–Aug.; call for prices). With dozens of internationally acclaimed musicians and a grand concert hall (the St. Francis Auditorium), the Santa Fe Chamber Music Festival is one of the town's biggest summer draws. Those who insist on the best come for the six-week season of more than 80 concerts, master classes, open rehearsals, youth concerts and more. Through its composer-in-residence program, the festival has brought in some of the foremost composers in the United States. Preconcert lectures by composers, musicologists, and instrumentalists give audiences a deeper appreciation of the music. Daytime rehearsals in St. Francis Auditorium are free.

Santa Fe Concert Association (505-984-8759; www.santafeconcerts.org; P.O. Box 4626, 321-G W. San Francisco St., Santa Fe, NM 87502; open Sept.–May; prices vary with concert; season tickets available). Since 1931, Santa Fe's oldest music organization has brought outstanding musicians from all over the world to perform from a repertoire of classical and modern concert music. Association traditions include the Youth Concerts series and the all-Mozart Christmas Eve special. Most concerts are held in the Lensic Performing Arts Center.

Santa Fe Desert Chorale (505-988-2282; www.desertchorale.org; 311 E. Palace Ave., Santa Fe, NM 87501; open July–Aug.; also Christmas concerts; call for prices). One of the few professional choruses in the United States, the chorale has been described by the *Albuquerque Journal* as "a definitive choral performing ensemble." Music director Joshua Habermann auditions between 24 and 30 singers each year. Twentieth-century works form the backbone of the chorale's repertory; however, major music from all periods is performed, particularly from the Renaissance and Baroque periods. World premiers have included Dominick Argento's *A Toccata of Galuppi's*, Brent Pierce's *El Pocito*, Steven Sametz's *O'Llama de Amor Viva*, and Grace Williams's *The Call of the Sea*. Santa Fe concerts are performed at several downtown locations. Holiday concerts at St. Francis Cathedral Basilica are a seasonal high point.

Santa Fe Opera (505-986-5900; 800-280-4654; www.santafeopera.org; P.O. Box 2408, Santa Fe, NM 87504-2408; open July–Aug.; expect to pay $100 minimum for a ticket; standing room may be available for less). When the Santa Fe Opera opened in 1957, it filled a musical void and gave the city international stature. *Connoisseur* magazine has called it "the premier summer opera festival in the United States . . . a daring, pioneering enterprise." The ambitious repertoire usually takes chances on lesser-known or new operas, along with a world premiere or nearly forgotten masterpiece.

The opera's elegant amphitheater contributes to the mystique. Seven miles north of Santa Fe on US 285, it sits on a hilltop with views of the Sangre de Cristo Mountains to the east and the Jemez sunsets to the west. The 2,128-seat facility, famous for its architectural design, excellent acoustics, and views of the stage, now has a complete roof. Curtain time is 9 PM in July and 8:30 in August. Take a warm coat and blankets; temperatures tend to plummet after dark. Preopera gourmet tailgate picnics are de riguer.

Santa Fe Pro Musica (505-988-4640; 800-960-6680; www.santafepromusica .com; P.O. Box 2091, Santa Fe, NM 87504; open Oct.–Apr. and Dec.; call for prices). Full orchestral performances are at the Loretto Chapel and the Lensic Performing Arts Center. The annual candlelight Baroque Christmas concerts in Loretto Chapelare so popular that visitors from all over the world include them in their Santa Fe holiday plans. In addition to concerts by its Chamber Orchestra and Baroque Ensemble, Santa Fe Pro Musica presents world-renowned solo artists such as Yo-Yo Ma, Lang Lang, and Ian Bostridge, while also offering audiences the opportunity to hear up-and-coming young performers like this season's Laura Lutzke and Conrad Tao.

Santa Fe Symphony Orchestra and Chorus (505-983-353; 800-480-1319; www.santafesymphony.org551; W. Cordova Rd., Ste. D, Santa Fe, NM 87505; open Oct.–May; $20–70; season tickets available). The Santa Fe Symphony Orchestra and Chorus, a lively group founded in 1984, performs under the direction of guest conductors. The season consists of eight subscription concerts of classical and contemporary compositions. Most performances are held at the Lensic Performing Arts Center. Imaginative programming is a hallmark of the symphony.

Taos

Taos Community Auditorium (575-758-4677; www.tcataos.org/calendar; 145 Paseo del Pueblo Norte, Taos, NM 87571-5901; open year-round; prices vary with performers, most $10–15). An enormous spectrum of fine, cutting-edge, innovative, multicultural music, drama, comedy, dance, and theater performances with regional and national talent.

Taos School of Music Summer Chamber Music Festival (575-776-2388; www.taosschoolofmusic.com; P.O. Box 2630, Taos, NM 87571; open mid-June– early Aug.; $20 individual, $10 under 16; $60 season tickets). Established in the 1960s, this chamber music academy draws an international group of talented young chamber music performers to study piano and stringed instruments at Taos Ski Valley. Weekly performances at Taos Community Auditorium feature the young artists as well as world-renowned faculty and groups such as the American String Quartet and Brentano String Quartet. Dinners followed by chamber music concerts at Hotel St. Bernard, the group's summer headquarters, are a Taos summer highlight.

Near Taos

Music from Angel Fire (575-377-3233; 888-377-3300; www.musicfromangelfire .org; P.O. Box 502, Angel Fire, NM 87110; open late Aug.–early Sept.; $20-35; series tickets available). Internationally known musicians perform superb renditions of classical, Romantic, Baroque, and contemporary works in a series of concerts in Angel Fire, Taos, Raton, and Santa Fe. Some concerts are free.

There's plenty to do, see, and hear of an evening in Santa Fe and Taos. Here are some of the latest hot spots. (For current happenings, check the Friday "Pasatiempo" section of the *Santa Fe New Mexican* and the weekly *Taos News* in Taos.)

Santa Fe

If you enjoy flamenco, head to the **Eldorado Court & Lounge** (505-988-4455; 309 W. San Francisco St.) to hear some of the best on weekends, as well as Cuban and Latin sounds. Look to the lovely room that is **Vanessie of Santa Fe** (505-982-9966; 434 W. San Francisco St.) for a cocktail-piano atmosphere and some sophisticated karaoke led by maestro Doug Montgomery.

    La Fonda's La Fiesta Lounge (505-982-5511; www.lafondasantafe.com; 100 E. San Francisco St.) is another favorite place for locals and visitors to listen to live music every night while taking a spin on the intimate dance floor. Entertainment ranges from small jazz groups, to flamenco guitar, to country and western. **El Farol** (505-983-9912; 808 Canyon Rd.) is a Santa Fe institution ensconced in an ancient adobe building. Cozy and dark with local landscape murals, it offers tapas bands both local and national, and dancing in a tight space. Diva Nacha Mendez, salsa, Latin, jazz, open mike—this "heartbeat of Santa Fe" has it all. At **La Casa Sena Cantina** (505-988-9232; 125 E. Palace Ave.) the waitstaff is a young group of professional singers who belt out jazz and best of Broadway. The cantina offers seating at 5:30 and 8 PM Fri. and Sat. and at 6:30 Sun.–Thurs. (See also chapter 6, *Restaurants and Food Purveyors.*)

    If you want camaraderie and conversation, popular spots range from the elegance of La Posada de Santa Fe's **Staab House Lounge** (505-986-0000; 330 E. Palace Ave.), with flamenco and South American rhythms, to the funk of **Evangelo's** (505-982-9015; 200 W. San Francisco St.), offering live country, jazz, and rock bands Friday and Saturday nights. The **Dragon Room**, the bar next door to the famous The Pink Adobe restaurant (505-983-7712; www.the pinkadobe.com/dragon; 406 Old Santa Fe Trail), is one of the town's best-known see-and-be-seen spots. If you just want to relax, head for the **Hotel Santa Fe** (505-825-9876; 753 Cerrillos Rd.) for classical guitar and Native flute music.

    A dozen or so restaurants in Santa Fe and environs boast convivial bars and fairly regular live entertainment, such as Spanish classical guitar, flamenco, mariachi trios, jazz, Latin rhythms, country and western, and big bands. Here are a few favorites: the **Cantina at El Meson** (505-983-6756; 213 Washington Ave.) for a weekly rotation of tango, jazz, and more jazz, to go with the tapas and excellent sherry; **Maria's**, with mariachis nightly during summer (505-983-7929; 555 W. Cordova Rd.); and **Tiny's** (505-983-9817; St. Francis Dr. and Cerrillos Rd. in the Pen Road Shopping Center), where you can give a listen to the Santa Fe Big Band. The popular **Second Street Brewery** (505-982-3030; www.secondstreetbrewery.com; 1814 Second St.)—and even better at the newer location at The Railyard (505-989-3278; 1607 Paseo De Peralta, #10)—offers a range of contemporary and folk Thurs.–Sun. to A lively hangout and meet-up spot, some would say, Santa Fe's best, is the bar and patio at Cowgirl BBQ & Western Grill (505-982-2565; 319 S. Guadalupe St.).

An excellent place to begin or end your evening is Taos' "living room"—the Taos Inn's **Adobe Bar** (575-758-2233; www.taosinn.com; 125 Paseo del Pueblo Norte). The inn itself is a lovingly restored historic landmark, There's live entertainment nightly, and you're likely to rub elbows with many Taoseños. **Fernando's Hideaway Lounge** at the Don Fernando de Taos Hotel & Suites (575-758-4444; 1005 Paseo del Pueblo Sur) is reputed to have the happiest happy hour in town, 5–7 PM weekdays. There's live music nightly at the **Sagebrush Inn** (575-758-2254; www.sage brushinn.com; 1508 Paseo de Pueblo Sur), where some of the best local country-and-western performers play. Local bands also play weekends at the **Best Western Kachina Lodge** (575-758-2275; 413 Paseo del Pueblo Norte). At **Ally Cantina** (575-758-2121; 121 Teresina Lane) tourists and locals crowd into this funky old space until the wee hours for live music nightly. **KTAO Solar Center** (575-9758-5826; 100 Ski Valley Rd.) has evolved into a supervenue for touring musicians and performers (think reggae, afro-beat), with happy hour Wed.–Sun. 5–7, a full bar, and food service. Very reasonable ticket prices ($5–7), kid-friendly, and the coolest place in town to hang out. **Caffe Tazza** (575-758-8706; 122 Kit Carson Rd.) is the place to hear poetry readings and more offbeat performers. If you just want to relax with a microbrew, you can't beat **Eske's Brew Pub** (575-758-1517; 106 Desgeorges Lane).

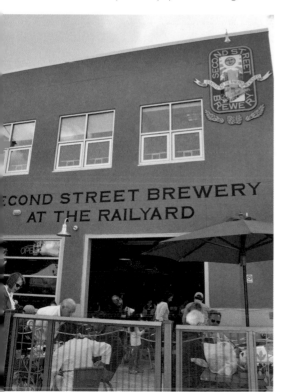

The Railyard is the Second Street Brewery's second home and quite the popular watering hole.

PUEBLOS

The ancestors of Indians living today on New Mexico's 19 Indian pueblos dwelled in the Southwest for many centuries; literally thousands of ruins dot the landscape. Their prehistoric period was marked by frequent migration and resettlement, but the 16th century opened a different era. During that time, Spanish conquistadors and settlers arrived. Concurrently, nomadic tribes of Athapaskan Indians began making periodic raids on the pueblos for slaves, food, and goods. Americans who came from the East in the 19th century brought more cultural, political, and economic pressures.

Today's Pueblo Indians are justly proud not only of their cultural and artistic traditions but also of their growing economic self-sufficiency. The pueblo villages are self-governing, sovereign entities with their own schools, clinics, and police forces. The Pueblo people operate numerous thriving businesses, in particular, resorts and casinos. Many offer bargain buffets as well.

Many Pueblo Indians speak English and Spanish in addition to their native tongues. Their artwork is in great demand by collectors all over the world, and their powerful legacy enriches this part of the world in untold ways.

Pueblo Etiquette

Here are some things to keep in mind when visiting a pueblo:

- Inquire ahead of time about visitors hours. Remember that some pueblos are closed to outsiders on certain days for religious activities.

- Drive slowly.

- Never bring drugs or alcoholic beverages to a pueblo.

- Stop at the visitors center or tribal office when you arrive. This is a requirement at all the pueblos. Some charge fees; others ask visitors to register.

- Do not walk into or on a kiva (circular ceremonial structures).

- Homes, kivas, and cemeteries are not open to non-Pueblo visitors. However, if you are invited to come into someone's home to eat, it is considered impolite to refuse. (It's also considered polite to eat and leave promptly so that others can come in and eat.) Most pueblos have food concessions on feast days, when visitors can sample Pueblo cooking.

- Remember that dances are religious ceremonies, not performances. Conduct yourself as if you were in a church. Revealing clothing, such as shorts and halter tops, is not acceptable. Don't talk or obstruct the view of others during the dances, don't applaud afterward, and don't approach the dancers or ask about the meaning of dances. The Pueblo people prefer not to discuss their beliefs with outsiders.

- Do not cut across the plaza or area where the dances are being performed. Always walk along the perimeter.

- For your comfort, bring along folding chairs to watch the dances from.

- Observe each pueblo's regulations on use of cameras, tape recorders, and drawing. Most pueblos forbid these activities during dances. (See pueblo listings for particulars.) If you want to photograph a pueblo resident, ask permission first and give a donation to the family.

One of the best times to visit is on a feast day, the major public celebration at each pueblo. Ostensibly, feast days are named for particular saints; however, the tradition predates the arrival of the Spanish priests, who applied the names of saints to what were already holy days for the Pueblo people.

Feast days usually start with a Mass at the Catholic Church. A priest may lead a procession of dancers to the church, and the dances begin sometime after Mass. In spring, summer, and early autumn, such dances as the Blue Corn Dance, Butterfly Dance, and Harvest Dance may be performed in observance of the planting and harvest. In winter, the hunting cycle is celebrated with Deer, Elk, and Buffalo dances. (See pueblo listings for dates of feast days.)

On Christmas Eve and Christmas Day, you may see the Matachines dance at Taos, Picuris, San Juan, Santa Clara, and San Ildefonso Pueblos. Dancers clothed in beaded head-dresses with scarves over their mouths move to 16th-century Spanish folk tunes played on guitars and violins. The origins of the Matachines dance are obscure, but it is probably rooted in Moorish customs brought from Spain. Similar dances are performed in neighboring Spanish villages and throughout the hemisphere.

Key Numbers

New Mexico Tourism Indian Affairs Department: 505-476-1600; www.iad .state.nm.us.

Indian Pueblo Cultural Center: 505-843-7270; 866-855-7902; www .indianpueblo.org; 2401 12th St. NW, Albuquerque, NM 87104.

Near Santa Fe

Cochiti Pueblo (505-465-2244; www .pueblodecochiti.org; tribal office: P.O. Box 70, Cochiti Pueblo, NM 87072, exit 264 from I-25, about 25 miles south of Santa Fe; Keresan language;

The mysterious Matachines dance is performed at Alcalde during the holiday season.

feast day: July 14, San Buenaventura; no admission fee; cameras not allowed). Cochiti Pueblo remains firmly rooted in its past while building a strong future. The church built in 1628 to honor San Buenaventura still stands. Not far away is Cochiti Lake, a recreational community built on land leased from the pueblo, which also operates Cochiti Lake services such as fishing. Cochiti Lake has an 18-hole golf course. (See also "Swimming" and "Water Sports" in chapter 7, *Recreation*.)

Cochiti Pueblo is best known for its drums and evocative clay storyteller fig-urines. The popular storyteller figure was created in 1964 by Cochiti potter Helen Cordero, who says she was inspired by her grandfather telling stories to children. Now many Pueblo potters make these popular storytellers in human and animal forms, but Cochiti storytellers are still the most highly prized. Cochiti drums, essential to the pueblo's ceremonies, are also widely coveted by collectors. Individ-ual pueblo artists sell crafts out of their home studios.

Nambe Pueblo (505-455-2034; 544 Np 101 Santa Fe, NM 87506: drive 15 miles north of Santa Fe on US 285, 3 miles east on NM 503 to sign for Nambe Falls, then 2 miles to pueblo entrance; Tewa language; feast day: Oct. 4, St. Fran-cis de Asis; fees: sketching $15, still cameras $5, movie/video cameras $10; fees subject to change). A small pueblo set near the Sangre de Cristo Mountains in a piñon and juniper valley, Nambe (nam-BAY) retains a few original buildings, including mission ruins. Many tribal members work at nearby Los Alamos National Laboratory, in Española, or in Santa Fe. Beautiful Nambe Falls, one of the state's few waterfalls, is the setting for the annual Fourth of July Ceremonials. Apr.–Oct. Nambe Falls Recreational Site (505-455-2304) offers fishing, picnicking, camping, boating, and sightseeing. Fees are charged for each activity. Many artists offer their pottery and wares for sale. For tours led by Native American guides, call **Buffalo Tours** (505-455-0526).

Pojoaque Pueblo (505-455-7660; 39 Camino del Rincon, Santa Fe, NM 87506; Tewa language; feast day: Dec. 12, Our Lady of Guadalupe; contact tribal governor's office at 505-455-3334 before sketching or filming). The 20 businesses that line the east side of US 285 at Pojoaque (po-WAH-kee) speak of an enterprising spirit and prosperity; you would not guess that Pojoaque is a pueblo that has pulled itself back from near extinction. Only mounds of earth remain of the original pueblo, and in the late 1800s the people themselves were almost wiped out by a smallpox epidemic.

In the 1930s, a new Pojoaque was founded, and a milestone was reached in 1983 when tribal members danced for the first time in more than 100 years. Now they celebrate Our Lady of Guadalupe Day and Reyes Day on Jan. 12.

Next to the Pojoaque Pueblo Tourist Information Center on US 285 is the **Poeh Center** (pronounced POE), a museum that hosts artist exhibits, weekend dance performances, and workshops (505-455-7136; www.poehcenter.com; 78 Cities of Gold Rd., Santa Fe, NM 87506; Mon.–Fri. 10–4, Sat. 10–2). The museum also serves as a training complex for Tewa artists, with archives and Tewa art collections. Also on Cities of Gold Road is **Cities of Gold Casino & Hotel** (800-455-3313; www.citiesofgold.com; 10-A Cities of Gold Rd.).

San Ildefonso Pueblo (505-455-2273; www.indianpueblo.org/19pueblos /sanildefonso.html; 36 Tunyo Place, Santa Fe, NM 87501: drive 15 miles north of Santa Fe on US 285, turn left at NM 502, then 6 miles to entrance on right; Tewa language; feast day: Jan. 23, San Ildefonso; fees: $5 per carload; sketching and painting $25; videotaping $20; still cameras $10; fees subject to change; no photography allowed on feast days). San Ildefonso is world famous for its black-on-black pottery, a technique developed by Maria Martinez and her husband, Julian, in the 1920s. Maria was also among the first Pueblo potters to sign her work. Her pots are prized by private collectors and museums nationwide, and her descendants still make pottery, both innovative and traditional. Other artisans sell wares out of their homes. Inquire at the visitors and information center.

San Ildefonso also operates the **Maria Martinez Museum** (505-455-3549, Mon.–Fri. 8–4) with displays of local arts, embroidery, photography, pottery-making techniques, and Pueblo history. A stocked fishing lake is open Mar.–Oct.; permits can be obtained at the lake.

Ohkay Owingeh Pueblo (505-852-4400; www.indianpueblo.org/19pueblos /ohkayowingeh.html; P.O. Box 1099, San Juan, NM 87566; drive 1 mile north of Española on NM 68, turn left onto US 74 at San Juan Pueblo sign, entrance is 1 mile farther; Tewa language; feast day: June 24, San Juan; cameras not allowed; contact tribal governor's office at 505-852-4400 to see whether pueblo is open). In 1598 conquistador Don Juan de Oñate declared this prosperous and friendly pueblo the first capital of New Mexico. When Spanish demands for gold and slaves became too insistent, the people asked Oñate to take his capital somewhere else. (It ended up in Santa Fe.) A native named Popé (Po-PAY) organized the Pueblo Revolt in 1680. (See chapter 1, *History*.)

The largest and northernmost of the Tewa-speaking pueblos, Ohkay Owingeh has two central plazas, with its Catholic Church and ceremonial kivas side by side. It also runs the **Ohkay Owingeh Arts & Crafts Cooperative**, a multipurpose complex where visitors can view and buy the pueblo's distinctive red incised pottery, a ware whose luster and geometric designs are coveted by collectors worldwide. San Juan artisans also excel at jewelry making, carving, weaving, and other arts.

The **Ohkay Casino and Restaurant** is a popular stop with a hotel and RV park. Fishing at the tribal lakes is open winter and summer; contact the tribal office for regulations. The powerful Turtle Dance is performed each Dec. 26.

Santa Clara Pueblo (505-753-7326; www.indianpueblo.org/19pueblos/ santaclara.html; P.O. Box 580, Española, NM 87532); 1.3 miles from Española, on NM 30; Tewa language; feast day: Aug. 12, Santa Clara; fees: $5 adults, $4 seniors and children, adult fee includes still-camera permit, no sketching or video cameras allowed). The **Santa Claran Hotel** (505-747-0059; www.santaclaran.com) offers rooms with adobe fireplaces, and espouses the values of the pueblo itself.

Set in the wide Rio Grande Valley, with vistas of mountains on either side, Santa Clara is home to 2,600 enterprising tribal members who farm, work at jobs outside the pueblo, and create stunning red and black polished pottery, sculpture, and paintings. They are the descendants of the ancient Puye cliff dwellers, and their name for their pueblo, Kha P'o, means "singing water."

Santa Clara potters are noted for their intricately carved pottery (sgraffito), particularly the etched miniatures. Look for POTTERY FOR SALE signs on houses; you'll be invited to come in and meet the artist. Santa Clara also offers guided tours of the pueblo and its historical church. On the tours, you'll be allowed to photograph, see pottery demonstrations, buy native foods, and perhaps see a dance. Tours are offered weekdays only, with five days' advance notice. Inquire at the tourism office or phone the number above.

Santa Clara Canyon Recreational Area, a rugged natural spot, is open to visitors Apr.–Oct. for camping, picnicking, and fishing. Inquire about fees at the tourism office.

The Conchas Fire of 2011 badly burned and damaged the pueblo and its watershed. Restoration is in process.

Santo Domingo Pueblo (505-465-2214; www.indianpueblo.org/19pueblos /santodomingo; P.O. Box 99, Santo Domingo Pueblo, NM 87052, about 34 miles S. of Santa Fe on I-25; Keresan language; feast day: Aug. 4, Santo Domingo; no cameras, sketching, or recording allowed; donations accepted). For information on the Santo Domingo Pueblo Arts & Crafts Market, held Labor Day weekend, call 505-465-0406. Santo Domingo is home to an amazing number of creative and enterprising artists. Many have transformed the traditional *heishi* and turquoise jewelry-making techniques into beautiful contemporary designs. Others have revived the ancient Santo Domingo pottery tradition and are producing superb blends of old and new. Santo Domingo jewelry is available from artists selling under the portal of the Palace of the Governors in Santa Fe and at shops at the pueblo. The Aug. 4 Feast Day Corn Dance is an unforgettable scene, with hundreds of dancers, singers, and clowns participating in all-day ceremonies. Santo Domingo hosts an annual arts-and-crafts market each Labor Day weekend, with 300 booths of jewelry, pottery, and other artwork along with Indian foods.

Tesuque Pueblo (505-955-0139; www.indianpueblo.org/19pueblos/tesuque; 503 Riverview Lane, Box, Pack and Mail, Espanola, NM 87532-2504, 9 miles north of Santa Fe on US 285, main village is 1 mile west of highway; Tewa language; feast day: Nov. 12, San Diego; no photography or video). Though close to Santa Fe and operating several successful businesses, Tesuque (te-SOO-kay) is one of the most conservative of the pueblos. The site was occupied as far back as 1250; however, the original pueblo was at another location that was abandoned after the Pueblo Revolt of 1680. (See chapter 1, *History*.)

The present pueblo was established in 1694. Listed on the National Register of Historic Places, Tesuque has a large central plaza with a Catholic Church. The tribe operates **Camel Rock Casino** (800-462-2635; www.camelrockcasino.com) on US 84/285, along with a store (505-983-2667) and the **Tesuque Natural Farm** (505-983-2667), where certified organic blue corn, chile, and other vegetables are grown. Several artists' studios are open to the public, selling mostly traditional Tesuque clay figurines, pottery, beadwork, drums, weavings, and carvings. Inquire at the tribal office.

Near Taos

Picuris Pueblo (505-587-2519; www.indianpueblo.org/19pueblos/picuris; P.O. Box 127, Peñasco, NM 87553; drive 17 miles north from Española to junction with NM 75, turn right and continue 13 miles to Picuris; Tewa language; feast day: Aug. 10, San Lorenzo; fees: sketching $20, still cameras $5, movie/video cameras $15, self-guided ruin tours $3, call in advance about tours; fees also for fishing and camping, inquire at Picuris Pueblo Fish & Game and Parks & Wildlife at 505-587-1601). In 1519, Picuris (pee-ku-REES) was the last pueblo to be discovered by the Spaniards; it is nearly hidden in the Sangre de Cristo Mountains. It was settled in the 1200s and about 200 years later had grown into a multistoried adobe complex. Picuris was abandoned after the 1680 Pueblo Revolt and reestablished in the 1700s. It has never made a treaty with another government and retains its status as a sovereign nation and tribe.

The smallest of the pueblos, Picuris operates several facilities for visitors. The Hidden Valley Shop and Restaurant includes a small convenience store and smoke shop, fishing equipment, and arts and crafts. Inquire at the tribal office about hours. Pu-Na and Tu-Tah Lakes are stocked ponds with a picnic area. The Picuris Pueblo Museum displays authentic Indian arts, crafts, and pottery.

Taos Pueblo (575-758-1028; www.taospueblo.com; 120 Veterans Highway, Taos, NM 87571, 2 miles north of Taos off NM 68; Tewa language; feast days: Sept. 29–30, San Geronimo; fees: $10 adults, $5 seniors, $5 students (13–college with ID), under 12 free; parties of 10 or more, $8 per person; sketching $15, painting $35, still camera $6; pueblo may be closed to non-Indians during Feb., March, and Aug., inquire at tribal office; no photography during feast days). Taos was well established long before Europe emerged from the Dark Ages. The present pueblo of multistoried adobe apartment buildings has been occupied since about A.D. 1450. Today, as then, the clear waters of the Rio Pueblo flow through the area from sacred Blue Lake in the Sangre de Cristo Mountains and residents draw their water from the stream. To honor their traditions, they live without indoor plumbing or electricity, just as their ancestors did. Beyond the borders at the village wall, these conveniences are available.

Architecturally, Taos Pueblo is the most spectacular of the area's pueblos, capturing the imaginations of countless artists. Its beauty is the outward manifestation of its spiritual strength. Taos was the seat of the Pueblo Revolt of 1680, when the Spaniards were driven out of New Mexico. It also played an active role in the 1847 uprising of Hispanics and Indians against the U.S. government. (See chapter 1, *History*.)

Taos Pueblo is governed by the governor and war chief. The economy is based on government services, tourism, arts and crafts, ranching, and farming. The Feast of San Geronimo is a highlight of the year, with a sunset dance on Sept. 29, footraces, an arts-and-crafts fair, a ritual pole climbing, traditional dances, and food. During the festivities, Chifonetes perform humorous acts.

Visitors are also welcome at the Taos Pueblo Pow Wow, held the second weekend of July each year. Native Americans from many tribes join in this colorful and popular social dance event. (The powwow is a Plains Indian tradition, but Taos has been influenced by contacts with Plains tribes for centuries.) Other dances open to the public (no cameras) are the Turtle Dance, Jan. 1; Buffalo or Deer Dance, Jan. 6; Feast of Santa Cruz Corn Dance, May 3; San Antonio Corn Dance, June 13; San Juan Corn Dance, June 24; and Deer Dance or Matachines, Christmas Day. Christmas Eve is a special time to visit, with bonfires and processions. July 25–26, the Feast of Santa Ana and Santiago, is an excellent time to visit and observe dancers from many tribes.

Taos Pueblo artists are noted for their mica-flecked (micaceous) pottery, tanned buckskin moccasins, and drums made of hides stretched over hollowed cottonwood logs. Many shops on the pueblo plaza sell these goods, along with fragrant breads freshly baked in outdoor adobe ovens called *hornos*.

SEASONAL EVENTS

Unless otherwise noted, admission is not charged for the following events.

Santa Fe

Christmas

Christmas in Santa Fe is a delight that belongs on every "bucket list." The Palace of the Governors usually sponsors Las Posadas, a traditional Spanish reenactment of Joseph and Mary's search for shelter on the night Jesus was born. The Plaza is the setting for the pageant, performed by an area church group, wherein the choir and audience members follow the Holy Couple around the Plaza. Other stellar events include Christmas at the Palace of the Governors, with hot cider, *biscochitos*, and Christmas music, the annual show of the Gustav Baumann Marionettes, and so much more.

Many area musical ensembles conduct seasonal concerts in Dec.; consult the Santa Fe Convention and Visitor Bureau or local newspapers for schedules. Also, many area pueblos hold special dances around Christmas (see the introduction to "Pueblos," above). On Christmas Eve, Santa Fe is alight with thousands of *farolitos*, glowing candles placed in paper bags. The scent of piñon bonfires, or

Taos Pow Wow

luminarias, fills the air as hundreds of people take to the streets in the Canyon Road neighborhood to see the *farolitos*, sing carols, and socialize.

Feast Day Dances
Each pueblo has a special Feast Day celebration annually on its patron saint's day. See "Pueblos," above.

Indian Market (505-983-5220; www.swaia.org; Southwestern Association for Indian Arts (SWIA), P.O. Box 969, Santa Fe, NM 87501; weekend following third Thurs. in Aug.; the Plaza and vicinity; free). Indian Market is the biggest weekend of the year in Santa Fe, when more than 1,000 Native American artists exhibit and sell their work at outdoor booths on and around the Plaza, and is the largest exhibition and sale of Indian art in the world. Begun more than 80 years ago as an effort to help Pueblo Indians revive their pottery and jewelry-making traditions, it has since been the springboard for many successful artistic careers. All participants are carefully screened; they must be Native American, and their work must be totally handmade.

Activity starts before dawn on Sat. with artists unloading work at their booths and eager collectors lining up to get first chance at a coveted pot or necklace when the market officially opens at 8 AM. Irresistible smells of fry bread, coffee, mutton stew, and Navajo tacos fill the air, and the Plaza slowly fills with people. Artists demonstrate skills such as sand painting or basket weaving, and the drums sound for social dances in the courtyard of the Palace of the Governors. The array of artwork is mind-boggling, from pottery, jewelry, beadwork, and weaving to basketry, paintings, drums, and rattles. There's something for everyone, from a $3 corn necklace to a $5,000 Navajo rug. The party begins earlier in the week with special events such as clothing design contests, numerous auctions, and galas. Contact SWIA for details.

La Fiesta de Santa Fe (800-777-2489, Santa Fe Convention and Visitors Bureau; www.santafefiesta.org; weekend after Labor Day; the Plaza and vicinity). The oldest continuously observed festival in the United States, La Fiesta is the quintessential celebration of New Mexico's Hispanic culture. The first Fiesta de Santa Fe was held in Sept. 1712, with processions, sermons, candle lighting, and pomp and circumstance in commemoration of Don Diego de Vargas's reentry into Santa Fe in 1692, following the 1680 Pueblo Revolt. (See chapter 1, *History*.)

Fiesta preparations begin long in advance, with the selection of a young woman as fiesta queen, along with her court, and a young man as Don Diego de Vargas and his 17-member retinue. All performers play roles in a reenactment of Vargas's return. On the weekend after Labor Day, La Fiesta begins with the Pregón de la Fiesta and Mass at Rosario Church.

An extremely popular addition to La Fiesta is Zozobra, or "Old Man Gloom," a 40-foot-tall papier-mâché puppet that stands in Fort Marcy Park on Thurs. night of La Fiesta. Zozobra was born in 1926, the brainchild of Will Shuster, one of Los Cinco Pintores, founders of the Santa Fe art colony. As fireworks flare and "the Gloomies," as they are known, gyrate wildly around him, Zozobra goes up in flames, symbolically burning away the year's troubles so that the celebrations can begin. The cheering crowd then heads for the Plaza for food, music, and dancing. Plaza festivities continue through the weekend. In recent times, this event has become much, much more commercialized.

Lannan Foundation (505-986-8160; www.lannan.org; 313 Read St., Santa Fe, NM 87501; $6 adults, $3 seniors and students). The Lannan Foundation sponsors the Readings & Conversations literary series on various Wed. evenings Sept.–May at the Lensic Theater and at Santa Fe School for the Deaf. National and international literary stars tend to headline. Poets and writers of fiction and nonfiction read and discuss their work. Tickets for these events go fast, so try to book them at least a month in advance by going to www.lensic.com or calling 505-988-1234.

Rodeo de Santa Fe (505-471-4300; www.rodeodesantafe.org; Rodeo Grounds, 2801 Rodeo Rd., Santa Fe, NM 87507; mid-July; call for details). See "Rodeos" in chapter 7, *Recreation.*

Santa Fe Film Festival (505-988-7414; www.santafefilmfestival.com; 60 W. San Francisco St., Ste. 307, Santa Fe, NM 87501; Oct.; individual tickets approximately $10; festival pass approximately $300). Independent, international, classic, and animated films; panel discussions; awards galas and banquets. The 12th annual festival, held in 2011, showcased an evolving array of filmmaking talent as well as established stars, like Emilio Estevez.

Santa Fe International Folk Art Market (505-992-7600; www.folkartmarket .org; second weekend in July, 9–5; Milner Plaza on Museum Hill). The world comes to Santa Fe! The growth of this event has been phenomenal. It now ranks as one of the most popular and best attended in the year, with juried exhibitors and artists from everywhere on the planet attending. The crowds, too, can be overwhelming, so if you have any aversion to them, go early in the day. The earlier the better, even if you pay a premium for your ticket as an Early Bird. The preopening evening gala is exceptional and, again, well worth the expense, if you want first shot at the art. Expect to wait in lines, even for the shuttle buses that leave from various sites around town. World music and entertainment plus an international food bazaar make this event, despite the crowds, a worthy highlight.

The art of *colcha* embroidery endures and is taught today.

Spanish Market (505-982-2226; fax 505-982-4585; info@spanish colonial.org; www.spanishcolonial.org; Spanish Colonial Arts Society, P.O. Box 5378, Santa Fe, NM 87502-5378; 750 Camino Lejo, Santa Fe, NM 87501; last full weekend in July; on the Plaza; free). During the centuries when New Mexico was a Spanish colony, its isolation from Spain and distance from Mexico fostered the growth of unique folk arts. Many of these arts and crafts helped serve the religious needs of the settlers. Beginning in the 1920s, largely due to the interest of writers and artists from the East Coast and California,

The work of Marie Romero Cash is on display at Spanish Market in Santa Fe.

they experienced a revival, and the work of New Mexican artisans is in great demand by collectors and museums.

At Spanish Market, which celebrated its 60th anniversary in 2011, you can see the finest Hispanic artwork produced in the region today: *santos, colcha* embroidery, woolen weavings, straw appliqué, carved and painted furniture, tinwork, forged iron, *reredos*, and more. Hundreds of artists exhibit in booths around the Plaza. The scene is complemented with native New Mexican folk music groups, flamenco dancers, food booths, and artist demonstrations. There's also a Winter Market in December.

Don't miss the **Contemporary Market**, on Lincoln Avenue, just off the Plaza. Exciting, innovative, and affordable work by Hispanic artists, including jewelry, fiber arts, painting, furniture, and crafts, is exhibited and sold at this show, which operates alongside the traditional market. And the artists delight in discussing their work with you.

Taos

Fiestas de Santiago y Santa Ana (575-758-3873; 800-348-0696; www.new-mexico -visitor.com; 1139 Paseo del Pueblo Sur Taos, NM 87571; late July; the Plaza; free). In the 1930s, the newly incorporated Town of Taos started the Fiestas for Santiago (St. James) and Santa Ana (St. Anne). Still celebrated today, Las Fiestas

Flamenco performed at the gazebo on Santa Fe Plaza.

de Santiago y Santa Ana continues to preserve and celebrate the cultures that have lived together in this valley for four centuries.

This fiesta honors Taos's patron saints. The joyous celebration begins with a Friday night Mass and candlelight procession to the Plaza. The weekend is filled with a satirical parade on local history, crowning of a Fiesta Queen, kids' parade, arts-and-crafts fair, and food booths. The event is not only a celebration; it is a way to pass on rich traditions.

Old Taos Trade Fair (575-758-0505; www.taoshistoricmuseums.org; 222 Ledoux St., Taos, NM 87571; late Sept.; $8 adults, $4 children under 16, Sun. free to Taos County residents). This two-day fair, which coincides with San Geronimo Day at Taos Pueblo (see "Pueblos," above), brings to life Spanish colonial culture in the 1820s. Held at the Martinez Hacienda (see "Buildings and Sites," above), the fair features mountain men, traditional craft demonstrations, native foods, caravans, muzzle-loading rifle demonstrations, and Hispanic and Indian music.

Taos Fall Arts Festival (505-758-3873; 800-732-8267; taosfallarts.com; P.O. Box 675, Taos Convention Center, 120 Civic Plaza Dr., Taos, NM 87571; late Sept.–early Oct.; free). A roundup of arts festivities, this yearly event celebrates the history, cultures, and art of Taos County. Events include gallery openings, invitational and juried art exhibitions, an arts-and-crafts fair. High-quality exhibits of art celebrating the region are always worthwhile. Plus, it is a glorious time of year to be in town. The Spring Arts Festival in Apr.–May is a similar experience.

Taos Solar Music Festival (800-732-TAOS; www.solarmusicfest.com; late June; Kit Carson Park, Paseo del Pueblo Sur and Civic Plaza Dr.; $20–80). Wow! This is the place to be to hear headliners and emerging artists in an atmosphere of pure fun. Plus, you can get an education on the latest in solar energy. Performers have included Michelle Shocked, Leo Kotke, Los Lobos, Robert Mirabal, Ottmar Liebert, Ani deFranco,and the Indigo Girls playing a variety of reggae, folk, western swing, Spanish, rock, and acoustic. (See also "Taos Pueblo" in this chapter.)

Yuletide in Taos/Lighting of LeDoux Street (575-758-3873; www.taos.org; Taos County Chamber of Commerce, P.O. Drawer I, Taos, NM 87571; mid-Dec; free). Imagine Taos Plaza edged in snow on a clear, crisp winter night, the scent of piñon smoke flavoring the air. This celebration incorporates Taos's Hispanic and Indian traditions in a series of community events: *farolito* tours, candlelight dinners, dance performances, ski area festivities, ethnic holiday foods, a crafts fair, caroling, and a Christmas parade and tree lighting on the Plaza. This is truly a meaningful and precious experience of the season, with the community, starting with the lighting of LeDoux Street with hundreds of dazzling *farolitos*.

The Wool Festival at Taos (800-684-0340; www.taoswoolfestival.org; P.O. Box 2754, Taos, NM, Kit Carson Park; first full weekend in Oct.). From live alpacas and churro sheep to demonstrations of weaving and needle arts to delectable for-sale items, such hand-dyed wools, felt hats, scarves, and handmade sheepskin

Calling all fiber fanatics to the annual Taos Wool Festival.

boots, this event is pure paradise for the crafter or wannabe. You can also enroll for classes. You'll find an outstanding regional wool market, featuring juried vendors displaying their wool fiber, yarns, and artistic creations. In other words, do not miss! This is one very family-friendly festival, and every year it just keeps getting better.

SUMMER INSTITUTES

Santa Fe

Santa Fe Photographic Workshops (505-983-1400; www.santafeworkshops.com; P.O. Box 9916, 50 Mt. Carmel Rd., Ste. F2, Santa Fe, NM 87504). Workshops in all aspects of photography, taught year-round and all over the world by photographers of national and international repute. Whether you want to learn photography, upgrade your skills, or specialize, you will find the serious yet collegial atmosphere here stimulating and your time will be well invested. Serious amateurs, take note!

Santa Fe School of Cooking (505-983-4511; www.santafeschoolofcooking .com; 116 W. San Francisco St., Santa Fe, NM 87501). In addition to classes on the traditional chile-flavored cuisine of New Mexico, this venerable cooking school can also show you how to prepare Spanish, vegetarian, Mexican, and contemporary southwestern dishes. You'll wow your family and dinner guests with your new skills.

Near Santa Fe

Ghost Ranch Education and Retreat Center (505-685-4333; www.ghostranch.org; HC 77 Box 11, Abiquiu, NM 87510). If you want to experience the magic of New Mexico and you are on a budget, it's a good bet you'll love Ghost Ranch. Here, you will find classes and seminars in photography, writing, pottery, silversmithing, watercolor, weaving, traditional arts such as natural indigo dyeing, history, spirituality, bodywork, renewable energy, health, and music year-round, with the biggest concentration of offerings during the summer months. Located in the heart of O'Keeffe's breathtaking red-rock country, rustic Ghost Ranch is a center of diversity. Visit the Web site for a downloadable catalog.

Taos

Taos Art School (575-758-0350; www.taosartschool.org). Located on "the Left Bank" of the Rio Grande, this two-decades-old art institute offers classes and workshops in painting, Navajo weaving, photography, and more, as well as tours of Chaco Canyon, Georgia O'Keeffe country, and just about any place in northern New Mexico worth exploring deeply.

THEATER

Santa Fe

Santa Fe Playhouse (505-988-4262; www.santafeplayhouse.org; 142 E. De Vargas St., Santa Fe, NM 87501; open year-round; prices vary, but tickets are usually quite reasonable). Founded in the 1920s, the Santa Fe Playhouse started as the Santa Fe Community Theater. It remains the longest-running theater group in

New Mexico, showcasing the work of dedicated amateurs. Today it seems very much at home in its own intimate adobe theater building in one of Santa Fe's oldest neighborhoods. A favorite each fall is the Fiesta Melodrama, staged the week of La Fiesta. (See "Seasonal Events," above.) One of the best-kept secrets that week is who among the city's prominent citizens will be skewered in this irreverent satire. The season includes a program of classic and contemporary works.

Taos

Taos Center for the Arts (575-758-2052; www.tcataos.org; 133 Paseo del Pueblo Norte, Taos, NM 87501). The Taos Center for the Arts has been in existence for more than 50 years and sponsors more than 50 performing arts events annually in the Taos Community Auditorium. At this cultural wellspring, find exciting dance, performance art, and all manner of well-executed entertainment designed to stimulate and uplift, usually at reasonable prices. Check out the packed schedule. In addition, Taos has added an evanescent, irregular and moveable small theater scene that can best be tracked down in the Tempo Magazine each Thursday. Outstanding here is Metta Theater, (575-758-1104; 147 Paseo del Pueblo Norte, Taos, NM 87501.)

5

Sacred Sites, Ancient Ruins, and Natural Wonders

GOD IS EVERYWHERE, BUT HIS ADDRESS IS IN ESPAÑOLA

NEW MEXICO IS HOME to a remarkable variety of spiritual paths. From Christian to Buddhist to Sikh, all have found the high mountains and desert expanses an inspiration to faith and practice. Contemporary spiritual seekers resonate with ancient Native American traditions, ongoing for thousands of years and still very much alive in New Mexico. The generations have imparted to the land itself a sense of the sacred, with the continuity of spiritual practice. Meditation, prayer, and song are performed in time with the cycles of the year and hours of the day. Here people of all faiths are inspired to solitary contemplation as well as participation in community gatherings.

New Mexico also has a tradition of pilgrimage. Each Holy Week, pilgrims may be seen walking the roads and highways to the Santuario de Chimayó, long considered a site of miraculous healing. Catholic roots go five centuries deep into the land.

Worship often extends outside the church or kiva into the plaza, the streets, and the homes of the community. Prayer is more often than not accompanied with feasting, music, and dance, considered vital elements of the ceremony. Gatherings, such as the Matachines Dances performed in the Hispanic villages as well as on the Indian pueblos, are often open to the public. Any slightly-more-than-casual observer will be struck not only with the depth of religious observance, involving the entire community, but also with the shared traditions, such as the mixtures of Catholic and Indian ceremony that occur here as well as throughout Mexico and Latin America. Such sharing is a natural evolution for cultures that have lived side by side for centuries.

LEFT: Sacred Taos Mountain as seen from the Martinez Hacienda

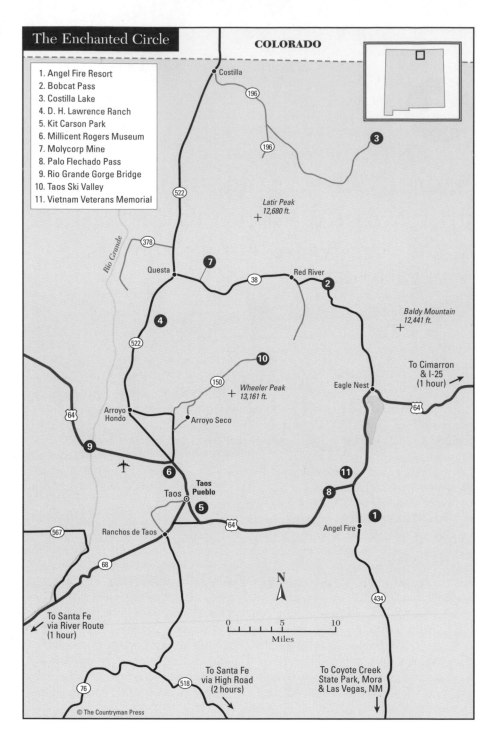

The Enchanted Circle

COLORADO

1. Angel Fire Resort
2. Bobcat Pass
3. Costilla Lake
4. D. H. Lawrence Ranch
5. Kit Carson Park
6. Millicent Rogers Museum
7. Molycorp Mine
8. Palo Flechado Pass
9. Rio Grande Gorge Bridge
10. Taos Ski Valley
11. Vietnam Veterans Memorial

Costilla

196

196

3

522

Rio Grande

378

*Latir Peak
12,680 ft.*

Questa

7

38

Red River

2

*Baldy Mountain
12,441 ft.*

4

522

10

150

*Wheeler Peak
13,161 ft.*

Eagle Nest

To Cimarron
& I-25
(1 hour)

64

64

Arroyo
Hondo

Arroyo Seco

9

6

Taos
Pueblo

Taos

5

11

8

1

567

64

Angel Fire

Ranchos de Taos

68

To Santa Fe
via River Route
(1 hour)

N

0   5   10
Miles

434

76

518

To Santa Fe
via High Road
(2 hours)

To Coyote Creek
State Park, Mora
& Las Vegas, NM

© The Countryman Press

But sacred sites in New Mexico encompass more than shrines and altars built by human hands. Many believe the ancient ruins that stand on this land occupy power or holy spots. Some of these ruins contain places that in the past were used for prayer and ritual. Many consider certain natural wonders to be their own personal power spots, reminders of the power of the Creator, where they are able to feel a connection with the Divine.

Whatever your own spiritual path, you need not travel very far in northern New Mexico to receive inspiration and revitalization. Because of the variety of spiritual paths that have found a home here, northern New Mexico also offers a spiritual "educational opportunity" not generally available elsewhere. Whatever sacred sites you choose to visit, you will be joined in spirit to the many others who have stood there before you.

Spiritual Explorations

Discovering the wonders of
Santa Fe and Taos

SACRED SITES

Santa Fe

Dar Al-Islam (505-685-4515; www .daralislam.org; off County Rd. 155 at Sign 42A, above Ghost Ranch; visitors are restricted: call for hours). Designed by Egyptian architect Hassan Fathy, reputed to be the world's foremost adobe architect, this imposing mosque is the center of a longstanding local Muslim community.

El Santuario de Chimayó (505-351-9961; www.holychimayo.us; 15 Santuario Drive, Chimayó, NM 87522; masses and visiting hours: Sun. Mass, noon; weekday Mass, Oct.–May 7 AM, June–Sept. 11 AM; open daily in summer 9–5, winter 9–4). This chapel is located about 25 miles northeast of Santa Fe on US 84/285 to Española; turn east on NM 76. Follow signs to Chimayó. The site of this chapel is believed to be a former healing place of Pueblo Indians. The church was built 1813–16 by Bernardo Abeyta and other residents of El Potrero. They later finished the adobe chapel honoring Nuestro Señor de Esquipulas. There are at least two versions of the legend of its origin: Don Bernardo Abeyta, while deathly ill, received a vision that beckoned him to a spot on the ground beneath the cottonwoods, where he was immediately cured. Or, in another variation of the story, he was saying his Friday evening prayers for healing when he saw a nearby illumination. At any rate, he built the chapel on

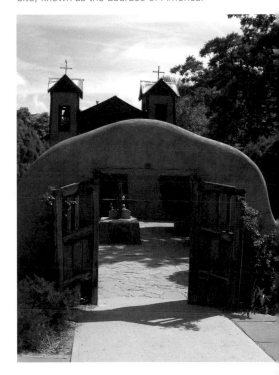

The Santuario de Chimayó is a pilgrimage site, known as the Lourdes of America.

that spot. For generations, Hispanic villagers in these remote mountains have attested to the miraculous healing powers of the "holy dirt" from a certain spot in the chapel floor. Testimonials and crutches lining the walls of the anteroom to the chapel give weight to the Santuario's reputation as the "Lourdes of America." Pilgrims bring prayers for healing to the Santuario all year long, but on Good Friday it is the destination of a pilgrimage when approximately 30,000 walk to Chimayó from all over the state to receive blessings. The twin-towered Santuario, a classic example of Spanish-Pueblo church architecture, is also a favorite subject of artists. At the time of this writing, a sanctuary inn where pilgrims may stay longer is under construction.

KSK Buddhist Center (505-471-5531; 505-471-5336 (KSK Noble Truth Bookstore); www.nobletruth.org; 3777 KSK Lane, Santa Fe, NM 87505: off Airport Road; open: Mon.–Fri. noon–6, weekends 10–6). Buddhist sitting meditations are held in this authentic Tibetan *stupa* (temple). This center of Tibetan Buddhism was founded by the Venerable Kalu Rinpoche in 1975. Its spire is visible as you drive down Airport Road. Visiting lamas and other teachers hold prayer and meditation services; they also give talks on Buddhist practices. The bookstore is a friendly, well-stocked place to find books by the Dalai Lama and other Buddhist thinkers. Resident Lama Karma Dorje leads sitting meditations. If you would like to visit the stupa at other times, please pick up the key at the bookstore. As of this writing, the KSK Center is in the process of constructing a pavilion for classes and other events.

The brothers at the Monastery of Christ in the Desert plant hops for Monk's Ale.

Monastery of Christ in the Desert (801-545-8567; cidguestmaster @christdesert.org; www.christdesert .org; P.O. Box 270, Abiquiu, NM 87510; 75 miles north of Santa Fe on US 84/285, go west on US 84 past Ghost Ranch Visitors Center, turn left on Forest Service Rd. 151; Sun. Mass, 9:15 AM, open to all; gift shop and bookstore open daily). A 13-mile winding dirt road takes you to the monastery grounds with its glorious rock-and-adobe church. This remote Benedictine monastery built along the Chama River was designed by Japanese architect George Nikashama. Visits give guests the opportunity to share in the life of this 40-member Benedictine order with the key elements of love, prayer, reading, study, silence, and manual labor. To reserve guest rooms for silent retreats, write the guest master (by postal mail or e-mail) well in advance, especially for Christmas and other Catholic holidays.

Mountain Cloud Zen Center (505-988-4396; www.mountaincloud.org; 7241 Old Santa Fe Trail, 1 mile south of intersection with Zia Rd., across from electric substation). This Zen center was founded in 1981 by students of Philip Kapleau's Rochester Zen Center. Formal sitting meditations in the Rinzai/Soto tradition are offered early each morning.

Sikh Dharma of New Mexico (505-753-6341; www.espanolaashram.com; 1 West Sombrillo Road, Española, NM 87532). Hacienda de Guru Ram Das, named for the builder of the Sikh's Golden Temple in India, is the location of this spiritual center, which is open to visitors. The annual Peace Prayer Day, which begins a weeklong celebration, is held on the Saturday before summer solstice. A recent theme was "Activating Compassion through Sacred Sound." Certain practices, yoga, classes, and meals are open to the public. To get to Sikh Dharma, take US 84/285 north from Santa Fe 26 miles. Before Española, go right on NM 106 at the stoplight, then take the first right onto Sombrillo. Go up and over hill. Look for the gold dome of the gurdwara (temple) on the left; parking lot is on west side of street.

Upaya Zen Center (505-986-8518; www.upaya.org; 1404 Cerro Gordo Rd., Santa Fe, NM 87501). A Buddhist retreat and learning center, Upaya offers weekday Zen meditation throughout the day beginning at 6 AM Wed.–Fri. and 7 AM every other day, with the last meditation beginning at 5:30 PM daily. On Wednesday, dharma talks by Joan Halifax Roshi, founder and head teacher, as well as other practitioners are included. Please call for a tour of the zendo or information on personal retreats. Please write for a schedule of Upaya courses on subjects such as healing, dreams, the neuroscience of meditation, and death and dying.

Taos

Lama Foundation (575-586-1269; info@lamafoundation.org; www.lamafoundation .org; Box 240, San Cristobal, NM 87564; weekdays, 10 AM–noon; please write or call for calendar of summer events). Founded in 1967, the Lama Foundation has endured beyond the "be here now" revelations of the 1960s to become an ecumenical spiritual center where teachers of many paths offer workshops. Since the Hondo Fire swept through the Ponderosa pines on Lama Mountain in 1996, Lama has lengthened its offerings of workshops on permaculture, creativity, sustainable agriculture, gender, and architecture as well. All are invited to share a vegetarian meal and participate in Dances of Universal Peace on visitors days, which occur on scheduled Sundays during the summer season. The mountain, long reputed to be a link on the Kiowa Peace Path, where all could pass freely and safely, is recovering from the fire, with meadows of wildflowers and stands of aspen shaping a new ecology. The name *Lama* comes from *la lama*, meaning "mud." A key Lama offering is the opportunity to make a solo self-sufficient retreat, or hermitage, in a secluded cabin on the mountain.

Neem Karoli Baba Ashram (575-751-4080; www.nkbashram.org; P.O. Box 1710, Taos, NM 87571; 416 Geronimo Lane, Taos, NM 87571; open daily 7 AM–9 PM, in winter 7 AM–8 PM; chanting Tues. 7 PM; Sun. 11 AM; morning and evening devotions). Inspired by the teachings of the Indian guru Neem Karoli Baba and his American disciple, Ram Dass (Richard Alpert), this ashram offers a quiet meditation room with an impressive statue of Hanuman, the monkey-faced Hindu god of service. The annual cycle of celebrations culminates with Majaraj-ji's Bhandara

Meditation circle in the Dome at the Lama Foundation

on the weekend in Sept. closest to the full moon. Chanting begins Sat. at 4 AM; that afternoon, around 4 PM, a vegetarian Indian feast is served to all. The ashram continues to evolve and expand, with the addition of a permaculture farm and more faciities.

Montefiore Cemetery (www.nmjewishhistory.org). This cemetery is located about 65 miles north of Santa Fe: Take I-25 to second Las Vegas exit. Go left to large cemetery. Jewish section is in back on right. In the old Jewish cemetery in Las Vegas, New Mexico, it is possible to be touched by the lives of Jewish pioneers of the West. You can also begin to get a sense of the strength of the Jewish merchant-rancher community instrumental in the development of the life of culture and commerce in northern New Mexico during the late 19th and early 20th centuries. The New Mexico Jewish Historical Society holds an annual cemetery-cleaning celebration. People of all ages tend the graves, and a picnic lunch is served.

For those who would like to learn more about Jewish pioneer life, contact the New Mexico Jewish Historical Society at 505-348-4471 or 5520 Wyoming Boulevard NE, Albuquerque, NM 87109, about their archive located at the State Road Center and Archives (at the intersection of Cerrillos Rd. and Camino Carlos Rey in Santa Fe).

ANCIENT RUINS

Bandelier National Monument (505-672-3861 ext. 517; www.nps.gov; 46 miles west of Santa Fe: take US 285 north to Pojoaque, west on NM 502, south on NM 4; open daily year-round, summer 8–6, winter 8–4:30; closed Christmas and New

Winter residents of Bandelier National Monument.

Year's; ruins trails open dawn–dusk; $12 per car, campsites $35 per night; gift shop, snack bar. (Since the 2011 Las Conchas Fire, access is by shuttle only from several signed access points along NM 4.) Once a lush little Shangri-la tucked in a deep canyon on the Pajarito (pa-ha-REE-toe) Plateau was home to the ancestors of some Pueblo tribes between A.D. 1100 and 1550. The residents irrigated their corn, beans, and squash with water from Frijoles (free-HOLE-ace) Creek and made their homes from the plentiful volcanic rock. Following the devastating La Conchas fire of 2011, certain trails as well as the visitors center have been reopened. You can visit cliff dwellings and view the village ruins and ceremonial kivas. The loop trail of the main Frijoles Canyon ruins takes about an hour. More agile visitors can climb ladders, as the residents once did, to enter Bandelier's restored dwellings—including a spectacular ceremonial cave with kiva. Ancestral Pueblo petroglyphs are visible on many trails. In summer, visitors can take ranger-led tours of the ruins after dark on special night walks.

Now the Newman Center on the campus of New Mexico Highlands University, this was originally the first synagogue in New Mexico: Temple Montefiore.

Bandelier's 33,000 acres are federally designated wilderness, with 70 miles of maintained trails that go up onto mesas, down into volcanic canyons, and through high-altitude pine forests. Those in good physical condition can take day hikes to more remote ruins. The visitors center and Frijoles Canyon ruins tend to be crowded, but solitude can be yours if you're willing to walk a bit. (See also "Hiking and Climbing" in chapter 7, *Recreation*.) Call for current conditions of backcountry trails. No pets on trails.

Pecos National Historical Park (505-757-7200; www.nps.gov/peco/index.htm; 1 Peach Tree Lane, Pecos, NM, 28 miles southeast of Santa Fe, off I-25; Open daily 8–4:30, Memorial Day–Labor Day 8–6; closed Christmas; $3 per person, free on certain holidays; bookstore). In 1540, before the Spaniards arrived, Pecos was a thriving Pueblo Indian village with apartment-like houses four or five stories high. In their green river valley, the Pecos people traded with other Pueblo villages and the Plains Indians to the east. Coronado's men visited in 1541, and by the early 1620s, the Franciscans had arrived to build a mission and convert the Indians to the Spanish way of life. The Franciscans also enlisted the Indians to help build a church, 150 feet from altar to entrance, with walls 22 feet thick in places. The foundations can still be seen, but the church and the Franciscans' efforts were destroyed in the Pueblo Revolt of 1680 (see chapter 1, *History*). A smaller church built atop the ruins in 1717 also lies in ruins.

What happened to the thriving village? Historians believe Pecos was decimated by European diseases and Comanche raids in the 17th century. The last residents left in 1838 to live with relatives at Jemez Pueblo, across the Rio Grande Valley. Today a 1.25-mile trail on gentle terrain rings the mission and pueblo ruins and includes a ceremonial kiva playing recorded Indian chants.

Signs of the old days in Pecos

A.D. 1200, this thriving culture suddenly faded away. The inhabitants are believed to be the ancestors of today's Pueblo people.

The ruins were known to Spaniards and Indians in the region at least as far back as 1840, and the first archaeological excavations were started in 1896. Today, you can spend a couple of days or more exploring the ruins along the Chaco Wash. There are even more ruins atop the mesas. Rangers are available for guided walks, and the visitors center offers a good introduction with films and displays. The ruins are in surprisingly good condition, so it's easy to imagine Chaco Canyon alive again with the laughter of children and the sounds of men and women at work in the courtyards and fields.

Note: Consult a good map before setting out, and call the park to check on road conditions, since roads can become impassable during rain or snow. Also, there's no lodging, gasoline, or food at the park; the nearest town, Bloomfield, is 60 miles away. Staples are available on weekdays at Blanco Trading Post or convenience stores on US 550. Campsites tend to fill quickly on weekends and most days during summer. The 9-mile auto tour is a good way to get an overview of the park.

NATURAL WONDERS

Rio Grande Gorge Bridge. At the intersection of NM 68 and NM 150 (Taos Ski Valley Rd.), go left 7 miles on US 64. This bridge, completed in 1965, the nation's second highest span, soars 2,000 feet from rim to rim and rests 650 feet above the Rio Grande. The view from here of the river swirling through basalt boulders below, plus the panorama of the winding Rio Grande Gorge—known as America's first preserved Wild and Scenic River—the Taos Plateau, and the Sangre de Cristo

Hiking among the hoodoos at Kasha-Katuwe Tent Rocks National Monument.

Puye Cliff Dwellings (505-753-7326; www.puyecliffs.com; NM 30 and Santa Clara Canyon Road; call for directions and hours; $5 per adult). About 40 miles northwest of Santa Fe, near Española, the Puye Cliffs are home to Santa Clara Pueblo. The tribe welcomes visitors, who can walk to the top of a mesa where a village once stood and take in the magnificent views, although access has been somewhat limited due to the Las Conchas fire of 2012, which destroyed much of the Pueblo. Here you will find cliff dwellings dating from the 1200s. This ancient pueblo, built 1450 to 1475, was once the center of numerous villages on the Pajarito Plateau. Many of the designs found on pottery here focus on a plumed serpent figure who guarded the springs, which provided life-giving water. The tourism office of Santa Clara Pueblo offers tours here, which is the only and best way to see the site. Ask for information at the gas station at the intersection above.

Tsankawi Ruin Trail (505-672-3861; open daily; closed Christmas and New Year's Day; free). To get to the trail, go about 30 miles west of Santa Fe on US 84/285 to NM 502, then get on NM 4 on the way to Bandelier, immediately south of White Rock. Look for sign and gate on the west side of NM 4, just south of Y-shaped stoplight intersection of east Jemez Rd. An easy walk to unexcavated ruins, a visit to Tsankawi (Sank-ah-WEEa) section of Bandelier National Monument offers a spectacular panoramic view across the Rio Grande Valley to Santa Fe and the Sangre de Cristo Mountains. Tsankawi is a simplifcation of the Tewa Indian name *saekewikwaje onwikege*, which means "village between two canyons at the clump of sharp, round cactus." The enclave protects an important Rio Grande ruin of the Anasazi—a prehistoric Puebloan people. Take the 1.5-mile loop trail that begins at the parking area along NM 4. Descendants of the Chaco Canyon Ancestral Pueblo people lived here about A.D. 1300–1580. Faint petroglyphs and hand- and toeholds of the original Tewa-speaking dwellers are visible along the climb, aided in places by ladders. Please do not disturb the shards of black-on-cream pottery lying on the ground.

Outside the Area

Chaco Culture National Historical Park (505-786-7014; www.nps.gov/chcu; open daily dawn–dusk; closed Christmas; visitors center open 8–5; $4 per individual, $8 per vehicle; campsites $10 per night, no hookups, no showers).

To get to this historical park, go 60 miles south of Bloomfield in northwest New Mexico, via CR 7900 (approximately 3 miles east of Nageezi Trading Post). From NM 57, go 21 miles north on unpaved road. All roads into the park are unpaved for the final 20–26 miles. Known as the Stonehenge of the West, Chaco is believed by many to be one of the great "power spots" on the globe. It is one of three UN World Heritage Sites in New Mexico. Humans have inhabited the area for 6,000 or more years. About A.D. 900 the Anasazi (now referred to as Ancestral Puebloan) culture began to flower, and Chaco Canyon was its crowning achievement: 6 large pueblos and as many as 75 smaller towns, all built in a relatively short time. The largest, Pueblo Bonito, was a community of four-story masonry apartment buildings with solar orientation, hundreds of rooms, and dozens of kivas. The Chacoan people farmed with an elaborate irrigation and terracing system and created stunning pottery and turquoise jewelry. They built an astonishing 400 miles of arrow-straight roads connecting the canyon with outlying settlements, and they traded with the people of Mesoamerica. Then, sometime around

Bandelier's 33,000 acres are federally designated wilderness, with 70 miles of maintained trails that go up onto mesas, down into volcanic canyons, and through high-altitude pine forests. Those in good physical condition can take day hikes to more remote ruins. The visitors center and Frijoles Canyon ruins tend to be crowded, but solitude can be yours if you're willing to walk a bit. (See also "Hiking and Climbing" in chapter 7, *Recreation*.) Call for current conditions of backcountry trails. No pets on trails.

Pecos National Historical Park (505-757-7200; www.nps.gov/peco/index.htm; 1 Peach Tree Lane, Pecos, NM, 28 miles southeast of Santa Fe, off I-25; Open daily 8–4:30, Memorial Day–Labor Day 8–6; closed Christmas; $3 per person, free on certain holidays; bookstore). In 1540, before the Spaniards arrived, Pecos was a thriving Pueblo Indian village with apartment-like houses four or five stories high. In their green river valley, the Pecos people traded with other Pueblo villages and the Plains Indians to the east. Coronado's men visited in 1541, and by the early 1620s, the Franciscans had arrived to build a mission and convert the Indians to the Spanish way of life. The Franciscans also enlisted the Indians to help build a church, 150 feet from altar to entrance, with walls 22 feet thick in places. The foundations can still be seen, but the church and the Franciscans' efforts were destroyed in the Pueblo Revolt of 1680 (see chapter 1, *History*). A smaller church built atop the ruins in 1717 also lies in ruins.

What happened to the thriving village? Historians believe Pecos was decimated by European diseases and Comanche raids in the 17th century. The last residents left in 1838 to live with relatives at Jemez Pueblo, across the Rio Grande Valley. Today a 1.25-mile trail on gentle terrain rings the mission and pueblo ruins and includes a ceremonial kiva playing recorded Indian chants.

Signs of the old days in Pecos

Winter residents of Bandelier National Monument.

Year's; ruins trails open dawn–dusk; $12 per car, campsites $35 per night; gift shop, snack bar. (Since the 2011 Las Conchas Fire, access is by shuttle only from several signed access points along NM 4.) Once a lush little Shangri-la tucked in a deep canyon on the Pajarito (pa-ha-REE-toe) Plateau was home to the ancestors of some Pueblo tribes between A.D. 1100 and 1550. The residents irrigated their corn, beans, and squash with water from Frijoles (free-HOLE-ace) Creek and made their homes from the plentiful volcanic rock. Following the devastating La Conchas fire of 2011, certain trails as well as the visitors center have been reopened. You can visit cliff dwellings and view the village ruins and ceremonial kivas. The loop trail of the main Frijoles Canyon ruins takes about an hour. More agile visitors can climb ladders, as the residents once did, to enter Bandelier's restored dwellings—including a spectacular ceremonial cave with kiva. Ancestral Pueblo petroglyphs are visible on many trails. In summer, visitors can take ranger-led tours of the ruins after dark on special night walks.

Now the Newman Center on the campus of New Mexico Highlands University, this was originally the first synagogue in New Mexico: Temple Montefiore.

Mountains, is a New Mexico must-see. From this height, river rafters are only tiny specks on the winding river. The gorge itself contains the Taos Box, a favorite whitewater run. Hang on to your hat! This is a mighty windy spot.

Kasha-Katuwe Tent Rocks National Monument (505-954-2000; www.blm .gov/nm/st/en/prog/recreation/rio_puerco/kasha_katuwe_tent_rocks.html; $5 per car; dogs not allowed). About 40 miles southwest of Santa Fe, just northwest of Cochiti Pueblo. Take I-25 south to Cochiti exit. This is the site of a fascinating miniature canyon. Soft, compressed volcanic rock has eroded into tent-shaped formations, many with a harder material balanced on top. Smaller bases supporting a larger boulder are called hoodoos. A favorite hiking and camping spot among locals, believed by many to be a very spiritual place.

Valles Caldera National Preserve (505-661-3333; www.vallescaldera.gov; 18161 NM 4, Jemez Springs, NM 87025). About 40 miles northwest of Santa Fe. Continue on NM 4 past Bandelier about 15 miles. This vast, astonishing green basin—all that remains of what was once considered the world's largest volcano— is an 89,000-acre caldera, or collapsed volcano, a basin formed during Pleistocene volcanic activity. Located on a 142-year-old land grant named Baca Location No. 1, also called Valle Grande or Baca Location, it is home to a herd of 45,000 elk. It is said that lava from the explosion that formed the caldera has been found as far away as Kansas. Since the area was named one of the country's newest national monuments, hiking, cross-country skiing, sleigh rides, fly-fishing, wildlife viewing, horseback riding, and hunting have become available for various fees on a reservations-only basis. Various use fees are in effect for recreational activities.

6

Restaurants and Food Purveyors
PLEASING THE PALATE

THE SANTA FE–TAOS AREA offers more than 300 restaurants serving everything from New Mexican, American, and Continental to French, Chinese, Japanese, and East Indian cuisine. In addition, scores of food purveyors offer unique drinks, pastries, baked goods, candies, and delicacies. The combination is enough to satisfy the most far-ranging or curious appetite.

We searched for a variety of places and price ranges—everything from Santa Fe's internationally acclaimed gourmet dining spots to corner taco stands. We looked for unique local dining experiences and so avoided fast-food and chain restaurants. Fortunately, we were free to write honest reviews, since we were in no way beholden to these establishments. The results, we are confident, will steer you to the best dining the area has to offer. We have attempted to provide a range of dining opportunities, from the casual pizza or sandwich to the world-famous new southwestern cuisine that has its home here. The combination of fresh local ingredients—inspired by growers' markets—and some of the most creative and well-traveled chefs in the world make this an exciting dining scene. Exploring the cuisine is one of the most memorable aspects of a visit here.

A note to smokers: Smoking is not allowed in Santa Fe or Taos restaurants. Some places permit smoking on the patio, and certainly some establishments that qualify more as bars than restaurants permit smoking. A few have separate smoking rooms.

One thing you'll find on your gastronomic travels in Santa Fe and Taos is a plethora of New Mexican restaurants. Remember: New Mexican cooking—particularly northern New Mexican cooking—is not Mexican or Tex-Mex; it's a

LEFT: Love a good fry bread? Find fabulous just-made Indian tacos at local arts festivals like the annual Dixon Studio Tour.

I think I like this one best!

unique mix of Spanish, Mexican, Pueblo Indian, and local cuisine that includes many familiar foods like burritos, enchiladas, and tacos, as well as less familiar foods such as *flautas, sopaipillas*, and *chicharrones*. This cuisine has its roots in the native foods of corn, chile, beans, and squash.

The most important single ingredient in northern New Mexican cuisine is chile, which should not be confused with chili, the tomato-sauce-based concoctions found in Texas, Ohio, and other parts of the country. New Mexican chile sauces have little or no tomato. They're flavorful, spicy, sometimes hot sauces made with a mix of chile peppers, garlic, oregano, and cumin, and they're served with almost every meal. Chile can be red or green, hot or mild, and there's no telling by color which is which. So when your waiter says, "Red or green?"—a query that happens to be the official state question—don't be afraid to ask which is hotter. If you say Christmas, you'll get some of both.

While the best-known Santa Fe restaurants may carry a well-earned reputation for being expensive, if you know where to go and follow our suggestions as well as your own traveler's instincts, you should be able to dine surprisingly well, even on a budget. We'll point you to the locals' favorites where both excellent food and fine service can be had for a modest price.

Before you leap into this diverse restaurant scene, we suggest you peruse the two restaurant charts in the appendix. One lists restaurants according to cuisine, the other according to price. The restaurants listed in this book are given a price code based on the average cost of a single meal including appetizer, entrée, dessert, tax, and tip, but not including alcoholic beverages.

the city limits of Santa Fe is listed under "Restaurants Near Santa Fe." Similarly, any establishment outside Taos town limits appears under "Restaurants Near Taos."

Dining Price Codes		*Key*	
Inexpensive	Up to $15	B	breakfast
Moderate	$15–30	L	lunch
Expensive	$30–75	D	dinner
Very Expensive	$75 or more	SB	Sunday brunch
		SSB	Saturday and Sunday brunch

Local Flavors
Taste of Santa Fe

Bumble Bee's Baja Grill (505-820-2862; 301 Jefferson St., Santa Fe, NM 87501; closed Thanksgiving, Christmas; inexpensive; Baja style; L, D; partial handicapped access; no reservations). Best fish tacos! The fresh salads, salsas, and homemade chips, Baja-style grilled fish and shrimp, and soft corn tacos—all prepared for maximum flavor and health consciousness, dished up at bargain prices—have made Bumble Bee's popular with Santa Fe diners and families. One burrito is big enough to share. Savory marinated roast chicken, served with black beans and cilantro-lime rice, is delectable. Phone your order in ahead and drive through for zero wait time.

Café Pasqual (505-983-9340; 121 Don Gaspar Ave., Santa Fe, NM 87501; closed Thanksgiving, Christmas; moderate–expensive; New Mexican, new southwestern cuisine; B, L, D; partial handicapped access; reservations strongly recommended for dinner; special features: community table, T-shirts, cookbooks). There's good reason for the lines down Water Street waiting to get into this legendary

Santa Fe eatery, much as there's ample reason why Café Pasqual's consistently makes lists of "best places to have breakfast in the U.S." That famous huge, delicious, Mexican-flavored breakfast is served all day, and no visit to Santa Fe is complete without it. Carefully prepared food; consistency; friendly service (once you get in); a bustling atmosphere with colorful murals, chile *ristras*, and bright Mexican banners make this cozy café memorable. To avoid the crowd, arrive in the off-hours or sit at the congenial community table.

Café Pasqual's is the place for a legendary breakfast in Santa Fe or a Meso-American-inspired dinner.

For breakfast, you'll *ooh* and *aah* over the Genovese omelet with sun-dried tomatoes and pine nuts. For lunch, savor the tangy taste of a zesty shrimp cocktail, a heavenly grilled salmon burrito, or a healthful Yucatán free-range chicken breast salad. You can slice dinner costs with half orders and still come away satisfied. And you'll drool over the rich assortment of desserts and pastries. (Hint: Try the toasted piñon ice cream with caramel sauce.) Owner Kathy Kagel is almost as well known for organizing to feed the hungry in northern New Mexico as she is as a chef!

The Compound (505-982-4353; 653 Canyon Rd., Santa Fe, NM 87501; closed major holidays; very expensive; Continental; no handicapped access; nonsmoking section; reservations strongly recommended; special features: full bar, patio). Chef-owner Mark Kiffin has racked up awards aplenty, including a recent James Beard honor. The Alexander Girard–designed white interior is the epitome of chic yet minimal Santa Fe style—although gentlemen are no longer required to wear ties as in days of yore. The Compound has perfected the art of welcoming, professional service. Here we have the concept of food as entertainment on a grand scale: Santa Fe's beautiful people, dressed to the nines, plus fresh ingredients from all over the world shipped overnight to be shaped by the chef's imagination. The menu changes seasonally. You can order sweetbreads and foie gras, blue-corn-dusted softshell crabs, slow-baked salmon, or grilled lamb rib eye, and be sure to leave room for the liquid chocolate cake. The Compound makes an unforgettable dining experience and ought to be on any visitor's "special splurge" list. A good place to propose.

Cowgirl Hall of Fame Bar-B-Q (505-982-2565; 319 S. Guadalupe St., Santa Fe, NM 87501; closed Thanksgiving, Christmas; moderate; barbecue, western; partial handicapped access; reservations recommended for dinner; special features: patio, fireplaces, takeout). The Cowgirl is known as a watering hole and place to meet as much as a restaurant. Beginnings include appetizers such as nachos, quesadillas, soups, and chile. Their forte is the mesquite-smoked barbecue, but you'll find burgers and fish platters; smoked chicken, black bean, and blue corn enchiladas; and good old T-bone steaks. Sprinkled throughout are choice vegetarian dishes, such as the vegetarian chile and butternut casserole. An unusual item on any menu is collard greens, and this dish is worth ordering at the Cowgirl. If you're particular about spicy food, ask. Finish up with chocolate espresso mud pie or peach cobbler, or, for laughs, order the Baked Potato, actually a chocolate sundae disguised as a spud, which kids of all ages adore. The place is usually jumping, frequented by a casual crowd, and on weekend nights, live music plays in the full bar. The spurs, saddles, and photographs of Prairie Rose, Faye Blessing, and other rodeo cowgirls on their rearing horses make a fine memorabilia collection. The comfortable bar is a magnet for an interesting group, and there are plenty of no-cover events. The occasional Sat. afternoon free bluegrass jam is a blast and draws some of NM's best-known musicians off duty.

Coyote Cafe (505-983-1615; 132 W. Water St., Santa Fe, NM 87501; open daily; very expensive; new southwestern; L [summer weekends], D; full handicapped access; smoking in bar only. reservations strongly recommended; special features: patio din-

Mojitos, anyone? It's Coyote Cafe's rooftop cantina for chips and salsa or a full menu of Mexican fare during the warm season.

ing). Santa Fe's Coyote Cafe is restaurateuring on a grand scale. Eric de Stefano, former chef at Geronimo, has taken over from virtuoso restaurateur Mark Miller. Each dish is an inspired blend of flavorful ingredients, usually with a spicy edge, and the results are some of the most creative food around.

In warm weather, the lighthearted rooftop patio serves delicious lower-priced fare, from satisfying enchiladas to an ample, savory Cuban sandwich; service is also available at the Coyote's main bar. While you're there, be sure to try a Chimayó cocktail, a wonderful concoction made with apple juice, tequila, and Cointreau. You're likely to find me there on a July afternoon. The perfect place to socialize. Come by and say hi!

El Farol Restaurant and Lounge (505-983-9912; 808 Canyon Rd., Santa Fe, NM 87501; closed major holidays; expensive; Spanish tapas; L, D; no handicapped access; reservations recommended; special features: patio dining, live music). The Santa Fe landmark bills itself as the city's oldest restaurant and cantina, and indeed, it dates from 1835 when canyon residents stopped by for a haircut and refreshments. El Farol taught Santa Fe to eat tapas and not a little about flamenco. The menu includes tapas *frias* (marinated white Spanish anchovies and chilled mussels in sherry vinaigrette) and tapas *calientes* (calamari, grilled baby chorizo with mashed potatoes, and pork tenderloin with figs and port). Or start with a soup like posole clam

.5 Mile

chowder and go on to an entrée such as herb-crusted halibut with Pernod saffron cream, the house special of paella Valencia, or grilled beef tenderloin fillet with portobello mushroom and asparagus. End with Spanish cheeses of Manchego and Cabrales. The flan is laced with lemon, rosemary, and caramel, and the steamed chocolate pudding is deliciously not-too-sweet. The wine list features one of the most extensive inventories of Spanish wines in New Mexico. Enjoy the Alfred Morang murals and the thick adobe walls that have welcomed prophets, poets, and punks. Parking can be challenging—try the city lot across the street. With tango, salsa, and Latin music, there's plenty of live song and dance here, drawing in the city's top performers, many with international reputations. Performances are held almost nightly, plus special flamenco-dinner shows.

French Pastry Shop (505-983-6697; La Fonda Hotel, 100 E. San Francisco St., Santa Fe, NM 87501; closed Christmas; inexpensive–moderate; French; B, L; partial handicapped access [enter from La Fonda Hotel]; no reservations; no credit cards). Chocolate éclairs, croissants, palmiers, napoleons, café au lait, espresso, fresh fruit tarts, chocolate mousse, dessert crêpes, fresh strawberries with crème Chantilly . . . are you drooling yet? This little shop of gastronomic delights has provided the Santa Fe community with authentic French cuisine since 1974, both for café au lait with pastry and for light lunch. A sign says ALL PASTRIES ARE MADE WITH PURE BUTTER AND ARE MADE FRESH DAILY. Famous, too, for breads baked in whimsical animal designs—you can order your own. The reasonably priced menu includes ratatouille, torte Milanaise, and French onion soup as well as quiche Lorraine. The perfect spot for a cozy cup of cocoa on a wintry afternoon. Bon appétit! The restaurant's iconic Santa Fe style was created by Mary Elizabeth Jane Colter, designer for the Fred Harvey Co.

Geronimo (505-982-1500; 724 Canyon Rd., Santa Fe, NM 87501; closed Mon. lunch; very expensive; contemporary Southwest; L, D, SB; partial handicapped access; reservations recommended; special features: fireplace, courtyard). Geronimo has been drawing raves since it opened in 1991. Housed in one of the city's finest old adobes, it's airy and elegant in drop-dead-gorgeous minimalist Santa Fe style, and the food is over-the-top spectacular. The menu consists of American staples updated with southwestern and other ethnic ingredients. Start with roast lobster bisque with red pepper crab cake, sautéed quail breast with Iroquois corn polenta cakes, or seared French foie gras, and go on from there to mesquite-grilled salmon with Meyer lemon and spinach ravioli or peppery elk tenderloin with applewood-smoked bacon.

To enjoy Geronimo without breaking your budget, try lunch. Desserts vary daily, and the entire menu changes at least once a season. For cool evenings, try the intimate bar with kiva fireplace and brass-topped tables.

Guadalupe Cafe (505-982-9762; 422 Old Santa Fe Trail, Santa Fe, NM 87501; closed Mon.; moderate; New Mexican; B, L, D, SB; full handicapped access; reservations for parties of 6 or more; special features: fireplaces, patio). If you're looking for authentic New Mexican cuisine, you'll want to get here early to avoid the long line of locals, including state legislators from the nearby Roundhouse, who appreciate hearty, well-prepared New Mexican classics. As the menu warns, the chile

.Smile

served in this cozy adobe is the real deal. And the freshly prepared enchiladas, burritos, and *chalupas* never fail to please. What they don't warn you about is the portions big enough to share. Those with more tender palates can enjoy daily specials and fish and chicken entrées, accompanied by garlic mashed potatoes and a satisfying corn pudding, or the monster salads. In winter the kiva fireplaces add a warmly romantic note; by summer the crowds move to the patio. The cinnamon rolls big as pie plates are quite possibly the best on the planet. Reasonable prices and accommodating service round out the experience; you'll probably want to stop by more than once. Do make reservations, though.

Il Piatto Italian Farmhouse Kitchen (505-984-1091; 95 W. Marcy St., Santa Fe, NM 87501; open daily; moderate–expensive; innovative Italian; L, D; full handicapped access; reservations recommended; special features: patio dining, take-out). Reinventing itself as an Italian farmhouse hasn't hurt Il Piatto a bit. Come here for the green-lipped mussels baked in garlic aioli, or the creamy wild mushroom risotto. The antipasto makes an excellent start to a meal. Small, unpretentious, with superb food, Il Piatto features fresh soups and crisp salads, a variety of tasty antipasti and pastas, traditional Italian specials such as chicken cacciatore, and grilled selections, all with homemade pasta. But the pasta dishes with delectable sauces are the real treat. The chef shops for seasonal local produce at the farmers' market and isn't shy about making seasonal menu changes. Homemade desserts include such delectables as tiramisu (sponge cake soaked in coffee liqueur) and baked chocolate mousse with blackberries. There's also a moderately priced wine list and a selection of

dessert wines and port. On warm days you can dine on the little streetside patio, and in the evening, Il Piatto creates a romantic mood with music and candlelight. Chef Matt Yohalem goes all out for his customers. The three-course prix fixe menu allows all kinds of flexibility in ordering. Special late afternoon bar menu with wine bargains, and later night hours add to the appeal. Can you tell I adore this place? Love to celebrate my birthday with those homemade pumpkin ravioli in sage cream sauce.

Il Vicino (505-986-8700; 321 W. San Francisco St., Santa Fe, NM 87501; closed major holidays; inexpensive; Italian; L, D; full handicapped access; no reservations; special features: patio). If you're downtown, it's close to midnight, and you're craving made-to-order wood-oven pizza and a growler of award-winning microbrewed beer, hurry on over to Il Vicino. Order take-out or dine in and enjoy the big salads, satisfying pizzas, calzone, and lasagna. Panini sandwiches are filled with roast chicken and red peppers or turkey and mozzarella; or you might sample the more exotic variations such as panino di Bosco, with portobello mushroom, red peppers, spinach, caramelized onion, provolone, and goat cheese. For dessert, there's cannoli and the wildly rich flourless chocolate cake. Lines form quickly here, especially before shows at the Lensic Performing Arts Center just down the block.

India Palace (505-986-5859; 227 Don Gaspar Ave., Santa Fe, NM 87501; open daily; inexpensive–moderate; East Indian; L, D; partial handicapped access; no smoking; reservations recommended for dinner; special features: patio dining, take-out, lunch buffet, Indian art). The India Palace offers the exquisite and complex tastes of the Indian subcontinent in an

.9 mile

intimate and luxurious setting with pink linen. A fountain plays and statues of gods smile serenely as diners sample delicacies from all regions of India.

Appetizers include the crisp fried patties called samosas and many Indian breads, from leavened naan to *paratha* stuffed with spinach, all baked fresh to order. Tandoori specialties include several kinds of chicken and lamb. Curries abound and can be prepared mild enough for any taste. There are also the vegetarian dishes for which India is famous, from creamed lentil dal to *bhindi masala*, or spiced okra. Lunch is the best time to go, when you can sample their reasonably priced buffet to your heart's content. The buffet provides a cross section of the menu—beautifully presented and a great bargain feast. You'll want a siesta afterward.

Jinja Asia Café (505-982-4321; 510 Guadalupe St., North DeVargas Center, Santa Fe, NM 87571; open daily; moderate; Asian; L, D; partial handicapped access; no reservations). With an emphasis on wraps, noodles, and pot stickers, Jinja creatively blends the flavors of Vietnamese, Thai, and Japanese cuisine and serves them up in dark wood surroundings with a luxurious feel and prices that won't devastate your wallet. Go for a full meal or an appetizer at the exotic bar. When the need for a noodle dish spiced with ginger or lemongrass strikes, this is the place. Wait: Is that Gene Hackman at the bar? He owns the place, after all.

La Plazuela Restaurant (505-982-5511; La Fonda Hotel, 100 E. San Francisco St., Santa Fe, NM 87501; open daily; moderate–expensive; Spanish, Mexican, New Mexican, Continental; B, L, D; full handicapped access; reservations recommended for dinner; special features: covered patio, hand-painted windows, hand-carved wood furniture, stone floor). The central courtyard of the landmark La Fonda Hotel was once a patio open to the sky. Now enclosed, the restaurant retains the charm of outdoor dining as diners sit beneath huge potted trees basking in filtered sun through the skylight. Color and light are everywhere— brightly painted panes of glass run from floor to ceiling, gaily covered with designs of birds and flowers by local artist Ernesto Martinez, who also created the hotel's hallway decorations, murals, and painted ballroom. The menu is known for its traditional northern New Mexico specialties, including a combination plate with tamales, cheese enchilada, and green chile relleno. The rellenos de La Fonda are homemade, served with posole and fluffy *sopaipillas*. Lamb, cedar-planked salmon, and steak are on the menu as well.

Chef Lane Warner's signature dishes include chipotle-glazed filet mignon and chicken breasts marinated in tequila and lime. Desserts, made on the premises, include Mexican chocolate streusel, the perennial favorite— a brownie served with homemade banana ice cream. Ice cream flavors change daily and may include everything from vanilla to prickly pear. The black bean soup is almost too beautiful to eat. Almost but not quite. Order the guacamole made tableside, and you may never go home. A great spot for a working breakfast, too.

Maria's New Mexican Kitchen (505-983-7929; 555 W. Cordova Rd., Santa Fe, NM 87501; closed Thanksgiving, Christmas; moderate; New Mexican; L, D; partial handicapped access; nonsmoking section; reservations recommended; special features: patio, fireplaces, mariachis). With 50 years in the same location, Maria's is a Santa Fe classic that continues to draw crowds of all ages from all neighborhoods. In an old adobe house with fireplaces tucked into corners and mariachi bands strolling between tables, this restaurant is known for its traditional Mexican dishes and atmosphere. Plates of enchiladas, tacos, and chile rellenos come steaming from the kitchen. Delicious tortillas are made right in the dining room while you watch. The food is based on traditional recipes and cooking styles: sizzling fajitas served on metal platters in a forest of green peppers and onions, tender and spicy *carne adovada*, authentic green chile stew to warm you up on even the coldest afternoon, and the classic blue corn red chile enchiladas; even the tacos are superb. Besides, there's some of the freshest guacamole salad in town, and a mountainous egg flan that will have you wishing for more. At Maria's, it's hard to decide between red or green; both are tasty and neither sports too much spice. I generally like the blue corn enchiladas with red; however, I have found them a wee bit on the salty side of late, and I am not the only one. Maria's remains a top choice to sip a margarita. Owner Al Lucero has written a definitive book about margaritas, and his bartenders can concoct better than 70 different kinds. Dinners can be ordered in the bar.

New York Deli (505-982-8900; 505-424-1200; 420 Catron St., Santa Fe, NM 87501; 4056 Cerrillos Rd., Santa Fe, NM 87505 at corner of Rodeo Rd.; closed Christmas; moderate; New York deli; B, L, D; partial Handicapped access; no reservations). My go-to place for a fresh bagel, scrambled eggs with lox and onion, corned beef and eggs, and a pastrami sandwich. Tasty deli food with a southwestern twist, an extensive menu, and reasonable prices make this eatery a real favorite. This Santa Fe standard

dishes up family recipes, and you can enjoy them al fresco in the "Central Park" patio at the Catron St. location. You'll find chicken soup with matzo balls, cheese blintzes, and a breakfast that's served anytime, with such flourishes as smoked salmon eggs Benedict and blue corn piñon pancakes. They serve excellent coffee, too.

The Pink Adobe (505-983-7712; 406 Old Santa Fe Trail, Santa Fe, NM 87501; closed major holidays; moderate–expensive; Continental, New Mexican with Cajun twist; L [Mon.–Fri.], D; partial handicapped access; reservations required for dinner; special features: fireplaces, patio dining). The Pink, as it is affectionately known, is located in Santa Fe's historic neighborhood, the Barrio de Analco, across the street from San Miguel Mission, the oldest church in the United States. The restaurant is set in a 300-year-old house, painted the distinctive hue for which it is named. Finding a more romantic spot on a chilly night when the fireplaces are alight is not easy. At the adjacent Dragon Room bar, politicians, cowboys, and artists mingle in a setting hospitable to locals and visitors alike, munching on popcorn and sipping margaritas.

Rosalea Murphy, who became a great Santa Fe personality, founded the Pink in 1944, and following a change in ownership, her family reopened the place. The menu does not change, nor would anyone want it to. Elegant appetizers such as lobster salad, escargots, and artichoke with green onion sauce begin a meal that may feature Continental dishes subtly altered for the Pink's special style. Steak Dunigan, my reliable favorite dish, adds green chile, and the spaghetti Bolognese is from an old family recipe. New Mexican dishes of blue corn enchiladas and tamales boast a particularly hot and spicy chile. The favorite dessert at The Pink Adobe is the famous French apple pie. The place for the quintessential Santa Fe experience. You will not be disappointed.

Plaza Café Downtown (505-982-1664; West Side of Santa Fe Plaza, Santa Fe, NM 87501; open daily 7 AM–9 PM; inexpensive–moderate; American, Greek, New Mexican; B, L, D; partial handicapped access). A shout of glee went up from the citizenry when the Plaza Café, a downtown fixture since 1905, reopened mid-2012 after a devastating kitchen fire. And it really does look the same—a trip back in time. As close as Santa Fe gets to a diner serving everything from cashew mole enchiladas to Greek salad, a mighty fine burger, gyros, club sandwich, and excellent green chile stew, the comfy Plaza Café is where folks love to meet up. Towering coconut cream pie and moist carrot cake will tempt you. You can't beat the breakfast of blue corn piñon pancakes or huevos rancheros.

Rio Chama Steakhouse (505-955-0765; 414 Old Santa Fe Trail, Santa Fe, NM 87501; closed Christmas; expensive; American; L, D; partial handicapped access; reservations recommended; special features: full bar, patio dining). Here's a good place to get back to the basics: prime dry-aged beef in the form of thick, tender, succulent rib eyes, filets, and luscious Black Angus prime rib; fabulous house-made onion rings, beefsteak tomato salad, rich creamed spinach, and shrimp cocktail. Now serving Heritage Ranch Beef, specially ranch raised, so you know where your meat is coming from. So you're going light or your sister-in-law is a vegetarian? Rio Chama also serves grilled chicken, lamb, tuna, and a veggie plate. This informally elegant eatery is enough to transform a vegetarian into an omnivore. An ooey-gooey fondue, served to be shared in the lively bar, warms up a chilly night. And don't forget that Rio Chama serves a contender for best burger.

San Francisco Street Bar & Grill (505-982-2044; 50 E. San Francisco St., Santa Fe, NM 87501; closed major holidays; inexpensive–moderate; American; L, D; no handicapped access; no reservations; special features: take-out). In its spiffy second-floor incarnation, the SFSB&G offers a menu that includes Middle Eastern specialties and has a distinctly tourist-friendly appeal, particularly when the tourist needs a convenient break from shopping. They've gone way beyond their famous burgers, which once garnered a favorable mention in the *New York Times*, to sesame ginger chicken breast; Asiago, basil, and roasted garlic ravioli; and a healthy selection of crisp salads. They're open until 11 nightly, no small convenience in a town that pretty much shuts down by 9:30.

Santa Fe Baking Co. & Café (505-988-4292; 504 W. Cordova Rd., Santa Fe, NM 87501; closed Christmas; inexpensive; American, Southwest; B, L; full handicapped access; no reservations; special features: patio). This popular breakfast spot is light, bright, friendly, delicious, and cheap. Located in the Coronado Shopping Center, it's off the beaten tourist path and offers plenty of parking. Here, you'll find standard American breakfasts and a variety of full-bodied coffees and juices, along with a case of irresistible freshly baked croissants, scones, and pastries. This makes a wonderful spot to read the newspaper and plan the weekend with a superb latte and chocolate croissant. Reliable Wi-Fi, smoothies, and fresh juices, too. Lunches include an assortment of delicious sandwiches both hot and cold, as well as a variety of salads and soups.

You can find me here on many a morning, enjoying the reasonable ($7.50 includes fresh coffee) burrito special.

The Shed (505-982-9030; 113½ E. Palace Ave., Santa Fe, NM 87501; closed Sun., Thanksgiving, Christmas, New Year's; moderate; Mexican, American; L, D; partial handicapped access; reservations recommended; special features: fireplaces, patio, enclosed in winter). Located in an adobe dating from 1692, this long-established restaurant is a landmark. The winding rooms and narrow hallways add to the historic atmosphere. Wear casual, or go stylish. Located off the street, tucked back into an enclosed patio, it appeals to Mexican food lovers. Aside from the many blue corn entrées, what sets this restaurant apart is the chile. Straight from the farm, the chiles are ground on the premises; for more subtle palates, the freshness is indeed noticeable. Selections of fish and beef dishes help widen the choice for those a little timid about Mexican food. Wine is served by the glass or the bottle; beer is on draft. In summer, the patio makes for perfect dining, and a table by one of the corner fireplaces can take the winter chill off and add to the romance of a good meal. You'll know you can't be anywhere on earth but Santa Fe. Usually crowded, so plan accordingly.

Tia Sophia's (505-983-9880; 210 W. San Francisco St., Santa Fe, NM 87501; closed Sun., major holidays; inexpensive–moderate; New Mexican; B, L; handicapped access; nonsmoking section; no reservations). Located in the heart of San Francisco Street, Tia Sophia's is an unassuming little restaurant that serves consistently good New Mexican meals in a family atmosphere. Daily breakfast and lunch specials are popular and affordable, and it's still patronized by loyal old-timers and politicos. This is the place for a classic Santa Fe breakfast. The breakfast burritos and huevos rancheros are worth ordering for those with a hearty morning appetite. For lunch, order one of the homemade stuffed *sopaipillas*. Please note that Tia Sophia's closes promptly at 2 PM. Eat, then shop.

Tiny's Restaurant and Lounge (505-983-9817; 1005 St. Francis Dr., Santa Fe, NM 87501; closed Sun. (except during football season), major holidays; inexpensive–moderate; New Mexican, American; L, D; full handicapped access; reservations recommended Wed., Fri., Sat.; special features: take-out, children's portions, patio, full-service lounge). Walter "Tiny" Moore and his son-in-law Jimmie Palermo opened Tiny's Dine and Dance in 1950. Since then, the location and name have slightly changed, but Tiny's has maintained its reputation for good food and for being a longtime favorite hangout for local politicos. The *carne adovada* is some of the best in town, and Tiny's is well known for its chicken guacamole tacos, pork chops, and posole. Plenty of *banco* seating, country-and-western background music, and hints of Italian proprietorship (including a huge Frank Sinatra picture) add to a comfortable dining experience. The lounge is the heart and soul of Tiny's, and it features one of the largest decanter collections in the Southwest. There's live entertainment Thurs.–Sat. Unpretentious and laid back, with dancing on weekends.

Tomasita's (505-983-5721; 500 S. Guadalupe St., Santa Fe, NM 87501; closed Sun., major holidays; inexpensive; northern New Mexican; L, D; handicapped access; no reservations; special features: take-out, adjoining lounge, children's portions). Tomasita's is housed within the red brick Guadalupe station of the Chile Line railroad, which connected northern

New Mexico pueblos and towns from 1880 to 1941. Handed down from generations, Tomasita's recipes produce a distinctly northern New Mexico cuisine that melds the corn, chile, beans, and fruit of the area. Specials include tamales, chile rellenos, blue corn chicken enchiladas, *carnitas* Antonio, and stuffed *sopaipillas*. The dining atmosphere is exuberant, the chile is hot, and the chips and salsa are bound to whet the appetite. A seat at the bar gets you new friends almost instantly. The delicious frozen margaritas are a signature item and rated highly by Santa Feans. Mexican, Spanish, or Irish coffee will warm you up if you've been out skiing all day. After-dinner treats include *natillas*, a delicious custard pudding, and ice cream–filled *sopaipillas* served with strawberries—Tomasita's version of a New Mexico strawberry shortcake. Ample seating easily accommodates large families. But be prepared to wait a little while for dinner; Tomasita's is very popular and a good value. Sit at the bar if you're looking for conversation. Live mariachis on Tues. evening add to the conviviality. The food can be iffy in high season.

Tortilla Flats (505-471-8685; 3139 Cerrillos Rd., Santa Fe, NM 87501; closed major holidays; inexpensive–moderate; New Mexican; B, L, D; partial handicapped access; no smoking; no reservations; special features: take-out, children's menu, full bar). Generous portions of everything from the iced tea to the *sopaipillas* make Tortilla Flats a favorite among Santa Feans—not to mention an ideal family restaurant. The chile is traditionally spicy and flavorful, evidenced by the menu's disclaimer: "We are not responsible if chile is too hot." Daily lunch specials include beef brisket tacos, *carne adovada*, Santa Fe Trail steak, and green chile pork chops. Burritos are enormous. The dining area is comfortable and casual and easy to converse in. And the restaurant's southwestern setting is roomy with an inside-an-adobe feel. Ample booths and tables can accommodate just about any size party. And for those who like to get up late, home-style New Mexican breakfasts are served until the dinner menu rolls out at 4 PM. A cozy, full-service cantina featuring 16-ounce margaritas connects to the dining room. Fresh ingredients, friendly service, reasonable prices, zesty chile, and hearty servings are the consistent trademarks of Tortilla Flats.

Upper Crust Pizza (505-982-0000; 329 Old Santa Fe Trail, Santa Fe, NM 87501; closed Thanksgiving; inexpensive; pizza, sandwiches; L, D; partial handicapped Access; no reservations; special features: free delivery, patio and front-porch dining, live music, parking in rear). Location, location, location. Consistently one of the best, most convenient to sightseeing bargain lunches in town. This clean, casual eatery is nestled in an old adobe structure with vigas, skylights, and Saltillo tile floors. Weekday lunches, you'll encounter a line out the door and down the street. Locals know that between 11 and 1 they can get a huge piece of pizza, salad, and a drink for a few bucks, made to order with fresh ingredients, and the service is prompt. Even high-maintenance people are accommodated with a smile. Pizzas such as the Grecian Gourmet are made with either traditional Italian or whole wheat crusts. Sandwiches and house specials come with a side salad and chips. Try the house special whole wheat calzone filled with a blend of three cheeses, spinach, pesto, and tomatoes. Be sure to order a side of mouthwatering garlic bread made with fresh diced garlic and herbs sautéed with butter.

Bobcat Bite Restaurant (505-983-5319; 418 Old Las Vegas Hwy., 4.1 miles E. of Old Pecos Trail; intersection; open Wed.–Sat.; inexpensive; hamburgers and more; L, D; full handicapped access; no reservations; no credit cards). Write your name on the blackboard. Wait until you are called. The Bobcat Bite is a small adobe that once served as a trading store and gun shop. The menu emphasizes beef: cheeseburgers, 13-ounce hamburger steaks, 13-ounce rib eyes, and special 8-ounce New York strip steaks with salad and garlic bread. Their burger is consistently mentioned as "the best burger" whenever such issues are up for debate. Portions are generous, and the mostly local crowd is congenial despite the small tables and counter space. The chef credits the delicious burgers to his well-seasoned and much-used grill. There is also strict attention paid to grilling each individual order, with the menu listing definitions of *rare* ("dark red—warm center") to *well done* ("fully cooked—no pink"). Quality is the name of the game here, and for that, it is worth the wait and dining in the "cute" crowded space.

Gabriel's (505-455-7000; 4 Banana Ln., Santa Fe, NM 87506-0910; closed Christmas, Thanksgiving; moderate; New Mexican, Mexican; L, D; full handicapped access; smoking at patio or bar; reservations recommended). Overlooking the Pojoaque Valley lies a restaurant offering delicious local fare. Expect generous portions of flavorful New Mexican– and Mexican-style dishes. Mesquite-smoked pork ribs, sizzling fajitas, chile stew, and frozen margaritas are just some of the superb concoctions available at this local favorite. Don't leave without partaking of the mouthwatering guacamole prepared tableside: It's their signature dish and also the floor show. The restaurant is just 15 miles north of Santa Fe, so a bit off the beaten path. This fact makes them work harder to please you. Stop in for lunch or dinner.

Rancho de Chimayó (505-984-2100; 300 County Rd. 98 Chimayó, NM 87522; closed: Mon., Nov.–May; moderate; northern New Mexican; L, D; full handicapped access; reservations recommended; special features: fireplaces, patio dining, musicians in summer). This is the single most important northern New Mexico restaurant to bring your visiting family and friends. It provides the ultimate New Mexico experience in both food and décor. This beautifully remodeled ranch house has been in the Jaramillo family since the 1880s. A restaurant since 1965, it still has the feel of old northern New Mexico, including wood floors, whitewashed adobe walls, hand-stripped vigas, and a lushly terraced patio. Moreover, the food is prepared from recipes that have been in the Jaramillo family for generations.

After many visits over the years, we've found the food consistent, the portions generous, and the service friendly and efficient. And despite their busy-ness, both service and food remain up to their consistent quality standards. It's lovely in wintertime to sip a margarita beside the blazing piñon fire. The menu includes about a dozen traditional northern New Mexican plates plus steak and trout amandine. The nachos are particularly crisp. A huge, flaky *sopaipilla* relleno is stuffed to bursting with beef, beans, and Spanish rice. And the Chimayó chicken is moist and flavorful. For dessert, we recommend the flan, a rich, creamy caramel custard with a pleasing tapioca consistency. A visit to the Santuario de Chimayó followed by a lunch at the Rancho de Chimayó will give you a better feeling for New Mexico tradition than just about anything else, as well as a true sense of well-being.

Tesuque Village Market (505-988-8848; 138 Tesuque Village Rd., Santa Fe, NM 87606, junction of NM 591 and Bishop's Lodge Rd.; open daily; inexpensive; New Mexican, American; B, L, D; partial handicapped access; no reservations; special features: patio dining, take-out). When you walk into Tesuque Village Market, you'll find an upscale grocery store with shelves and coolers stocked with beer, cookies, ice cream, candies, canned goods, and elaborate selections of mustards and salsas. There's an entire room full of California and local wines. The deli bar offers an inviting assortment of gourmet cheeses, meats, cakes, and breads for take-out.

The menu includes a varied selection of New Mexican and American offerings, from huevos rancheros and bean burritos to sandwiches and seafoods. Sunday morning brunch with the *New York Times* is a tradition for many locals—go with the blue corn pancakes. Popular lunches include a huge green chile burger with spicy fries and a tasty green chile stew. Desserts, made fresh daily, include Glurpy Cakes, pies, cobblers, éclairs, cheesecakes, and more. Indoors or outside on the front porch, you'll find a great place to hang out with a coffee and read.

Local Flavors

Taste of Taos

Hunan Chinese Restaurant (575-751-0474; 1023 Paseo del Pueblo Sur, Taos, NM 87571; closed Tues., major holidays; inexpensive; Chinese; L, D; partial handicapped access; nonsmoking section; no reservations; special features: take-out). Hunan Chinese Restaurant is the place to refresh your palate after all your New Mexican dining experiences. Here you can indulge in delicious pot stickers, hot-and-sour soup, pepper steak, mu shu duck, and imperial shrimp, and there's a great bargain-priced lunch special served every day 11–3. Those who know and love Chinese food will be able to appease their cravings at Hunan.

Taos Diner (575-758-2374; 908 Paseo del Pueblo Norte, Taos, NM 87571; inexpensive; open daily; contemporary American; B, L; partial handicapped access; no reservations). Although Taos Diner has opened a second kitchen on the south end of town, I prefer the original location for huevos rancheros with red chile, Cobb salad, local natural burgers, and general deliciousness. You can order half a salad. Much of the food is locally sourced. The red chile is good and hot. No wonder locals flock here.

Lambert's of Taos (575-758-1009; 309 Paseo del Pueblo Sur, Taos, NM 87571; open daily; expensive–very expensive; contemporary American; D; partial handicapped access; reservations recommended. special features: private dining, patio dining, take-out). In addition to having what is widely considered the most complete and intriguing wine list in town, Lambert's delivers a fine meal in a relaxing atmosphere conducive to high enjoyment. This is one of those rare places that will feel like a bargain despite the considerable tab. Appetizers featuring fresh lobster and other seasonally available ingredients are creative, light, and scrumptious. The house special of pepper-crusted lamb loin with red wine demi-glace, the medallions of beef tenderloin with blue cheese mashed potatoes, and the pistachio-crusted chicken breast with roasted shallot sherry sauce are but a few examples of the grace and flair demonstrated here. The menu changes seasonally. Sitting at the bar is where you're likely to find the locals.

Michael's Kitchen Café & Bakery (575-758-4178; 304C Paseo del Pueblo Norte, 0.3 mile north of the Plaza; open daily 7 AM–8:30 PM; closed Nov., major holidays; inexpensive–moderate; American, New Mexican; B, L, D; partial handicapped access; no reservations; special features: fresh-baked pastries and desserts, counter seating, children's menu, take-out). You can't avoid Michael's Kitchen while you are in Taos. The menu has something for everyone, the doughnuts are beloved, the red chile is just right, and parking is no problem. And the price is right, too. Don't be put off if there is a line. It moves quickly. Michael's Kitchen serves delicious hearty dishes from fried chicken to enchiladas, chosen from a tabloid-sized menu. As you walk in the door, you will notice the large display cases full of breakfast pastries, breads, pies, and other mouthwatering desserts baked fresh daily at the restaurant. Once you finish gawking at the salad-plate-sized cinnamon rolls with cream cheese icing and confetti sprinkles on top, have a seat at the counter or at a table in one of the main dining rooms and settle in for a while.

Orlando's New Mexican Café (555-751-1450; 1114 Don Juan Valdez Ln., 1.8 miles north of the Plaza on left; closed Sun., Christmas; inexpensive; northern New Mexican; L, D; no handicapped access; smoking on patio; no reservations; no credit cards; special features: patio). If you're in the market for authentic northern New Mexico cooking without the lard, you can't do better than Orlando's. The décor of colorful Mexican folk art, in lime and hot pink, accentuated with punched tinwork, and the scrumptious desserts all contribute to a delightful experience. Try the chile bowl "with everything," or go for one of the best Frito pies in northern New Mexico. Summer dining on the patio is a joy, though it can be very crowded during peak times, so plan accordingly. Success has not spoiled Orlando's, and it has come far from its humble beginnings as a hot dog cart on the Plaza.

Graham's Grill (575-751-1350; 106 Paseo Del Pueblo Norte, Taos, NM 87571; open seven days; moderate). Chef Lesley Fay and her husband maitre'd Peter work hard to keep their restaurant in the former JC Penney's running smoothly and pleasing customers. And their hard work pays off. A convivial dining spot that attracts locals as well as visitors, their seasonal menu has broad appeal. The food is not edgy, but whether you order lamb, beef, fish, or fowl, you will be guaranteed a tasty meal, well served, at a price that is not unreasonable—though the hype is a bit unreal. Just do not sit near either the front or back door during cold weather, as the narrow space can be drafty.

Five Star Burger (575-758-8484, 1032 Paseo del Pueblo Sur, Taos, NM 87571; open seven days; inexpensive). Get your burger in bison, lamb, turkey, veggie, or the old-fashioned way, with green chile, cheese, and Harris Ranch beef. Go for the crispy sweet potato fries. A bit pricier than your chain burger, but oh so worth it. Truly satisfying and, ultimately, a reasonable place to take the family for lunch or dinner. Money can't buy happiness, but it can buy satisfaction. At least here it can. The décor is a bit sterile and chainlike, but don't let that deter you.

Love Apple (575-751-0050; 803 Paseo Del Pueblo Norte, Taos, NM 87571; reservations strongly recommended). The food is quirky, the menu limited, and everything served from the tiny kitchen in this crumbling adobe former chapel is delish, starting with the cornbread all the way to the chocolate mousse. Free range and

locally sourced ingredients, intriguing salad combinations, New Mexican traditional dishes made with nontraditional ingredients, all served with casual elegance by candlelight make this one romantic adventure. Call ahead to be sure the menu is diverse enough for your party. The steaks are scrumptious, and, for the daring, so is the wild boar. The menu changes often. Wines are excellent, and do save room for the homemade desserts, particularly whatever is chocolate. One memorable evening guaranteed. The "love apple" refers to an antique moniker for the tomato.

Local Flavors

Restaurants near Taos

The Bavarian Ski Restaurant & Lodge (575-776-8020; Taos Ski Valley, Taos, NM 87525; open 7 days during winter; call for summer hours; expensive; German; L, D, après ski; handicapped access; reservations recommended). This is one hopping place at lunchtime during ski season. Warm and cozy as a German beer hall, it is the place to dine and unwind. You can ski to this midmountain European log lodge or call for a van to pick you up at Taos Ski Valley. Featuring German and European specialties such as Wiener schnitzel, bratwurst, Hungarian goulash soup, apple strudel, and beer imported from the oldest brewery in Munich. Bask in the winter sunshine on the beautiful sundeck surrounding this re-creation of an Alpine ski lodge.

Ranchos Plaza Grill (575-758-5788; 60 St. Francis Plaza, Ranchos de Taos, NM 87557; closed Mon.; inexpensive; traditional American with

Southwest flavor; B, L; partial handicapped access; reservations recommended; no credit cards; special features: patio, fireplace). Sit out on the patio, in view of the most painted and photographed church in America, the old Ranchos San Francisco de Asis Church made famous by Georgia O'Keeffe and Ansel Adams. Then dig into some of the most savory red chile you'll find anywhere. The Ranchos Plaza Grill specializes, most appropriately, in classic New Mexico cooking, served in an ancient rambling adobe hacienda.

Roasted Clove (575-377-0636; 48 N. Angel Fire Rd., Angel Fire, NM 87710; closed Mon.; expensive–very expensive; American, Continental; D; partial handicapped access; reservations recommended; special features: patio). If you've spent the day on the slopes or taken a drive to see the aspens in fall and want to finish your tour with an evening of pampering, this is the place. Not just another high-end restaurant, Roasted Clove serves with panache its classic Caesar and coconut shrimp appetizers, chicken in pesto

The Bavarian atop Taos Ski Valley invites skiers to warm up with its European-style hearty food and drink.

cream, wild mushroom *à la forestière* (mushrooms in butter, wine, herbs, and cream over fettuccine), *coquille moutard* (scallops sautéed in Dijon mustard and cream over linguine), filet mignon, and chipotle chicken, as well all the other creative and well-prepared dishes, with flair and care. The lovely Mediterranean-style setting elevates the surroundings to suit the cuisine. Suitable for a special occasion.

Taos Pizza Out Back (575-758-3112; 712 Paseo del Pueblo Norte, Taos, NM 87571; closed Thanksgiving, Christmas; inexpensive–moderate; pizza; L, D; partial handicapped access; no reservations; special features: take-out). Don't miss this funky little pizza joint slightly outside the Taos town limits. Don't be put off by its "back in the day" appearance. The undisputed local favorite pizzeria, Out Back is one of the hippest pizza parlors you've ever seen, complete with an old-fashioned

gas pump in the corner and customers' crayoned works of art hanging on the walls. It specializes in "Taos-style gourmet pizza," lovingly made to order from organic Colorado wheat. Because the place is so often packed, you may want to order in advance or do take-out. Try the Florentine, with chicken, garlic, and herbs sautéed in white wine, or the portobello mushroom pie. Servings are more than generous, and they don't scrimp on the toppings. One slice will fill you up, but it's so delicious, you'll want more. The salads are fresh and generous as well.

Trading Post Café (575-758-5089; 4179 NM 68 at NM 518, Ranchos de Taos, NM 87557; closed Sun., Christmas, New Year's; moderate–expensive; European; L, D; partial handicapped access; reservations recommended for parties of five or more; special features: fireplace, patio dining). Don't get confused. Despite the "Italian" sign out front, this is still the same Trading Post Café serving a freewheeling mix of Continental fare. Located right along the Taos Highway, this bustling, well-run eatery opened in Nov. 1994 on the old Ranchos Trading Post. Up until 1981, the trading post had been the largest general store in the Taos area and was also the area's most popular meeting place. Today the owners of the Trading Post Café have revived that community spirit, inviting residents and travelers alike to come in and warm their feet by the kiva fireplace, nestle into a comfy corner table, or sit counter side on tall, wrought-iron swivel stools. If you are dining solo, this is a most comfortable place to sit at the bar and watch your food being prepared.

The menu includes a wide array of lunch and dinner offerings—generous portions to suit everyone's palate, at a variety of prices. Salads, fish, pastas, soups—including the house special chicken noodle soup—Creole pepper shrimp, roast duck, chicken Vesuvio, and *bistecca Fiorentina,* a 10-ounce rib eye. How about a paella with a glass of Vouvray? The pasta specials are reliable, and the menu is always varied with daily specials. Do ask about the price in advance, however, as some of the special salads can be surprisingly pricey. Service is professional, and there's an excellent and moderately priced list of red and white wines by the glass, as well as an array of wonderful, homemade desserts. The patio is glorious in warm weather.

Food Purveyors

As agricultural communities, Santa Fe and Taos have been bastions of local produce and home cooking for the better part of 400 years. And vendors still sell seasonal fare, from sweet corn and chile to apples and *bizcochitos* (the anise-flavored "state cookie") at roadside stands. During past decades, specialty establishments, including ice cream and candy shops, delis, bakeries, and gourmet markets, have become better established. Farmers' or growers' markets continue to earn popularity, offering fresh, locally grown produce in-season and inspiring chefs as well as home cooks. Following are some of the special places and products, both old and new, that make the modern Santa Fe–Taos area such a gastronomic delight. And if you are fortunate to drive past one of the still-existing old-time general stores, such as Bode's in Abiquiu, do venture in. It's possible to find gourmet delights, a handmade tamale in the crockpot, or a great bowl of chile amid the pots and pans, hardware, and sacks of beans.

BAKERIES

Santa Fe

Dulce Bakery (505-989-9966; 1100 Don Diego Ave., Santa Fe, NM 87505). No shame to love sugar here in this minimalist café. Or butter. Masterful baking and cases loaded with turnovers and Danishes fresh from the oven. Resistance is futile. Cinnamon rolls with all the icing you can stand.

French Pastry Shop (505-983-6697; La Fonda Hotel, 100 E. San Francisco St., Santa Fe, NM 87501; closed Christmas; no credit cards). George Zadeyan and his brother started their first French Pastry Shop in Santa Fe in 1972. Two years later, they moved to La Fonda Hotel on the Plaza. The location, along with a delicious array of pastries and crêpes, has made this little café the quintessential Santa Fe experience. The reasons are obvious enough once you've been there: croissants, raisin rolls, apple turnovers, napoleons, strawberry tarts, éclairs, quiches, sandwiches, coffees, cappuccinos—you get the idea. Crêpes sweet and savory are the specialty de la maison.

Plaza Bakery/Häagen-Dazs (505-988-3858; 56 E. San Francisco St., Santa Fe, NM 87501; closed Thanksgiving, Christmas). You know about the ice cream, but do you know about the baked goodies? Stuffed chocolate croissants, cream cheese brownies, fruit pies, bear claws, strudel, scones, and herb baguettes are just a few of the delectables offered—along with 33 flavors of ice cream. Sandwiches, coffee, tea, and a variety of espresso drinks are also served. Located on the Plaza, this is a great people watching spot and usually very crowded. Rumored to be the nation's number 1 grossing Häagen-Dazs.

Sage Bakehouse (505-820-7243; 535-C Cerrillos Rd., Santa Fe, NM 87501; closed major holidays). When Sage Bakehouse first opened its doors, it changed Santa Feans' concepts of the staff of life to the finest crunchy-crusted artisan delight. From their special ovens come loaves of kalamata olive and pecan breads, all made of the purest, most basic ingredients. Try a sandwich of Black Forest ham and Gruyère cheese for lunch, and by all means taste their hearth breads.

Taos

El Gamal (575-613-0311; 112 Dona Luz St., Taos, NM 87571). Craving a fresh hot bagel? Feed your urge at this humble little Middle Eastern spot where you can also find baklava, hummus, baba ganoush, and much more.

Yes, you can get fresh hot bagels in Taos, at El Gamal.

Santa Fe

Santa Fe Brewing Pub and Grill (505-424-3333; 35 Fire Pl., Santa Fe, NM 87508; closed Sun.). In 1988, a wine bottle distributor named Mike Levis opened New Mexico's first commercial brewery on his 65-acre ranch outside Galisteo. Today, the brewery's best-known product is Santa Fe Pale Ale, available in bars, restaurants, and liquor and grocery stores. The company makes seven other beers that are available only at the brewery itself: Fiesta Ale, Porter, Wheat Beer, Barley Wine, Nut Brown Ale, Raspberry Ale, and Russian Imperial Stout. Tour the brewery (no reservations required) and pick up a T-shirt, cap, or poster emblazoned with the company label. Guided tours of the "top of the Turquoise Trail" facility on Saturdays at noon end with tasting samples of their brew. Or check out their new **Eldorado Taphouse** (505-466-6938; 7 Caliente Rd., Eldorado), about 15 minutes from Santa Fe.

Second Street Brewery (505-982-3030; 1814 Second St., Santa Fe, NM 87501; closed Christmas, Easter, Thanksgiving). A strong entry in the microbrewery scene, this one consistently wins major awards for its custom suds. The brewery is a success with locals, who enjoy the relaxed pub and its fish-and-chips, soups, and salads after work or on the weekends, with their families, when they can hear live music in the evening. The second location, Second Street Brewery at The Railyard, 1607 Paseo de Peralta, often has live music and reasonable pub food and has emerged as a popular gathering spot.

Taos

Eske's Brew Pub (575-758-1517; 106 Desgeorges Lane, Taos, NM 87571; closed Christmas). Ever try a green chile beer or an apricot ale? This is the place, where the fresh home-brewed beers are served with a menu of green chile stew, bratwurst, and delicious grilled sandwiches. A hangout where you really can kick back.

BUTCHERS

There are a number of small groceries and health food markets in Santa Fe and Taos that offer specialty and custom-cut meats. The following are some of the better ones (see also "Health Food Stores," below).

Santa Fe

Close to the center of town, you'll find **Kaune Foodtown** (505-982-2629; 511 Old Santa Fe Trail), one of the oldest groceries around. It offers a wide variety of meats, including natural beef and poultry, Colorado lamb, and game meats from venison and buffalo to rabbit and pheasant. The only place in Santa Fe you can purchase prime beef. You can also find a variety of natural meats, fish, and poultry at Santa Fe's four health food stores, **Whole Foods** (505-992-1700; 753 Cerrillos Rd.); **La Montanita Co-op** (505-984-2852; 627 W. Alameda); **Whole Foods** (505-983-5333; 1090 S. St. Francis Dr.); and **Trader Joe's** (505-995-8145; 530 W. Cordova Rd.).

Taos

Cid's Food Market (575-758-1148; 623 Paseo Del Pueblo Norte, Taos, NM 87571) has the best butcher department in town. You get what you pay for. Here you'll find

Coleman natural beef and lamb from Colorado, as well as Shelton's grain-fed, hormone-free chicken.

CANDY AND ICE CREAM SHOPS

In addition to **Plaza Bakery/Häagen-Dazs** (505-988-3858; 56 E. San Francisco St., Santa Fe; discussed under "Bakeries," above) and **Baskin-Robbins** found on Cerrillos Rd. (505-982-9031; 1841 Cerrillos Rd. and 505-474-3131; 4056 Cerrillos Rd., Santa Fe) and in the **DeVargas Center** (www.devargascenter.com; 564 N. Guadalupe St., Santa Fe), Santa Fe and Taos have other sweet-tooth centers worth mentioning.

Todos Santos (505-982-3855; 125 E. Palace Ave., Sena Plaza, Santa Fe, NM 87501). A candy shop like none other: a touch of New Orleans, a touch of Day of the Dead, glitzy gold-clad chocolates, and a whole lot of artisanal chocolate to tickle your fancy, many in over-the-top wrappings. The place for a special treat, or the place to go to woo a chocoholic.

Señor Murphy Candymaker (505-982-0461; La Fonda Hotel, 200 San Francisco St., Santa Fe, NM 87501; closed Sun., major holidays). The specialty here is anything with piñon nuts, for example, piñon toffee and piñon fudge—as well as spicy chile concoctions with peanut brittle and chocolate cream. They also make chile jellies and outstanding condiments for meats and hors d'oeuvres. Great gifts for yourself, those back home, or friends abroad. Another location is at Santa Fe Place mall at the south end of town.

Taos Cow Café & Deli (575-776-5640; 485 NM 150, Arroyo Seco, NM 87529; closed Thanksgiving, Christmas, New Year's). There is such a thing as insisting on going to the source, and if you're an ice cream lover, you'll want to make the pilgrimage up the Taos Ski Valley Road to the ice creamery known as Taos Cow for the creamiest, most exquisite ice cream you've ever tasted, in delectable seasonal flavors such as lavender and peach. Great breakfasts, sandwiches, and snacks, too, plus relaxed, Taos-funky riverside tables.

Taos Cow Café &, Deli in Arroyo Seco makes the best natural ice cream.

CATERERS

Santa Fe
Cowgirl Hall of Fame. See under "Restaurants" above. A favorite for BBQ beef and fajitas.

Walter Burke Catering (505-473-9600; 1209 Calle de Commercio, Santa Fe, NM 87505; open daily). If you want absolutely impeccable catering for any occasion, call Walter Burke. In Santa Fe, the name speaks for itself. About the only thing they don't provide is a location, but they can help you find one. In business since 1981, they're one of the largest catering firms in town, and they've prepared just about every kind of cuisine imaginable.

COFFEE SHOPS

There are so many good places to sip coffee in Santa Fe and Taos that it's difficult to list them all, much less do them justice. Here we simply call your attention to a number of choice spots where you can find good, fresh coffees, teas, espressos, and cappuccinos. Many also serve wonderful food, and some offer evening entertainment—from live music to open mike to Tarot readings. The rest is up to you.

Santa Fe

Counter Culture (505-995-1105; 930 Baca St., adjacent to The Railyard neighborhood) is a cool lunch and breakfast stop with grilled sandwiches, Asian noodles, and great soups, patio, and now serves well-prepared, tasty, and reasonably priced dinners. The **Chocolate Maven Bakery & Café** (505-984-1980; 821 San Mateo, Unit C) offers monster chocolate croissants, breakfasts so good they will make you cry, and unbelievable sandwiches; parking in their narrow lot is the drawback. **Downtown Subscription** (505-983-3085; 376 Garcia St.) in the Canyon Road neighborhood, the grandma of them all, is a spacious, cheerful bar and patio with rack upon rack of newspapers and magazines to browse, plus good coffees and pastries. **Plaza Bakery/Häagen-Dazs** (505-988-3858; 56 E. San Francisco St. on the Plaza) has rich, deep coffee, sublime pastries, and, of course, legendary ice cream. **Ohori's** (505-988-9692, 507 Old Santa Fe Trail; 505-982-9692, 1098 S. St. Francis Dr.) serves fresh-roasted beans, and you get a free cup of java if you buy a pound of beans. For my money, it's the best and the most expensive coffee in town. **Harry's Roadhouse** (505-989-4629; 98 Old Las Vegas Hwy.) is easy to find. Just look for all the cars parked out front, especially at Sun. brunch time. Delicious, hearty breakfasts, sandwiches, and homemade soups and specials, plus pizzas and salads. The **Teahouse** (505-992-0972; 821 Canyon Rd.) serves an amazing selection of fine teas, coffees, and light meals with a Zen spin. The hearty oatmeal is popular. Other favorite breakfast spots include the **Pantry Restaurant** (505-986-0022; 1820 Cerrillos Rd.)—go for the stuffed pancakes, the fresh corned beef and eggs, or anything with chile. Open until 9 PM, it has excellent daily specials. **Tecolote Café** (505-988-1362; 1203 Cerrillos Rd.) serves up delicious low-cholesterol alternatives to its substantial helpings of French toast and fresh-baked muffins,

For more quick bargain lunches while out and about, try **Cleopatra Café** (505-820-7381; 418 Cerrillos Rd.) in the Design Center for delicious moussaka, falafel, baba ganoush, and baklava; **El Teosoro Café** (505-988-3886; 500 Montezuma Ave.) in the Sanbusco mall has tasty warm spinach salad, sandwiches, and enchiladas; and **Back Street Bistro** (505-982-3500; 513 Camino de los Marquez) serves up a variety of homemade gourmet soups daily, as well as salads and sandwiches; the Hungarian mushroom is a fave. **Ramblin' Café** (505-989-1272; 1420 Second St.) has fantastic quesadillas and sandwiches with fresh-roasted turkey; really, when you've got to have a great sandwich, you'll do well here at bargain prices. At **Del Charro Saloon** (505-954-0320; 101 W. Alameda St.), where you can get a yummy lunch for less than $8, including homemade fries, creamy green chile chicken soup, burgers, and enchiladas that taste far more costly, you can also sip a margarita or Guinness on tap. Dine at the bar or on the heated patio with large outdoor fireplace. **Jambo Café** (505-473-1269; 2010 Cerrillos Rd.) serves Afro-Caribbean food that wins awards annually. Highly recommended.

When on the road between Santa Fe and Taos, you can satisfy your hunger at the roadside **Sugar's BBQ and Burger** (505-852-0604; 1799 NM 68, Mile Marker 18, Embudo) with delectable smoked ribs. Burgers aren't shabby, either.

Taos

In Taos good sipping spots include the **Bent Street Deli & Cafe** (575-758-5787; 120 Bent St. in the Dunn House complex) with adequate, not knockout, soups, salads, and sandwiches; the classic **Caffe Tazza** (575-758-8706; 122 Kit Carson Rd.) with its ramshackle patio; **World Cup Café** (575-737-5299; on the Plaza) serves only one kind of coffee—a strong, dark, espresso roast, and it is grand. And the grown-up feeling **Elevation Coffee** (575-779-6078; 1110 Paseo del Pueblo Norte) pours a fabulous cup and beautifully foams their lattes. But **Wired? Cyber Cafe**

Wired? Cyber Cafe is a cool, off-the-beaten path Taos hangout.

(575-751-9473; 705 Felicidad Lane), behind Albertson's, is probably now the numero uno coffee/hangout spot, with its rambling garden and multileveled work spaces. **Dragonfly Café & Bakery** (575-737-5859; 402 Paseo del Pueblo Norte) has a patio steeped in Taos charm with scrumptious baked goods and breakfasts. For an earthier spin, follow the locals to the **Taos Diner** (575-758-2374; 908 Paseo del Pueblo Norte) for generous breakfasts, burgers supreme, monster salads, and good old American fare with a healthy gloss.

COOKING SCHOOL

Santa Fe School of Cooking (505-983-4511; 116 W. San Francisco St., Santa Fe, NM 87501; closed Easter, Christmas, New Year's). If you're interested in learning to cook traditional New Mexican and contemporary southwestern food, take a lesson from the Santa Fe School of Cooking. The school and its food market, under the deft direction of Susan Curtis, are located on the upper level of the Plaza Mercado, a block from the Santa Fe Plaza. Curtis offers regional cooking classes almost daily for under $100 including a meal. The class packs in 2.5 hours' worth of technique, information, hints, and farmers' wisdom. Classes are held several times weekly; call for reservations.

FARMERS' MARKETS

At harvest time, the Santa Fe–Taos area is rich with roadside stands strung with red chile *ristras* and offering a variety of fresh-picked home-grown fruits, vegetables, preserves, and piñon nuts. In-season, the most abundant cluster of such spots can be found on NM 68 between Velarde and Dixon. From time to time, families even gather to cook and sell their freshly harvested green chile in shopping centers. Keep in mind that not all the produce is locally grown. When in doubt, ask the vendor.

Between June and October, there are a number of excellent farmers' markets in the Santa Fe–Taos area. The largest is the **Santa Fe Area Farmers' Market** (505-983-4098; 1607 Paseo de Peralta), held Tues. and Sat., 7–11:30 AM in the Santa Fe Railyard, a hot collection of specialty retail shops, galleries, and restaurants. Here you can get ultrafresh, locally grown produce (much of it organic), specialty vegetables like baby squash, as well as pre-

Expect live music at the farmers' market.

Watch Mariachis perform and shop where the chefs shop—at the Santa Fe Area Farmers' Market.

pared foods such as salsas, jams, and jellies—even fresh-squeezed apple cider and honey. Grab a pastry or a breakfast burrito to go with your fresh coffee, and you'll be a happy camper.

Saturday mornings are an event, with live music, tastings, and cooking demonstrations. Beware, however, as there is no guarantee the produce is either local or organic. The market is so popular that parking can be a real hassle. Don't say we didn't warn you. The market also has winter hours on weekends.

Three other regional markets offer similarly fresh local produce and specialty items July–Oct. These are the **Taos Farmers' Market** (575-751-7575), which meets Sat. around 7 AM near the county courthouse in back of Civic Plaza; the **Española Farmers' Market** (505-753-5340), which meets Mon., 10 AM–5 PM at 1005 N. Railroad Ave.; and the **Los Alamos Farmers' Market** (505-581-4651), held Thurs., 7 AM–noon at the Mesa Public Library parking lot, 20th and Central, and the second Thurs. of each month at Fuller Lodge, 8 AM–12:30 PM. Call for specific information.

FAST FOOD

As in most places, fast-food spots are abundant in the Santa Fe–Taos area. Some chains are so ubiquitous and predictable as to need no mention, and they are equally easy to find. Others, particularly those unique to the area, are worth looking for.

Santa Fe

One of the best and most popular places in Santa Fe is the **Burrito Company Café** (505-982-4453; 111 Washington Ave.), less than a block from the Plaza. Breakfast and lunch menus feature such favorites as fast burritos, Mexican plates, hot dogs, hamburgers, and New Mexico–style chile dogs. Here you can get a good blue corn chicken enchilada for a song. They also sell their own salsa and chile by the quart. It's a convenient local hangout, highly recommended for families and folks in a hurry.

While on the Plaza, you can get a delicious lunch as well as the quintessential Santa Fe experience for about $6, at **Roque's Carnitas**. Just follow the delicious aroma to Roque's cart on the corner of Washington and Palace Avenue, then claim a bench on the Plaza for some people-watching.

Possibly the most popular Mexican food take-out stand in town is **Baja Tacos & Burgers** (505-471-8762; 2621 Cerrillos Rd.) with its healthy ingredients, tasty ample portions, and "happy-hour" discounts. Specializes in tofu and

Baja Tacos still rules Cerrillos Road with tasty take-out.

vegetarian Mexican food. Also excellent for a quick Mexican food fix is **Felipe's Tacos** (505-473-9397; 1711 Llano), for healthy authentic quesadillas, burritos, and tacos, with a choice of fresh salsas to accompany.

If you're after a quick burger, try **Blake's Lotaburger**, a New Mexico chain that's popular for quick-and-easy family outings. Blake's raises their own beef, and if you want a New Mexico chile cheeseburger, this is a good place to find one. In or near Santa Fe, there are Lotaburgers (Airport Rd., Cerrillos Rd., St. Michael's Dr., and N. Guadalupe St.), as well as in Pojoaque. Near Taos you'll find Lotaburgers on Paseo del Pueblo Sur and in El Prado, just north of town. While not exactly fast food—more "rapid gourmet"—custom sandwiches and salad selections to-go are available at **Saveur** (505-989-4200; 204 Montezuma St., at the intersection with Cerrillos Rd., just beyond downtown).

Airport Road is now lined with food carts serving the authentic street food of Mexico. Go wherever you see the most cars parked—that's my method. Another spot worth mention-

Scrumptious street food, like savory grilled carnitas, is always available on the Santa Fe Plaza.

Leonel's is the big red truck with the famous tamales.

ing is **Bert's Burger Bowl** (505-982-0215; 235 N. Guadalupe St.) in Santa Fe, where the menu is written half in English and half in Spanish and the burger is legendary.

Taos

Look for **Monte's Chow Cart** (575-758-3632; 402 Paseo del Pueblo Sur), where the specialty of the casa is the chile relleno, and the breakfast burrito will fill you up with the authentic flavors of northern New Mexico. You must go to **Leonel's Fresh Tamales**, 519 Paseo del Pueblo Sur. In Arroyo Seco, **Abe's Cocina** (575-776-8516; 489 NM 150) is the place to pick up a breakfast burrito. When traveling to and from Santa Fe and Taos, do as the locals do and stop at **El Parasol** (505-753-8852; 602 Santa Cruz Rd., Española) for the take-out version of the next-door restaurant, El Paragua. There's no better place to take in the local color or the red chile; the chicken-guacamole tacos made them famous, and they are the best. Also with locations in Santa Fe and Pojoaque. Lowriders and movie stars alike flock here.

GOURMET SHOPS

Kaune Foodtown (505-982-2629; 511 Old Santa Fe Trail, Santa Fe, NM 87505; closed Sun., major holidays). If this little community grocery store looks a bit outdated, that shouldn't be surprising; it's about 50 years old. What is surprising is that it offers a dazzling array of gourmet foods, from imported prosciutto, truffle mousse, and vegetarian terrines to exotic spices and high-end canned goods such as hearts of palm and white asparagus and an entire wall of mustards. In addition, it has gourmet ice creams and fresh breads, jellies, and teas. This is where Santa Fe old-timers choose to shop. It also has a variety of fresh meats (see "Butchers," above) and is the only place in town where you can purchase prime beef.

HEALTH FOOD STORES

Santa Fe

La Montanita Co-op (505-984-2852; 913 W. Alameda St., Santa Fe, NM 87501; closed major holidays). Fresh, fair, and local is their motto; unfortunately, this can be expensive. However, the wide aisles of La Montanita provide a "shop local" alternative to big boy Whole Foods. They specialize in wholesome natural foods that are largely free of chemical preservatives, including local organic produce and nonsugar products. They also feature a range of gourmet and deli items (specialty cheeses and the like); chemical-free meats and fish; lots of bulk grains, herbs, and coffees; plus a wide variety of vitamins and health and beauty aids. Still retains its air of a neighborhood market.

Whole Foods (505-992-1700; 753 Cerrillos Rd., Santa Fe, NM 87505; closed Thanksgiving, Christmas). The national superstore of healthy foods has an on-site bakery, plenty of take-out selections, a wine shop, a cheese shop, fresh fish delivered daily, and everything you could want to prepare a picnic or gourmet meal. The awkward parking lot can make parking somewhat difficult, and watch out for that sharp turnoff to Cerrillos when driving in.

Taos

Cid's Food Market (575-758-1148; 623 Paseo del Pueblo Norte, Taos, NM 87571; closed Sun., major holidays). Since Cid's opened in 1986, owners Cid and Betty Backer have made it a point to purchase the freshest, purest food available. In addition to an array of organic, locally sourced fruits and vegetables and gourmet items, Cid's offers natural soaps, herbs, vitamins, non-animal-tested cosmetics, and biodegradable cleansers. At the same time, it has a great selection of treats such as Lindt chocolates and locally made salsas. Cid's has a first-rate meat department (see "Butchers," above), with bison, fresh fish, and the best cuts of lamb, beef, and pork. Those looking for sugar-free or gluten-free products will find them here. It's also the place to run into everyone you know in town and catch up on the latest. There's a salad and hot food bar where you can eat in or take out. You can sip your smoothie in the little glassed-in café space out front.

WINE AND LIQUOR STORES

Following are some convenient places to find that great bottle of wine and more in Santa Fe and Taos. Most of them sell a wide selection of beers, wines, and hard liquor—and many have employees who can make recommendations and help you find what you're looking for.

Santa Fe

Cliff's Packaged Liquor Store: 505-988-1790; 903 Old Pecos Trail, Santa Fe, NM 87501.

Kaune's Grocery Co.: 505-982-2629; 511 Old Santa Fe Trail, Santa Fe, NM 87501.

Lamplighter Liquor Store: 505-438-9132; 2411 Cerrillos Rd., Santa Fe, NM 87505.

Owl Liquors: 505-982-1751; 913 Hickox St., Santa Fe, NM 87501.

Rodeo Plaza Liquors: 505-473-2867; 2801 Rodeo Rd., Santa Fe, NM 87507.

Susan's Fine Wines & Spirits: 505-984-1582; 1001 Pen Rd., Santa Fe, NM 87501. Now with a new wine bar!

Near Santa Fe
Del Norte Lounge: 575-758-8904; 1574 S. Santa Fe. Rd., Ranchos de Taos, NM 87557.

Kokoman Wines & Liquors: 505-455-2219; Pojoaque, on US 285, 15 miles north of Santa Fe. One of the largest selections of fine wines, beers, and liquors.

Tesuque Village Market: 505-988-8848; Tesuque, NM, about 5 miles north of Santa Fe off US 285.

Taos
El Prado Liquor Store: 575-758-8254; El Prado, NM, 1 mile north of Taos on NM 3.

Wine Shop at the Old Blinking Light: 575-776-8787; Mile Marker 1, Ski Valley Rd., Taos, NM 87571.

Near Taos
Wineries
The first grapevines in the Rio Grande Valley were planted by missionaries in the 1500s, from cuttings originally brought from Spain to make sacramental wine. Thanks to the valley's long, warm days and cool nights, winemaking flourished here for hundreds of years—all the way up to prohibition in the 1920s. Finally in the early 1970s, after a hiatus of 50 years, commercial wine production began making a comeback—partly with the help of French, German, and Swiss investments. Today, New Mexico has dozens of wineries scattered throughout the state, a few of them located in the mountainous Santa Fe–Taos area. Most have tasting rooms and welcome visitors.

Black Mesa Winery (505-852-2820; www.blackmesawinery.com; 1502 NM 68, Mile Marker 15 Velarde, NM 87582; closed major holidays). Jerry and Lynda Burd live on the road to Taos in fruit country where grapes have grown for four centuries. Perhaps too well known for their Black Beauty, a chocolate-scented red, Black Mesa has matured into a producer of a grand range of highly respectable wines. Their tasting room is a comfortable place to get acquainted and "nose some juice." I am a fan of the Antelope, but it's all good.

La Chiripada Winery (505-579-4437; NM 75 Dr., #1119-8, Dixon, NM 87525, about 3 miles east of NM 68; open daily). Sometime when you're shuttling between Santa Fe and Taos on NM 68, take a quick detour at the Dixon turnoff for a taste of heaven in a traditional adobe and viga tasting room. Mike and Patrick Johnson started this little family vineyard in 1977 and began making wine in 1981. At 6,100 feet, La Chiripada is the highest commercial vineyard in the United States, where they successfully cultivate the heartiest of grapes (two Pinot noir hybrids, for example) that ripen into intense flavors. Each year they crush 20 to 30 tons of fruit. The combined results, several of which have won bronze medals in the *Dallas Morning News* National Wine Competition, speak for themselves. These wines are surprisingly good. We recommend the Primavera, a blend of Riesling and French hybrids, served at the Santa Fe School of Cooking. They also operate a wine shop in Taos on Bent Street, a block from the Plaza.

Recreation

FOR THE FUN OF IT

WITH HIGH-MOUNTAIN TERRAIN, clear blue skies, and several million acres of forestlands, the Santa Fe–Taos area offers a bountiful backdrop for year-round outdoor fun. Fishing, hunting, camping, golfing, boating, biking, horseback riding, running—every sport has its place and season. In spring, rafters buck the frothing rapids of the Rio Grande and balloonists float high over scenic hills. Summer hikers roam backcountry trails between 7,000 and 13,000 feet, while windsurfers sweep across the choppy waters of wide-open lakes. In fall, hunters and anglers take to rivers and hills with visions of lunker trout, kokanee salmon, and trophy deer and elk. The winter mountains become a snowy wonderland, offering world-class ski areas, myriad cross-country trails, and challenging snowmobile highways.

Active Pursuits

In and around **Santa Fe** and **Taos**

BALLOONING

For a blessedly quiet bird's-eye view of the Santa Fe–Taos area, there's nothing better than hopping in a basket and casting your fate to the wind. In Santa Fe, the place to call for a ride May-Oct. is **Santa Fe Balloons** (505-699-7555), available at $275 per person, including pickup and drop-off at your hotel. **Santa Fe Detours** (505-983-6565; 800-338-6877; 54½ E. San Francisco St., on the Plaza above Häagen-Dazs) can arrange a ballooning experience for $135 a person.

In Taos, **Pueblo Balloon Company** (575-751-9877; www. Puebloballoon .com; P.O. Box 361, Taos, NM 87571) is available to take you aloft, offering Rio Grande Gorge flights at $250 ($220 cash).

LEFT: Sipapu is a favorite with local snowboarders.

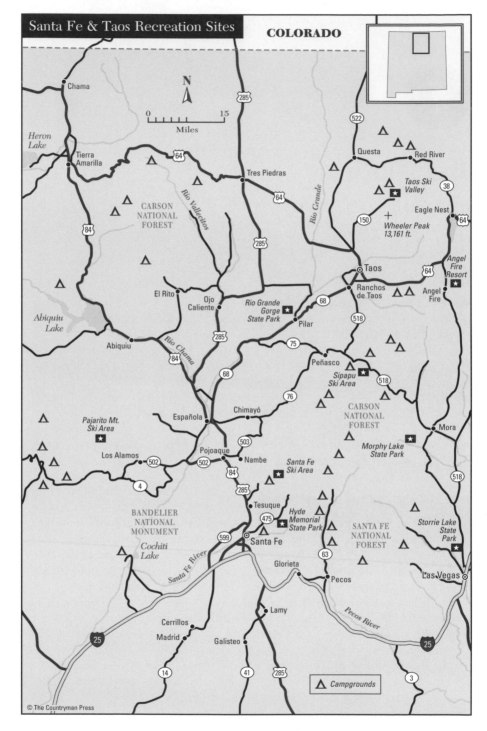

Santa Fe & Taos Recreation Sites

COLORADO

Chama

N

0 Miles 15

Heron
Lake

Tierra
Amarilla

Questa

Red River

522

Taos Ski
Valley

38

CARSON
NATIONAL
FOREST

64

Tres Piedras

64

Rio Vallecitos

Rio Grande

285

150

Wheeler Peak
13,161 ft.

Eagle Nest

64

Angel
Fire
Resort

84

El Rito

Ojo
Caliente

Rio Grande
Gorge
State Park

68

Taos

Ranchos
de Taos

64

Angel
Fire

Abiquiu
Lake

Abiquiu

Rio Chama

285

Pilar

518

84

68

75

Peñasco

Sipapu
Ski Area

518

Pajarito Mt.
Ski Area

Española

Chimayó

76

CARSON
NATIONAL
FOREST

Mora

Los Alamos

502

Pojoaque

503

Nambe

Santa Fe
Ski Area

Morphy Lake
State Park

518

4

502

84

285

Tesuque

475

Hyde
Memorial
State Park

SANTA FE
NATIONAL
FOREST

Storrie Lake
State Park

BANDELIER
NATIONAL
MONUMENT

Cochiti
Lake

599

Santa Fe

63

Glorieta

Las Vegas

Santa Fe River

Pecos

Cerrillos

Lamy

Pecos River

25

Madrid

Galisteo

14

41

285

Campgrounds

3

25

© The Countryman Press

If you're not in great shape, you will be by the time you bike along the Hondo River to Taos Ski Valley.

BICYCLING

From smooth country highways to rugged mountain trails, you can't beat the Santa Fe–Taos area for road biking and knobby-tired mountain bike adventures. If your heart is set on road biking, be sure to bring your own bike; it's almost impossible to get touring rentals in Santa Fe or Taos. And if you're mountain biking, remember: (1) Mountain bikes are not allowed in wilderness areas; (2) be considerate of hikers and those on horseback; (3) trails are usually steeper and more difficult than forest roads; and (4) trail conditions change markedly with the weather.

Santa Fe Area

One of the best ways to start pedaling in Santa Fe is to get hold of a **Santa Fe Bicycle Map** in the **Public Works office** at City Hall (505-995-6621; 120 S. Federal Pl., Santa Fe, NM 87501) or at one of the bicycle dealerships listed below. This map, compiled by the members of the Sangre de Cristo Cycling Club, shows both recreational and utilitarian routes in and around the city. Other good publications are the *New Mexico Bicyclist's Guide* compiled by the state highway department and *Santa Fe on Foot: Walking, Running and Bicycling Routes in the City Different* by Elaine Pinkerton. Both of these are available at most local bookstores and sports shops.

There are some great mountain biking trails minutes from downtown Santa Fe and a couple of places to rent the sturdy-framed, low-geared contraptions. Camino La Tierra accesses a number of easy trails on city-owned land close to town. For more aggressive riding, try the arroyo behind St. John's College, the Chamiso Trail, Pacheco Canyon Road, or any of the myriad trails off the Aspen Vista parking lot near the top of the Ski Basin Road. Dale Ball Trails, praised as rideable yet challenging for all levels, can be accessed in town at Cerro Gordo and Upper Canyon Road. For other good routes, call the Santa Fe National Forest at 505-438-5380. *Mountain Biking Northern New Mexico* by Bob D'Antonio (Falcon Publishing) provides an up-to-date guide.

To book a bike tour in the Santa Fe area, try **Bike N Sport** (505-820-0809; 524 W. Cordova Rd.). For rentals, at around $60 per day, Mello Velo is conveniently located at 621 Old Santa Fe Trail (505-995-6396).

Taos Area

Mountain biking trails in the Carson National Forest off US 64 will take you all the way to Angel Fire. A favorite route for families is Rio Chiquito, a long forest service road off NM 518 that connects with Garcia Park, including beaver ponds and good picnicking. Picuris Peak, also with access off NM 518, is a good intermediate-to-expert route with a steep grade but a great view. For more detailed recommendations, call or stop in at the Carson National Forest office (575-758-6200; 208 Cruz Alta Rd., Taos, NM 87571).

Bicycle Dealers

Santa Fe

Ace Mountain Wear and Bikes (505-982-8079; 825 Early St., Ste. B, Santa Fe, NM 87505-1680). Mountain bike repairs and information.

rob and charlie's (505-471-9119; 1632 St. Michael's Dr., Santa Fe, NM 87505). Specialists in retail parts and repair, with more than 4,000 parts in stock; good biking info and BMX stud bikes for kids.

Santa Fe Mountain Sports (505-988-3337; 1221 Flagman Way, 1221 Flagman Way, Ste. B1, Santa Fe, NM 87505). Offers new suspension bikes; open every day. Rents ski equipment as well.

Taos Area

Cottam's Ski Shop (575-758-2822; 207A Paseo del Pueblo Sur, Taos, NM 87571). Offers a selection of specialized bikes, right by the Plaza.

Gearing Up (575-751-0365; 129 Paseo del Pueblo Sur, Taos, NM 87571). Centrally located sales and service; mountain, road, hybrid, and tandem bike rentals; books, maps, and info. Geared toward general bike users.

Cottam's Rio Grande Rafting (575-758-2882; 800-753-7559; 1335 Paseo del Pueblo Sur, Taos, NM 87571). Mountain bike sales, rental, service, tours, and info.

Taos Mountain Outfitters (575-758-9292; 114 S. Plaza, Taos, NM 87571).

BOATING

See "Water Sports."

See also "Hiking and Climbing."

Many first-time visitors are surprised and delighted to find a land of lush mountain wilderness, including scores of idyllic campsites. Public, vehicle-accessible sites in national forest and state park areas are usually open May–Oct. and available on a first-come, first-served basis. There are also myriad backcountry campsites for those on the trail (usually requiring overnight permits), plus a number of private camping areas that offer trailer hookups and tent sites with all the amenities. For maps and specifics on public areas, contact the government agencies listed under "Hiking and Climbing." For information and reservations at private RV campgrounds, contact the following:

Private Campgrounds

Near Santa Fe

Los Campos Recreation Vehicle Park (505-473-1949; 3574 Cerrillos Rd., Santa Fe, NM 87501, only five minutes from the Plaza). One of two full-service RV parks within the city limits, with 94 full hookups, four tent sites, restrooms, shower, laundry, swimming pool, and car rentals.

Rancheros de Santa Fe Camping Park (505-466-3482; 736 Old Las Vegas Hwy., Santa Fe, NM 87505, exit 290 off I-25, 1 mile east on Old Las Vegas Hwy.). Wooded and open sites for tents, trailers, and motor homes with pool, showers, restrooms, groceries, hiking trail, laundry, and propane. Camping cabins also available. Open mid-Mar.–Nov. 1.

Near Taos

Golden Eagle RV Park (575-377-6188; 800-388-6188; P.O. Box 458, Eagle Nest, NM 87718, off US 64 in Eagle Nest at 540 W. Therma Blvd.). A 531-space RV park, including 29 pull-throughs, restrooms, showers, RV supplies, propane, and game room.

Gold Pan Motel & Gift Shop (575-377-2286; 800-377-2286; 50 US 64, Eagle Nest, NM 87718). Ten RV spaces and nine motel rooms. The café on the premises is a local hangout that serves three squares, seven days a week.

Questa Lodge (575-586-9913; P.O. Box 282, Questa, NM 87556, 0.25 mile off NM 522 in Questa, on the Red River). Motel and RV park with 26 full-service hookups, five cabins, tent sites, Laundromat, restrooms, and children's playground. Open May–Oct.

Roadrunner RV Resort (575-754-2286; 1371 E. Main St., Red River, NM 87558). Camping for 150 vehicles with 89 full hookups, laundry, showers, tennis court, restrooms, cable TV, playground, barbecue area, picnic tables, fire ring, tepees, and gazebo.

Valley RV Park and Campground (575-578-4469; Box 7204, NDCBU, 120 Estes Rd., Taos, NM 87571). Complete commercial campground including 35 full hookups, 75 water and electric hookups, 18 tent sites, playground, rec room, showers, phones, convenience store, and laundromat. Open Mar. 15–Oct. 31; Nov. 1–Mar. 15 with limited services available.

RECREATION

You can't drive very far in northern New Mexico without running into an Indian-run gambling casino. While the pros and cons of gambling are hotly debated on the streets and in the courts, the casinos remain up and running, with packed parking lots. If you yearn to try your luck without going all the way to Las Vegas, Nevada, just join the crowd. Many also serve lavish, low-cost buffets.

Buffalo Thunder Resort and Casino (505-455-5555; 30 Buffalo Thunder Trail, on US 84/285 north of Santa Fe). The newest and most exciting place to try and win your fortune.

Camel Rock Casino (505-984-8414; on US 84/285, 10 minutes north of downtown Santa Fe). Run by Tesuque Pueblo, Camel Rock offers slots, blackjack, bingo, roulette, and a restaurant.

Cities of Gold Casino (505-455-3313; on US 84/285, 15 miles north of Santa Fe). Cities of Gold is run by Pojoaque Pueblo and has more than 700 slot machines, in addition to other games, as well as an "extravagant" 24-hour buffet spread.

Ohkay Casino (505-747-1668; on US 84/285, just north of Española). Operated by San Juan Pueblo, this popular casino is well known for its breakfast buffet.

Taos Mountain Casino (575-737-0777; 700 Veterans Hwy., Taos, NM 87571). The only nonsmoking casino in the state, Taos Mountain offers slots but no bingo.

FITNESS CENTERS

Whether it's weight training, aerobics, racquetball, stretching, swimming, or yoga, rest assured there are plenty of gyms available. Most of them also employ fitness experts who are ready and eager to help you with a program tailored to meet your needs. Membership rates range $45–75 a month or $330–720 a year; rates for non-members run $5–12 a day.

Santa Fe

Bulldog Gym (505-988-5117; 1512 Paseo de Peralta, Santa Fe, NM 87505). Specializes in one-on-one personal fitness training.

Carl and Sandra's Physical Conditioning Center (505-982-6760; 153-A Paseo de Peralta, in the DeVargas Center). Run by Olympic trainer Carl Miller and his wife, this gym specializes in individualized personal weight training, aerobics, nutrition, stress management, and exercises for pregnant women.

Club International Family Fitness Center (505-473-9807; 1931 Warner Ave., Santa Fe, NM 87505). Separate rooms specialize in Nautilus, free weights, aerobics (including bench step), and cardiovascular exercise. Also offers lap pool with water exercises, six racquetball courts, treadmills, StairMasters, Lifecycles, Bio Cycles, CombiCycles, whirlpool, individualized fitness programs, sauna, steam room, and child care.

Fitness Plus (505-473-7315; 1119 Calle del Cielo, Santa Fe, NM 87507, off Cerrillos Rd.). A club for women only, with varied fitness classes, Nautilus, free weights, toning tables, massages, facials, acupuncture, and body wraps.

Fort Marcy Recreation Complex (505-955-2500; 490 Bishops Lodge Rd., Santa Fe, NM 87501). The city's major sports complex, with gym, weight room, jogging course, racquetball courts, aerobic and workout room, and classes galore. $4 per visit; $2 seniors, with a $150/year membership card. Nonmember and student rates also available.

Mandrill Gym (505-988-2986; 708 W. San Mateo Rd. Santa Fe, NM 87505). A serious weight-training center with free weights, Flex machines, aerobics, women's body-shaping classes, and sports massage.

Santa Fe Spa (505-984-8727; 786 N. St. Francis Dr. Santa Fe, NM 87501). Includes free weights, Nautilus and Cybex equipment, treadmills, StairMasters, yoga classes, individual training, sauna, and steam rooms, plus an extensive schedule of classes.

Taos Area

Northside Health and Fitness (575-751-1242; 1307 Paseo de Pueblo Norte, El Prado, NM 87527). A friendly, accessible, community-oriented fitness center with indoor and outdoor pools, four tennis courts, Cybex weight equipment, aerobics classes, cardiovascular room with Cybex rowers and NordicTrack skiers, physical therapy, kids' activities, and great drumming classes! Day passes available for $10.

Taos Spa & Tennis Club (575-758-1980; 111 Dona Ana Dr., Taos, NM 87571, across from Sagebrush Inn). Includes racquetball, tennis, indoor and outdoor pools, aerobics, weight room with free weights and machines, personalized instruction, hot tubs, sauna, steam rooms, and child care. Day passes available for $12.

GOLF

Most people don't think of New Mexico as a golf haven, but the sport is becoming increasingly popular in these parts. Local courses, varying between 6,000 and 8,600 feet in elevation, offer some of the highest fairways in the world, with terrain ranging from brushy plains to rolling hills thick with conifers. Most clubs hold seasonal tourneys, with schedules available at the pro shops.

Golf Clubs

Santa Fe

Santa Fe Country Club (505-471-2626), 436 A Country Club Rd., Santa Fe, NM 87502). Designed by one of the first PGA members more than 50 years ago, this 18-hole, par-72 course features tree-shaded golfing close to town. Usually open March–Nov., it has four sets of tees with distances between 6,703 and 7,091 yards and a ladies' course measuring 5,955 yards. It also includes a driving and chipping range and a practice putting green. Resident greens fees $34 weekdays, $44 weekends. The pro on duty is Joe Tiano.

Near Santa Fe

The Cochiti Lake Golf Course (505-465-2239; 5200 Cochiti Hwy., Santo Domingo, NM 87083) is rated number 5 in the state and among the top 25 public courses in the country. Set against a stunning backdrop of red-rock mesas and steep canyons, it features an 18-hole, par-72 course of 6,450 yards along with a driving range, putting green, pro shop, and restaurant complete with green chile cheeseburgers. The pro on duty is Jude Suina. Greens fees $48 weekdays, $55 weekends; both include a cart. Open all year, weather permitting.

Los Alamos Golf Course (505-662-8139; 4250 Diamond Dr., Los Alamos, NM 87544). This course is 18 holes, par 71, 6,500 yards. It includes driving range, putting green, bar, and snack bar. The pro on duty is Donny Torrez. Greens fees $31–$35.

Pendaries Village Golf & Country Club (505-425-6076; P.O. Box 820, Rociada, NM 87742). About an hour and a half out of Santa Fe, on the north side of Las Vegas. With a well-deserved reputation as one of the state's most beautiful golf courses, Pendaries is an 18-hole, par-72 mountain course at 7,200 feet. Greens fees $32 weekdays, $40 weekends, with a $24 golf cart rental charge. Has a pro shop, snack bar, and restaurant with bar. The pro on duty is Donald Torres. Open Apr. 15–Oct. 15.

Near Taos

Angel Fire Golf Course (575-377-3055; 800-633-7463; Angel Fire Resort, Drawer B, Angel Fire, NM 87710). At 8,600 feet, this is one of the highest and most lushly wooded regulation courses in the world. Usually open mid-May to mid-Oct., it's an 18-hole, par-72 course with driving range and putting greens, club and cart rentals, and a restaurant, snack bar, and bar. The new clubhouse is glorious. Greens fee $50 weekdays, $65 weekends, plus cart fee.

HIKING AND CLIMBING

Cradled by mountains containing two national forests and numerous wilderness areas and state parks, north central New Mexico offers more than 3 million acres of public forestland with hundreds of miles of lakeshores and cold mountain streams. Most of this land is truly wild and forested. It is also laced with more than 1,000 miles of well-maintained trails that vary from a half-hour guided nature walk to a two-week pack trip.

The primary recreation areas are the Santa Fe and Carson National Forests. A few of the gems within these two massive preserves include the 223,333-acre Pecos Wilderness, east of Santa Fe with magnificent aspen and evergreen forests; the 5,200-acre Dome Wilderness in the volcanic Jemez Mountains to the west; the 41,132-acre San Pedro Parks Wilderness with rolling, spruce-studded mountaintops and open meadows; and the rugged Wheeler Peak and lake-strewn Latir Peak Wilderness areas northeast of Taos.

Books, Maps, and Organizations

For an excellent introduction to some of the fine trails in the Santa Fe–Taos area, we suggest you contact the Santa Fe (The Northern Group) Sierra Club (505-983-2703; 1807 Second St., Unit 45, Santa Fe, NM 87501). During spring and summer months, they run two or three trips of varying difficulty every weekend. They've also published a book titled *Day Hikes in the Santa Fe Area*, detailing numerous short hikes, many of which can be made into overnight journeys. Another good hiking contact is the Randall Davey Audubon Center (505-983-4609; 1800 Upper Canyon Rd., Santa Fe, NM 87501). There, right in town, you can access the excellent Dale Ball Trails system.

You can also get topo maps of the northern New Mexico area at the Public Lands Information Center (505-954-2002; 301 Dinosaur Tr., Santa Fe, NM

87508) and at the same address, the Bureau of Land Management (505-954-2000) has an invaluable series of 1:100,000 scale maps based on the USGS series showing roads, trails, and landownership by color.

Taos Area
In Taos, one of the best wilderness contacts is Taos Mountain Outfitters (575-758-9292; 114 S. Plaza, Taos, NM 87571). In addition to routes and rentals, most of their salespeople are avid hikers and climbers. They also have a little publication called *Taos Rock*, which will steer you toward the best rock climbing in the area. Another good bet is Cottam's Rio Grande Rafting (575-758-2882; 1335 Paseo del Pueblo Sur, Taos, NM 87571), which rents backcountry gear and offers a variety of wilderness treks. Sipapu Lodge and Ski Area (575-587-2240; 5224 NM 518, Vadito, NM 87579) also offers hiking opportunities.

National Forest Offices

Santa Fe Area
Santa Fe National Forest (505-438-5300 supervisor's office; 11 Forest Lane, Santa Fe, NM 87508). Contact this office for general information, maps of the Santa Fe National Forest, and detailed topo maps of Pecos and San Pedro Parks Wilderness Areas.

Coyote Ranger District (505-638-5526, in Santa Fe; HC 78 Box 1, Coyote, NM 87012). Handles San Pedro Parks Wilderness Area.

Española Ranger District (505-753-7331; 1710 Riverside, Española, NM 87532 or P.O. Box 3307, Española, NM 87533, corner of Santa Clara St. and Los Alamos Hwy.).

Jemez Ranger District (505-829-3535; P.O. Box 150, Jemez Springs, NM 87025, between Los Alamos and Jemez Springs on NM 4).

Pecos Ranger District (505-757-6121; P.O. Drawer 429, Pecos, NM 87552, exit 299 for Glorieta/Pecos to NM 50).

Taos Area
Carson National Forest (575-758-6200 supervisor's office; 208 Cruz Alta Rd., Taos, NM 87571). Call the supervisor's office for information on the districts below:

El Rito Ranger District: 575-581-4554; P.O. Box 56, El Rito, NM 87530, at the junction of NM 110 and NM 96.

Peñasco Ranger District: 575-587-2255; P.O. Box 68, Peñasco, NM 87553.

Questa Ranger District: 575-586-0520; P.O. Box 110, Questa, NM 87556, 2 miles east of Questa on NM 38. Handles 20,000-acre Latir Peaks Wilderness Area north of Red River.

Tres Piedras Ranger District: 575-758-8678; P.O. Box 38, Tres Piedras, NM 87577, 1 mile west of the junction of US 64 and US 285.

National Monuments

Near Santa Fe
Bandelier National Monument (505-672-3861; www.nps.gov/band; National Park Service, Entrance Rd., Los Alamos, NM 87544) includes nearly 50 square miles of mesa and canyon country with myriad walking, hiking, and overnight camping

opportunities in the land of the Anasazi. Short trails in Frijoles Canyon lead through ancient ruins and cliff dwellings; longer trails lead south through canyons and west to the Dome Wilderness. Tsankawi (SANK-a-wee) located off NM 4, a smaller monument area near White Rock, offers several miles of trails through unexcavated ruins. Due to the massive Conchas Fire of 2011, trail access may be limited.

Pecos National Historical Park (505-757-7200; www.nps.gov/peco; National Park Service, P.O. Box 418, Pecos, NM 87552, 2 miles south of Pecos off NM 63). It includes a handicapped-accessible, self-guided trail through the ruins of the old Pecos Pueblo and church. Here you can find Civil War enactments, tours of Glorieta Battlefield, and many more seasonally scheduled activities. (For more information on Pecos or Bandelier, see chapter 5, *Sacred Sites*.)

State Parks
Santa Fe
New Mexico State Parks Division (505-476-3355; 888-667-2757; nmparks@state.nm.us; www.emnrd.state.nm.us/nm parks; 1220 S. St. Francis Dr., Santa Fe, NM 87504).

Near Santa Fe
Hyde Memorial State Park (contact state park number above, 12 miles northeast of Santa Fe via Hyde Park Rd.). Offers 350 acres of mountains and streams with trails and camping and picnic areas.

Santa Fe River Watershed Association (505-820-1696). Includes five narrow acres of greenery with a few picnic tables along Alameda Street, a few blocks from the center of town.

Get after the German browns in Cimarron Canyon State Park.

Taos Area
Cimarron Canyon (575-377-6271; P.O. 28869 US Highway 64, Eagle Nest, NM 87718, 3 miles east of Eagle Nest via US 64). A 33,000-acre mountainous preserve with numerous wonderful trails and camping and picnic areas.

Kit Carson Memorial Park (575-758-8234; 211 Paseo del Pueblo Norte, Taos, NM 87571). Offers short walks and a playground on 22 acres.

Rio Grande Gorge State Park (contact state parks number above; 16 miles southwest of Taos on NM 570). Includes shelter, barbecues, trails, drinking water, and campgrounds along the road by the river.

See also "Hunting and Fishing."

Horse travel may not be as common today as it was in the days of yore, but it's definitely alive and well. You can still get a whiff of the Old West as you saddle up and head on out, whether for a few turns around the corral, a picnic ride, or a weeklong pack trip. Following are some local outfitters. Prices range $20–35 per hour, with special rates for longer trips.

Santa Fe Area

Bear Creek Adventures (505-757-6229; HC 74 Box 21-D, Pecos, NM 87552). Operating out of the Glorieta Conference Center, Eric Roybal and his family offer a variety of horseback and horse-drawn experiences, from trail rides to sleigh rides and hayrides. Weddings, too!

The Bishop's Lodge (505-819-4013; 1297 Bishops Lodge Rd., Santa Fe, NM 87507). Approximately two-hour guided trail rides within the lodge's 1,000-acre grounds. Special wrangler rides for children under eight. Call for reservations and fees.

Broken Saddle Riding Co. (505-424-7774; 26 Vicksville Rd., Cerrillos, NM 87010, 26 miles from Santa Fe Plaza in Cerrillos). Enjoy 360-degree views along the Turquoise Trail.

Four Seasons Resort Rancho Encantado Santa Fe (505-946-5700; 198 NM 592, Santa Fe, NM 87506, about 8 miles north of Santa Fe off NM 592). Fifty-seven acres bordering the Santa Fe National Forest. Trail rides for guests only.

Terrero General Stores and Riding Stables (505-757-6193; P.O. Box 12, Terrero, NM 87573). Owners Huie and Sherry Ley run sightseeing and photography trips, as well as seasonal hunting, fishing, and pack trips into the Santa Fe National Forest and the Pecos Wilderness.

Taos Area

Cieneguilla Stables (575-751-2815; 2961 NM 68, near the village of Pilar, 13 miles south of the Taos visitors center). Custom rides available, or ride to the miner's cabin in Rio Grande Gorge canyon country.

Cimarroncita Ranch (866-376-2376; www.cimarroncita.com; 29820 US Highway 64 Ute Park, NM 87749). This glorious old place, only recently renovated and opened, offers guests riding and pack trips, plus fly-fishing, photo adventures, and a true getaway.

Taos Indian Horse Ranch (575-758-3212; 800-659-3210; Pinon Rd., Arroyo Seco, NM 87514, off NM 150). This well-established outfitter offers tracking rides, horseback rides, and overnight camping trips. Reservations required.

HUNTING AND FISHING

The Santa Fe–Taos area is a hunting and fishing paradise. Gun or bow hunters can bag not only deer, elk, squirrels, game birds, and waterfowl but also wild turkey, antelope, elk, bighorn sheep, and javelina—even exotic species such as ibex and oryx. Lake fish include bass, perch, catfish, and walleye. Kokanee salmon (introduced from the Pacific Coast) and five species of trout abound in stocked lakes and streams.

Before you go, be sure to get licenses and current rules and regulations from the **New Mexico Department of Game and Fish** (505-476-8000; www.wildlife.state.nm.us/contact; One Wildlife Way, Santa Fe, NM 87504) or from a local sporting goods store. You may also call or write them for their list of registered guides and outfitters. For information on hunting and fishing on Indian lands, see "Pueblos" in chapter 4, *Culture*. You don't need a license to hunt or fish there, but you must have written permission and an official tribal document showing legal possession of any game or fish taken.

For information on conditions and places to go, talk to any local guide or outfitter. They can take you to prime fishing and hunting territory, both public and private. If you decide to use a guide, check with the National Forest Service or the Bureau of Land Management to make sure the outfit has proper permits and insurance. Prices for guides and outfitters vary widely, depending on the quarry and kind of hunting, the destination and accommodations, and the length of time. Prices range from $220 for a day of fishing to around $4,000 for a five-day elk hunt, with the most luxurious trips going as high as $15,000.

Guides and Outfitters

Santa Fe

High Desert Angler (505-988-7688; 460 Cerrillos Rd., Santa Fe, NM 87501). This is the fly-fishing center of Santa Fe, including instruction and guide service, rentals, equipment sales, and expert, friendly advice. It's the opposite of intimidation.

Known World Guide Service (800-983-7756; 825 Early Street, Santa Fe, NM 87505). This service takes you to the Wild and Scenic Rio Grande, Red River, Pecos River, and Santa Fe National Forest.

Oshman's Sporting Goods (505-473-3555; 4250 Cerrillos Rd., Santa Fe, NM 87501). Here you'll find everything from spinning and fly rods to rifles and shotguns with all the eggs, lures, flies, and accessories you'll ever need.

The Outdoorsman of Santa Fe (505-983-3432; 530 N. Guadalupe St., Santa Fe, NM 87501). An archery and bow-hunting headquarters with an indoor archery range.

The Reel Life (505-995-8114; 500 Montezuma St., Santa Fe 87501). One-stop shopping for clothing, equipment, guide service, instruction, and travel information you need to make your next fly-fishing adventure a memorable one.

Ron Peterson Guns (505-471-4411; 509 Airport Rd., Santa Fe 87505). Guns, ammo, rods, reels, bows, black powder, scopes—the works. Also the home for Imperial Taxidermy, which does game heads, fish, reptiles, and life-sized animals.

Santa Fe Flyfishing School & Guide Service (713-502-1809; 79 Camino Rincon, Pecos, 87552). Learn how it's done on the glorious Pecos.

Near Santa Fe

Bear Creek Adventures (505-757-6229; Rte. 1, Box 21-D, Pecos, NM 87552). Hunting and fishing trips into the Sangre de Cristos for all experience levels.

Terrero General Stores and Riding Stables, Inc. (505-757-6193; P.O. Box 12, Terrero, NM 87573). Owner Huie Ley leads day trips, hourly rides, and overnight trips for hunting and fishing into the wildest areas of the Sangre de Cristo Mountains. A native of Terrero, he's one of the best outfitter-guides.

Los Rios Anglers (575-758-2798; 126 W. Plaza Dr., Taos, NM 87571). The professional fly-fishing guides here are some of the best in the state. A complete fly-fishing shop offering gear, information, and year-round pack-and-float trips—including trips into the Rio Grande Gorge and isolated fishing on private lands.

Solitary Angler (575-758-5653; 204 B Paseo del Pueblo Norte, Taos, NM 87571). To book a guided trip on local public water or on the Solitary Angler's 11 private miles of Culebra Creek or the Cimarron Holy Water, give a call.

Near Taos

Bitter Creek Guest Ranch (575-754-2587; P.O. Box 310, Red River, NM 87558). Fully licensed outfitter and guide, featuring deer and elk hunts into the mountain area of Valle Vidal.

Deep Creek Wilderness (575-776-8423; P.O. Box 721, El Prado, NM 87529). Hunting, fishing, horseback, camping, and sightseeing trips in the Carson National Forest, Latir Lakes Wilderness, and Valle Vidal area, with one of the biggest elk herds in the country.

Eagle Nest Marina and Mountain View Cabins (575-377-6941; NM 64, Eagle Nest, NM 87718). They offer fishing equipment and trips for cutthroats, rainbows, cohos, and kokanee all seasons at Eagle Nest Lake, including ice fishing in winter.

High Mountain Outfitters (575-751-7000; P.O. Box 2439, Ranchos de Taos, NM 87557). Run by Pete Trujillo, one of the best licensed hunting guides in northern New Mexico. He specializes in big-game trophy hunts with gun and bow for elk, deer, antelope, sheep, bear, mountain lion, and turkey, plus summer fishing and backpacking trips. All hunts include food, lodging, guides, and transportation.

Rio Costilla Park (575-586-0542; 72 NM 196, Costilla, NM 87524). Fishing and hunting trips on a 79,000-acre private reserve in the Latir Lakes area about 40 miles north of Taos. Trespass fee required for private hunting; call to arrange for guided trips.

PARKS IN TOWN

Following is a list of parks in Santa Fe and Taos that offer open space, quiet, and recreational opportunities for everyone. For maps and further information, contact the **Santa Fe Parks and Recreation Division** (505-476-3355; 1220 S. St. Francis Dr., Santa Fe, NM 87501) or the **Taos Parks and Recreation Department** (575-758-8234).

Santa Fe

Amelia White (Old Santa Fe Trail and Corrales Rd.). A small, natural park with pleasant sitting spots, walking paths, and access for the handicapped.

Ashbaugh (Cerrillos Rd. and San Jose Ave.). A long, narrow finger of green next to the Santa Fe Indian Hospital. Includes picnic tables, tennis court, baseball and soccer fields, walking paths, basketball court, and access for the handicapped.

Cathedral (Palace Ave. and Cathedral Pl.). A quiet, fence-enclosed lunch spot with picnic tables a block east of the Plaza.

Fort Marcy-Magers Field (Washington Ave. and Murales Rd., north of Paseo de Peralta). A major facility complete with picnic tables, restrooms, grills, tennis court, baseball field, indoor swimming pool, fitness room, gymnasium, playground, walking paths, par course, and handicapped access.

Gen. Franklin E. Miles (Siringo Rd. and Camino Carlos Rey). Many square blocks' worth of sports fields and fun, including restrooms, picnic tables, shelter, softball field, indoor swimming pool, paths, playground, and handicapped access.

Larragoite (Agua Fria Rd. and Potencia St., near Larragoite Elementary School). A neighborhood park offering picnic tables, tennis courts, and softball field.

The Plaza. The city's oldest and most used facility, with benches and trees in the very heart of town.

Ragle (W. Zia Rd. and Yucca St.). Many acres of athletic fields near Santa Fe High School, offering picnic tables, grills, shelter, restrooms, baseball fields, pathways, playground, and handicapped access.

Randall Davey Audubon Center. See "Historic Buildings and Sites" in chapter 4, *Culture*.

Salvador Perez (Alta Vista and Letrado Sts.). A square block of open, green playground with picnic tables, restrooms, tennis courts, softball field, indoor swimming pool, horseshoe pit, racquetball, volleyball, fitness room, trails, and handicapped access.

Santa Fe River (along Alameda St.). A refreshing sliver of green with picnic tables bordering the Santa Fe River. Trails have been recently upgraded, and the river usually has water running in it, thanks to watershed restoration.

Frank S.Ortiz Dog Park (160 Camino de las Crucitas, Santa Fe, 87501). Acres of off-leash heaven for pets and their human companions to hike, visit, explore. Fabulous views of the city and the Sangre de Cristos. Moderate to easy trails.

Washington (Washington Ave. and S. Federal St.). A quiet, landscaped park with benches and big shade trees right next to the post office and courthouse. A great picnic spot.

Taos

Filemon Sanchez Park (slightly outside the south side of town). Includes baseball diamonds and other recreation facilities.

Fred Baca Memorial Park (575-758-8234; Camino del Media, just outside the town limits). A four-acre municipal park with picnic tables, restrooms, two tennis courts, basketball court, soccer field, volleyball court, and playground.

Kit Carson Park (575-758-8234; N. Pueblo Rd., a block from the Plaza). A 20-acre park with bike and walking path, picnic tables, grills, playground, tennis court, basketball court, amphitheater, and ice skating. Includes the graves of Kit Carson, Mabel Dodge Luhan, Padre Martinez, and other famous Taoseños.

RAFTING, CANOEING, KAYAKING

Northern New Mexico's wild, scenic waters provide some of the best whitewater thrills in the country. The best time for such trips is usually late May through late July, but stretches along the Rio Grande from the Colorado border all the way to Cochiti Dam are negotiable all year. You can also float several stretches of the

Pecos River between Cowles and Las Vegas. For current information on river flows, go to streamflow.allaboutrivers.com/New_Mexico/river_flow-sNM.html. For maps and information on permits, seasons, and conditions, contact the **Bureau of Land Management** (575-758-8851; 226 Cruz Alta Rd., Taos, NM 87571). The BLM maintains a Web site, with information on public lands including New Mexico, at www.nm.blm.gov. Please be aware of the potential serious danger that may occur on raft trips, particularly when the water is high.

Most commercial float companies provide half-day, full-day, and overnight rafting trips on the Rio Grande and the Chama. A relatively serene float, ideal for families, is the Lower Rio Grande Gorge. Two of the most popular whitewater stretches are the Racecourse and the Taos Box on the Upper Rio Grande, with foaming Class IV waters that are bound to awaken your wild side. The Chama's Wild and Scenic waters offer beautiful overnight trips. $38–45 for half-day trips, $84–97 for a full day with lunch, and around $225 for overnights with all equipment and meals provided. Three-day trips and special discounts are also available. With increasing restrictions on river use, early booking is advised.

Commercial Float Trips and Rentals

Santa Fe

New Wave Rafting Company (505-984-1444; www.newwaverafting.com; 1101 Cerrillos Rd., Santa Fe, NM 87506). One of the largest and most reputable rafting outfitters in the area.

Rafting the Rio Grande below Taos is an exceptional adventure.

Santa Fe Detours (505-983-6565; 800-338-6877; www.sfdetours.com; 52½ E. San Francisco St., Santa Fe, NM 87501). Books tours with numerous rafting companies.

Santa Fe Rafting (505-988-4914; 800-467-7238; www.santaferafting.com; 1000 Cerrillos Rd., Santa Fe, NM 87505).

Whitewater Information and Reservations (www.sdcmountainworks.com /water/whitewater.php). Clearinghouse that books approved local rafting companies. For a list of all accredited rafting companies, go to raftnewmexico.org.

Taos Area

Cottam's Rio Grande Rafting (800-322-8267; 800-753-7559; www.cottams riograndrafting.com; 1335 Paseo del Pueblo Sur, Taos, NM 87571-5972).

Los Rios River Runners (575-776-8854; 800-544-1181; www.losriosriver runners.com; P.O. Box 2734, Taos, NM 87571). In business more than 40 years.

RODEOS

The Santa Fe–Taos area has its roots in the Old West. No event emphasizes this more clearly than the rodeo, which harks back to the 19th century when much of New Mexico was dominated by the cattle industry and its rough-and-tumble cowboys.

In July, you can attend the Rodeo de Santa Fe (505-471-4300), with some of the best riding and roping anywhere. A downtown parade of riders from all over the country kicks off the festivities.

Toward the end of July, you can drift on down to the Rodeo de Galisteo, a somewhat smaller though no less exciting Wild West event. Up north toward the end of June take in the Rodeo de Taos (575-758-5700) at the Taos County Fairgrounds.

RUNNING

Runners here enjoy an exceptional variety of terrain and unusually clean, clear skies. From mountain highways and trails to secluded city byways, there's no better place to develop your legs and lungs while enjoying the unspoiled open spaces. For a comprehensive listing of races throughout the state, contact the New Mexico USA Track and Field (505-328-3825; www.usatf.org/clubs/search/info.asp?associationNumber=42).

Santa Fe

The Santa Fe Striders running club (505-983-2144; www.santafestriders.org; P.O. Box 1818, Santa Fe, NM 87504) starts fun runs from the Plaza every Wed. at 6 PM in summer months. Contact them for information on seasonal running events. A few good running spots in Santa Fe include the east side, the banks of the Santa Fe River along Alameda Street, the Old Santa Fe Trail, and the St. Catherine's cross-country course. For more information on these and other good routes, consult Striders or Santa Fe on Foot by Elaine Pinkerton. For longer jaunts, try the Ski Basin Road and some of the routes listed under "Biking."

Each year, Taos hosts at least one 10-kilometer race, plus a triathlon in fall and a marathon in June. Since there's no organized running club, your best bet is to check for dates and times with the **Taos County Chamber of Commerce** (575-751-8800; www.taoschamber.com; 515 Gusdorf Rd., Ste. 6, Taos, NM 87571). For training runs, the outskirts of Taos quickly lead to fairly flat, wide-open spaces, particularly toward the north, east, and west.

SKIING

Downhill Skiing

The Santa Fe–Taos area is a skier's paradise, boasting half a dozen areas with some of the most popular world-class slopes in the country. Many of the ski areas start at 9,000 to 10,000 feet and rise to 12,000 or more, making for vertical drops in excess of 2,500 feet with annual snowfalls of up to 300 inches.

A few hardy souls began skiing at the Santa Fe Ski Basin shortly after World War II, and Lloyd and Olive Bolander set up the first rope tow at Sipapu in 1952. The sport really began to take off in 1955, when pioneer Ernie Blake began carving out a mountain niche for families at the Taos Ski Valley. Other spots such as Red River and Angel Fire followed during the 1960s. Since then, lifts, lodges, lounges, snowmaking, and myriad cross-country trails have created a major resort area that now draws skiers from all over the world.

In general, you can count on some of the beginner and intermediate runs to be open by late November, the remaining runs by the middle of December. Snowmaking usually creates a number of good trails by Thanksgiving at Angel Fire, Red River, Santa Fe, and Taos Ski Valley. All areas are open daily 9–4 with the exception of Pajarito Mountain near Los Alamos, which is open only on Wed., weekends, and federal holidays. Rates quoted are for one full day unless otherwise stated; check ski area Web sites for full details on special rates and packages.

For New Mexico ski information, visit **New Mexico Snow Report** (www.onthe snow.com or www.skinewmexico.com/Snow_Reports/Main/Snow_Reports) for the most up-to-date information.

Near Santa Fe

Pajarito Mountain Ski Area (505-662-5725 information; 505-662-SNOW snow report; www.skiparajito.com; 7 miles west of Los Alamos via NM 502 and FR 1; 10,441 ft. peak elevation; 1,200 ft. vertical drop; 153 in. average snowfall; no snowmaking; trails: 37 downhill [20 percent beginner, 50 percent intermediate, 30 percent advanced]; no cross-country; lifts: 5 chairlifts [3 double, 1 triple, 1 quad], 1 rope tow, terrain park; $57 adults, $4 half day, $34 children, $46 seniors, 6 and under $9, 75 and over free). Pajarito was started in 1957 by a group of Los Alamos National Laboratory employees who wanted a convenient place to ski. The area is owned and operated by the Los Alamos Ski Club, whose members are mainly Los Alamos employees or residents; however, it's also open to the public.

With 40 trails and 300 skiable acres, Pajarito is geared toward the serious day skier. Its runs are steeper, shorter, and rougher than most areas, which can be frustrating for beginners. On the other hand, some experts consider its runs the most challenging in the state. "If you can ski bumps, you're in heaven," says one of our friends. "If you're a novice who gets stuck on a bumpy run or goes into the trees, it's just hell." In recent years, there's been an effort to increase grooming to accommodate all levels of skiers.

There's no resort atmosphere at Pajarito—you won't find bars, lounges, or daycare for the kids—but you will find a three-story lodge with ski rentals and a nice cafeteria. You'll also find one of the rarest pluses of any ski area: no lift lines. Also, with only three skiing days a week, the snow at Pajarito lasts a relatively long time. Because of this and its small-town family atmosphere, many consider it an undiscovered gem.

Ski Santa Fe (505-982-4429 information; skisantafe.com/index.php?page= snow-report snow report; www.skisantafe.com; 2209 Brothers Rd., Ste. 220, Santa Fe, NM 87505, 15 miles northeast of Santa Fe via NM 475 [Ski Basin Rd.]; 12,053 ft. peak elevation; 1,703 ft. vertical drop; 225 in. average snowfall; snowmaking 30 percent of area; trails: 44 downhill [20 percent beginner, 40 percent intermediate, 40 percent advanced]; no cross-country; lifts: 4 chairlifts [1 quad, 1 triple, 2 double], 1 poma, 2 Mitey Mites; $66 adults, $48 half day; $48 13–20; $43 seniors and children; 72 and over free). Ski Santa Fe got its start in the 1930s with sheep and Indian trails as the basis for runs. The first ski area was developed a few miles down from its present site, at Hyde Park. By 1947, two dogleg rope tows with Cadillac engines lugged a few hardy skiers to the top of a nearby hill. In the early 1950s, the first chairlift was built at the present site—using army air corps surplus seats from a B-24 bomber and a 50-year-old cable from a nearby mine.

Currently, five modern lifts ferry skiers to 12,000 feet, the second highest slope in the country. At the top of the triple chair, you can take in 80,000 square miles of awe-inspiring views. You'll also find relatively short lift lines and some of the best family skiing in the state. Beginner and intermediate skiers can always find comfortable slopes, while advanced stretches such as Parachute and Wizard—not to mention Tequila Sunrise and Big Rocks, with their deep powder and ungroomed moguls—provide challenges and thrills for the very best.

The ski school at the basin, which includes Telemark and snowboard classes, will take children as young as three. For adaptive ski lessons, contact 505-995-9858 or visit www.adaptiveski.org. You can get daycare for the younger kids if you arrange for it in advance. There's also the on-slope Totemoff Bar and Grill, La Casa Mall at the base of the mountain, a cafeteria, a boutique, and more than 1,500 pairs of rental skis. In addition, a terrain park is now open to the public.

Near Taos

Angel Fire Resort (575-377-6401; 800-633-7463 information, snow report, and reservations; www.angelfireresort.com; 10 Miller Lane, Angel Fire, NM 87710; 22 miles E. of Taos via US 64 and NM 434; 10,677 ft. peak elevation; 2,077 ft. vertical drop; 210 in. average snowfall; snowmaking 52 percent of area; trails: 67 downhill [31 percent beginner, 48 percent intermediate, 21 percent advanced]; groomed 35-kilometer cross-country track; lifts: 5 chairlifts [2 high-speed quads, 3 doubles, 2 Sunkid Wondercarpets]; $64 adults, $48 half day; $44 ages 7–12; 6 and under/70 and over free; sightseers may purchase a single lift ride to the summit for $20). Texan Roy H. Lebus started Angel Fire Resort in 1967 with little more than a dream and a handful of dedicated workers. Today, it is known as a family resort and a "cruiser's mountain," featuring a variety of long, well-groomed trails (the longest is 3.5 miles). Angel Fire is predominantly tailored to beginning and inter-mediate skiers; however, it also offers a number of outstanding expert runs, includ-ing the addition of a new expert trail called C-4. A short 15-minute hike from the top of the Southwest Flyer chairlift, C-4 will top the adventurous skier and boarder's must-hit list on any fresh powder day. And they are so confident of their conditions and snowmaking machines, that if you are dissatisfied they will automat-ically return your ticket within one hour, if you want to come back another day. Widespread snowmaking guarantees 2,000 vertical feet of skiing even in the driest of years, and only in the very busiest of times does the lift line require more than a 5- or 10-minute wait. Another plus is the large picnic pavilion on the mountain that can accommodate several hundred skiers at a time.

With 3,000 beds, Angel Fire has one of the largest, most affordable lodging bases in the state. The resort also boasts more major (and offbeat) events than almost any other area—for example, the world shovel race championships, featur-ing the wild antics of riders careening down the mountain at more than 60 miles an hour on scoop shovels.

Angel Fire Resort has also bolstered its freestyle parks with exciting new fea-tures, helping to cement Angel Fire's position as the snowboarding capital of the state. They have added more than a dozen high-quality freestyle rails and fun box features, including the most popular flat rails, rainbows, double-kinks, C-rails, tabletops, and a few surprises—open challenges to freestyle skiers, as well as boarders. Angel Fire Resort was the site of the USASA Snowboard Nationals in 2004, and Liberation Park was picked as the 2008 Terrain Park of the Year in North America by On The Snow.

What's new at Angel Fire is the fantastic Angel Fire Resort Nordic Center offering 10 kilometers of groomed classic and skate cross-country ski trails, plus snowshoeing lanes and a family snow play hill for sledding. Lessons, equipment rental, retail, and pull-sleds are available in the full-service winter sports shop downstairs. When you're done playing outside and need to warm up, come into the Club and grab a hot chocolate and enjoy the beautiful views of the Sangre de Cristo Mountains. Snowboarding lessons are available at the ski school.

Red River Ski Area (575-754-2223 information, snow report; 800-331-SNOW reservations; www.redriverskiarea.com; P.O. Box 900, Red River, NM 87558, 37 miles north of Taos via NM 522 and NM 38; 10,350 ft. peak elevation; 1,600 ft. vertical drop; 214 in. average snowfall; snowmaking 85 percent of area; trails: 57 downhill [32 percent beginner, 38 percent intermediate, 30 percent advanced]; cross-country available nearby at Enchanted Forest; lifts: 7 lifts [2 double chairs, 3 triple chairs, 2 surface tow]; $64 adults, $49 half day; $58 teens; $49 children and seniors, over 70 and under 3 free). Red River was started in 1961 by a well-loved oilman and character named John Bolton, and its first lift consisted of used der-ricks and cables Bolton imported from an oil field in Texas. Located in the north-ern arc of the Enchanted Circle, Red River is another family-friendly ski area, a great place to learn, with extensive snowmaking and numerous wide beginner and intermediate trails. Runs such as Kit Carson and Broadway allow plenty of room for everybody to fall down, while expert speedways like Cat Skinner and Landing Strip are enough to get anyone's adrenaline pumping. The area rents about 1,000 pairs of skis, with another 2,000 pairs available in Red River. It also hosts on-slope bars and restaurants.

Along the Enchanted Circle in Eagle Nest, D&D makes a great stop for homemade breakfast, lunch, and dinner.

"That was sick" is the phrase you hear out here. Red River has three terrain parks tiered for every level of expertise, and its modern park designs will keep you coming back for more. Graduate from Pot O Gold Terrain Park, located on Gold Rush Hill, cruise into Bobcat Terrain Park, located on Bobcat Run, or head over to Hollywood Terrain Park, where your freshest tricks can be seen from the new triple chair.

Red River features a 4,500-bed lodging base less than a block from the ski area. During February's Mardi Gras in the Mountains, the whole town turns to cooking Cajun food and dresses in festive southern garb. There's a moonlight ski and snowshoe event, and Spring Break Torchlight and Fireworks show. Red River has a Kinderski school for ages 4 to 10 and Buckaroo Child Care for ages 6 months to 4 years.

Great powder, a variety of challenges, and plenty of facilities for the young ones make affordable Red River more attractive than ever.

Sipapu Ski and Summer Resort (800-587-2240; www.sipapunm.com; 5224 NM 518, Vadito, NM 87579, 25 miles southeast of Taos via NM 68 and NM 518; 9,225 ft. peak elevation; 1,055 ft. vertical drop; 190 in. average snowfall; snowmaking 70 percent of area; trails: 31 downhill [20 percent novice, 40 percent intermediate, 25 percent advanced]; cross-country available in nearby Carson National Forest; lifts: 1 triple chair, 2 pomas, 1 Magic Carpet; $44 adults, $33 half day; $37 ages 12 and under; $29 65–69; 70 and over free). Sipapu was started by Lloyd and

Olive Bolander, who first brought a small portable rope tow to the area in 1952. The next year they offered 30 pairs of rental skis with bear-trap bindings. Now, more than 50 years later, Sipapu is many times its original size. The area's laid-back atmosphere helps everyone feel at home, and the terrain parks are a haven for locals.

This refreshingly small, quiet ski area focuses mainly on beginner and intermediate fun, though they have added trails to appeal to experts, too. It is also known as a Telemark mountain. Lots of times after a pleasant run, you can jump right back on the lift with no wait at all. The area includes a restaurant and a snack bar, about 750 pairs of rental skis, on-slope lodging for nearly 200, and another 375 beds nearby. Delightful Sipapu is just about custom-made for families on a budget.

Taos Ski Valley (575-776-2291; 866-968-7386; www.skitaos.org; P.O. Box 90, Taos Ski Valley, NM 87525,18 miles northeast of Taos via US 64 and NM 150; 11,819 ft. peak elevation; 2,612 ft. vertical drop; 305 in. average snowfall; snow-making 100 percent beginner and intermediate; trails: 110 downhill [24 percent beginner, 25 percent intermediate, 51 percent advanced], no cross-country; lifts: 10 chairlifts [4 quad, 1 triple, 5 double], 2 surface lifts; $75 adults; $65 13–17 and 65–79; $45 children). Dreaming of his own resort, the indefatigable founder of Taos Ski Valley (TSV), Ernie Blake, spent countless hours flying his small plane over the Sangre de Cristo Mountains, scouting for the perfect site. The valley he finally located got an inauspicious start as a ski resort, with unreliable investors and near inaccessibility. But Blake persevered. When TSV opened as a fledgling family ski area in 1955, a 300-foot, diesel-driven T-bar was its first lift. TSV has never looked back. A long-standing dilemma was resolved a few years back, for good or not, depending on your point of view, when snowboarding was finally allowed at TSV.

The tradition at TSV is service, and that begins with excellent engineering and design. From lift-line management to trail marking, cafeteria food, and ski school programming, the pattern is consistently high quality. Even with a record-breaking abundance of snow and people, the whole system usually works flawlessly. Exceptions are the parking lots, which because of the lay of the valley tend to be long and narrow.

Lowlanders will definitely feel the elevation here. Drink plenty of water (no alcohol) and take frequent rests. The views across the valley and over to neighboring Kachina Peak (12,481 ft.) are worth a pause. The skiing is challenging, even for experts, but there are plenty of intermediate and novice slopes as well, including a few from the very top. The combination of trails called Honeysuckle, Winklereid, and Rubezahl can bring even a first-day skier down safely from the peak. If you're into pushing the envelope, you'll do no better than to bump and pump your way down such mogul-studded trails as the infamous Al's Run (under the #1 and #5 lifts), or to try the steep trails off the West Basin Ridge.

Amenities are provided at midstation snack bars (Phoenix and Whistlestop) and in numerous lodges and restaurants at the base. Families are efficiently accommodated, with daycare for tots ages six weeks and up, ski school for the kids, convenient lockers and storage baskets, and a most welcome addition: ski patrollers who actually patrol the slopes and slow traffic down in tight quarters. In or near the base lodge, you'll find about 2,000 pairs of rental skis, lodging for more than 1,000 skiers, all manner of books and souvenirs, and numerous festive events.

Where to Buy and Rent Ski Equipment

All the ski areas listed offer a good supply of on-slope rental equipment. You can also find ski rentals, sales, and service at numerous shops in Santa Fe, Taos, and other towns near the ski areas.

Santa Fe

Ace Mountain Wear (505-982-8079; 825 Early St., Ste. B, Santa Fe, NM 87505-1680). Custom clothing for skiers and snowboarders.

Alpine Sports (505-983-5155; 121 Sandoval St., Ste. B, Santa Fe, NM 87501). Downhill and cross-country sales and rentals.

rob and charlie's (505-471-9119; http//:robandcharlies.com; 1632 St. Michael's Dr., Santa Fe, NM 87505). Snowboard sales and rentals.

Skier's Edge (505-983-1025; 1836 Cerrillos Rd., Santa Fe, NM 87501). Downhill, cross-country, and snowboard rentals.

Ski Tech Ski Rentals (505-983-5512; 905 S. St. Francis Dr., Santa Fe, NM 87505). Cross-country rentals, fast computerized service.

Wild Mountain Outfitters (505-986-1152; 453 Cerrillos Rd., Santa Fe, NM 87501). Cross-country and Telemark sales.

Near Santa Fe

Cottam's Ski Rentals (505-982-0495; 740 Hyde Park Rd., Santa Fe, NM 87501). Downhill and cross-country rental and accessories, snowboards, inner tubes, and sleds.

Taos

Adventure Ski Shops (575-758-1167; www.adventureskishops.com; 1335A Paseo del Pueblo Sur, Taos, NM 87571). Downhill and cross-country sales, service, and repairs.

Cottam's Ski Shops (575-758-2822; 207 Paseo del Pueblo Sur, Taos, NM 87571). Downhill and cross-country rentals and service, and snowboards.

Taos Mountain Outfitters (575-758-9292; 114 S. Plaza, Taos, NM 87571). Cross-country rentals only.

Near Taos

Bumps! Ski Shop (575-377-3146; 48 N. Angel Fire Rd., Angel Fire, NM 87710). Front-entry boots, upgraded skis and accessories.

High Country Ski Rentals (575-377-6424; 3453 Mountain View Blvd., Angel Fire, NM 87710).

Terry Sports (575-776-8292; 11 Ernie Blake Rd., Taos Ski Valley, NM 87525). Downhill and cross-country sales, rentals, and repair.

Winter Sports Ski Shop (575-377-6162; 12 Aspen St., Angel Fire, NM 87710). A complete selection of sophisticated gear for skiers.

Downhill Rentals and Service

Mickey's Ski Rental (575-377-2501; 350 E. Therma Dr., Eagle Nest). Downhill ski rentals and repair.

Millers Crossing Ski and Sportswear (575-754-2374; 29 Sangre De Cristo Blvd., Red River). Cross-country sales, service, rentals, and lessons.

Mountain Sports (575-613-0416; 3375 NM 434, Angel Fire, NM 87710, next to Valley Market). Downhill ski sales and rentals, boots, clothing, snowboards.

Roadrunner Tours Ltd. (575-377-6416; Mountain View Blvd., Angel Fire, NM 87710). Downhill ski and clothing rentals.

Sitzmark Sports & Lodge (575-754-2456; 416 Main St., Red River, NM 87558). Downhill ski and snowboard sales, rentals, repair, and clothing.

Wild Bill's Ski and Snowboard Shop (575-754-2428; 325 W. Main St., Red River). Downhill ski rentals and repair.

Cross-Country Skiing

If you're looking for solitude and the quiet sound of skis sliding over backcountry trails, take a break from the lift lines and go touring or Nordic. Almost anytime Dec.–March, you can find myriad snow-covered trails lacing national forests and wilderness areas, plus countless public trails and a few privately groomed trails within the area. For current snow conditions and maps, contact the national forest offices listed below or www.nmroads.com Some of the more popular books on the subject include: *Ski Touring in Northern New Mexico* by Sam Beard; *Skiing the Sun* by Jim Burns and Cheryl Lemanski; and *Cross-Country Skiing in Northern New Mexico* by Kay Matthews.

Santa Fe Area

Some of the best ski touring in the Santa Fe area is in the **Santa Fe National Forest** (Santa Fe office 505-438-5300; 11 Forest Lane, , Santa Fe, NM 87501). A few of the more popular trails include those starting from Black Canyon Campground, about 9 miles from town via the Ski Basin Rd.; Borrega and Aspen Vista Trails about 13 miles up the Ski Basin Rd.; and Winsor Trail just off the Ski Basin parking lot. These and other trails in the area are administered by the Española Ranger District (505-438-5300). Ask for recreation staff.

In the Jemez Mountains, Peralta Canyon Rd., the East Fork of the Jemez, and Corral Canyon are all good touring areas, as are Fenton Hill and Jemez Falls in the Jemez Ranger District (505-829-3535).

Taos Area

The **Carson National Forest** offers numerous public ski-touring trails, some of them located right next to the Taos, Red River, and Sipapu ski areas. One of the more popular areas in the Camino Real Ranger District (505-587-2255) is **Amole Canyon** off NM 518 between Taos and Sipapu. Here the national forest, in cooperation with the Taos Norski Club, maintains set tracks and signs along a 3-mile loop that's closed to snowmobiles and ideal for skating. There are also 6- and 7-mile unmaintained loop trails at the same location. Another popular snowmobile-free route off NM 518 is **Picuris Lookout**, with exceptional mountain views. **Capulin/La Sombra**, about 5 miles east of Taos off US 64, is a flat, 1.5-mile trail that's great for skating.

Popular routes in the **Tres Piedras Ranger District** (575-758-8678) include Maquinita Canyon, Biscara Trail, Burned Mountain, and Forest Road 795. In the

Questa Ranger District (575-586-0520), try East Fork, Ditch Cabin, Long Canyon, or Goose Creek.

Detailed guides for many of the trails listed are available at Carson National Forest offices. Remember that some trails are designated for skiers or snowmobilers only, and some are shared. Restrictions are posted, but be sure to check with the forest service for detailed information. Also get hold of the forest service's *Winter Recreation Safety Guide*, which lists winter hazards and how to prepare for them.

Tours and Private Touring Centers

For instruction, tours, and overnight ski-touring packages in the Santa Fe area, **Santa Fe Detours** (505-983-6565) will arrange half- or full-day trips. **Southwest Wilderness Adventures** (505-983-7262; P.O. Box 9380 Santa Fe, NM 87504) also offers Nordic ski programs with rentals, clinics, and tours.

For cross-country ski instruction and tours in the Taos area, your best bet is to call **Millers Crossing** (575-754-2374; 800-966-9381; 417 W. Main St., Red River, NM 87558). The place to go touring near Taos is the **Enchanted Forest Cross Country Ski Area** (575-754-2374; 29 Sangre de Cristo Dr., Red River, NM 87558). Just east of Red River atop Bobcat Pass, it offers 30 kilometers of groomed and ungroomed trails amid 600 forested acres. Here, you'll find not only dog-friendly trails and prime ski terrain for classical, freestyle, and Telemark, but also instructors, patrols, warming huts, and rentals, plus snowshoeing and special events. $10 a day; rentals $12 a day; or $27 for three days.

SNOWMOBILING

There's an exhilarating network of trails for snowmobilers through both the Santa Fe and Carson National Forests. Many of these regularly groomed minihighways twist and turn through thick forests to high-alpine meadows where speedsters can zoom across wide-open spaces to their hearts' content. Be sure to check with district forest service offices (listed under "Public Ski Touring," above) before you choose a trail. Remember to slow down and stay clear of skiers and snowshoers. For maximum safety and fun, choose a trail that's designated for snowmobiles only. Three of the best are Fourth of July Canyon, Old Red River Pass, and Greenie Peak in the **Questa Ranger District** (575-758-6200) near Red River. A number of businesses in Red River also provide safe, guided snowmobile tours, complete with mountaintop hot dog cookouts. And in January, the **Angel Fire Ski Area** (575-377-3055) hosts the Angel Fire Snowmobile Festival, with races, free rides, buffet dinner, and prizes.

SPAS AND HOT SPRINGS

Still bubbling and steaming in the aftermath of its relatively recent volcanic activity, northern New Mexico is dotted with natural hot springs. Private bathhouses have been built over two such spots, at Ojo Caliente and Jemez Springs (outside the area), and numerous other gurgling hot spots can be found in the open air. Just outside Santa Fe there's even a Japanese bathhouse offering everything you could want in a natural spring, and more.

Ten Thousand Waves (505-982-5003; www.tenthousandwaves.com; 3451 Hyde Park Rd., Santa Fe, NM 87501; open daily; reservations strongly recommended). Only 10 minutes' drive from the Santa Fe Plaza, Ten Thousand Waves is the premier spa in the Santa Fe–Taos area. Disengagement from everyday cares begins when you park in the lot and walk up a winding path illuminated at night by ground-level Japanese lanterns. Up top, gurgling water and giant goldfish slip by as you cross a bridge and ascend to the lobby. Here, you may sign in for any of a host of pleasures, including public or private hot tubs, with special men's and women's tub hours scheduled.

Some of the mountainside tubs, though discreetly screened, have lovely views through the pines. The public tubs (including coed and women's tubs) are convivial places where idle conversation and subdued jollity prevail, while private tubs have the allure of romance or the challenge of solitary meditation. Locker rooms are handsome, with extras ranging from kimonos and thongs to soap, shampoo, and cedar lotion. Massage therapy runs the gamut from Swedish to shiatsu and every sort of body work and skin treatment you can imagine.

There are salt rubs, herbal wraps, and more. A well-stocked health food snack bar in the lobby and a cozy fireplace make lingering an added pleasure. Services are not cheap (in 2012 private tubs ran $29–49 per person per hour; communal and women's tubs were around $25 for unlimited time; massages $99 and up an hour, and facials $99–139). A 10-bath punch card, valid for communal tubs Mon.–Thurs., sells for $169. Warning: While the Waves is a popular destination—some say a Santa Fe must-do—I personally find the water here extremely hot.

Soak your bones and cure what ails you at Ojo Caliente.

Near Taos

Ojo Caliente Mineral Springs Resort & Spa (505-583-2233; 800-222-9162; www.ojospa.com; 50 Los Baños Dr., P.O. Ojo Caliente, NM 87549, southwest of Taos or north of Española on US 285; closed Christmas; reservations required for private tubs). A delightful getaway for all. This is the most popular mineral springs spa in northern New Mexico, featuring natural hot waters with therapeutic iron, arsenic, and lithium. Attendants in separate men's and women's locker areas pamper and guide you either to individual cubicles with fresh water for 15-minute arsenic soaks (great for arthritis and rheumatism) or to a large, enclosed outdoor grotto area with hot iron water. There's also a coed bathhouse with individual rooms for couples. After your soak, an attendant will put you on a table and cover you head to toe with steaming hot cotton blankets (aka the mummy wrap) for further relaxation or in preparation for a full-body massage.

Before returning to the world, you're invited to take a shower, a swim in the heated outdoor pool, or a peaceful walk beside giant cottonwoods—hike up to see the petroglyphs, or to fill canisters with any of the three mineral waters. You can even go riding if you want.

Ojo used to be rather latter-day-hippie funky, in a good way, but gentrification has definitely set in. Although they bill themselves now as "unpretentious," those of us who soaked here back in the day beg to differ. Locals find it disappointingly pricey, and prices keep going up here. As of 2012, they were: $18 for an all-day pass Mon.–Thurs.; $28 for the same on weekends and holidays; $16 sunset rate (after 6 PM) on Mon.–Thurs. and weekends. Expect to pay between $100–200 for body work. The inn here (see "Lodging Near Taos," in chapter 3, *Lodging*) also offers overnight packages for couples, including breakfast and two mineral baths apiece. If you are a local New Mexican, you are eligible to purchase the New Mexico Club card, entitling you to nine soaks for $119, Mon.–Thurs., which really is the best deal you can get.

SWIMMING

Opportunities for swimming abound in the Santa Fe–Taos area, from lakes and rivers to numerous fine municipal and private pools. Please see numbers listed below for Windsurfing. Swimming in the Rio Grande is discouraged, due to the rocky bottom and strong undertow, but you can spend time near the river at the Wild Rivers Recreation Area north of Taos and the **Orilla Verde Recreation Area** on the south end of Taos (575-758-8851). Beware of rattlesnakes in all rocky areas near the river, and guard your pets. Heron Lake (575-588-7470) north of Abiquiu in Heron Lake State Park is the favorite swimming area.

Santa Fe
In Santa Fe, you'll find four indoor public pools and one outdoor pool available for a small fee for adults and free for children seven and under. For details on times, classes, and activities, call the city recreation division: 505-955-2602. For numbers and addresses of private pools, see "Fitness Centers" and individual entries in chapter 3, *Lodging*. Municipal pools include:

Bicentennial Pool: 505-955-2510; 1121 Alto St. Open only in summer.

Fort Marcy Pool: 505-955-2511; 490 Bishop's Lodge Rd.

Salvador Perez Pool: 505-955-2604; 601 Alta Vista.

Taos
For swimming opportunities in Taos, there's one municipal pool (575-758-9171; 120 Civic Plaza), which charges a small fee for a swim and shower. There are also the **Don Fernando Pool** (575-737-2622) and the **Taos Spa & Tennis Club** (575-

758-1980; http://taospa.com; 111 Dona Ana Dr. Taos, NM 87571) available to non-members for $12 a day. Other pools are available in various hotels and motels (see individual entries in chapter 3, *Lodging*).

TENNIS

With clean air and clear skies most of the year, courts in the Santa Fe–Taos area are usually popping with tennis balls—except when they're snow covered during winter. Even then, both towns have numerous private indoor courts that can be rented any time of year.

Santa Fe

The city of Santa Fe offers some 27 public tennis courts and 4 major private tennis facilities, including indoor, outdoor, and lighted courts. Some public parks with tennis courts include Fort Marcy Complex, Genoveva Chavez Community Center Ortiz, and Salvador Perez Recreation Center. For specifics and other locations, call the **City Recreation Department** (505-955-4480 for tennis lesson information).

Santa Fe–area clubs with tennis courts include the following:

Bishop's Lodge: 505-983-6377; 1297 Bishop's Lodge Rd, Santa Fe, NM 87506.

El Gancho: 505-988-5000; 104 Old Las Vegas Hwy., Santa Fe, NM 87505.

Sangre de Cristo Racquet Club: 505-983-7978; 1755 Camino Corrales, Santa Fe, NM 87505.

Santa Fe Country Club: 505-471-2626; 4360-A Country Club Rd., Santa Fe, NM 87501.

Taos

The **Taos Parks and Recreation Department** (575-758-8234; 575-758-1980) maintains tennis courts at Kit Carson Park and Fred Baca Park. There are more outdoor courts at the **Taos Spa & Tennis Club** (575-758-1980; 111 Dona Ana Dr., Taos, NM 87571-4108). $12 an hour per person.

WATER SPORTS

See also "Hunting and Fishing."

Surprisingly, New Mexico boasts more small boats per capita than almost any other state in the Union. Some say it's because of the yearning for water in a state so high and dry. Others say it's because of the spirit of a land once covered by inland seas. But those who really know say it's simply because New Mexico has a lot of good boating. Canoeing, waterskiing, and fishing as well as boating activity can be found at the following lakes:

Near Santa Fe

Cochiti Lake (505-465-0307; Army Corps of Engineers, 82 Dam Crest Rd., Pena Blanca, NM 87041-5015). About half an hour southwest of Santa Fe off I-25, Cochiti is a no-wake lake with free public boat ramps and rentals of canoes, rowboats, and fishing boats. There's also a recreation center about half a mile from the lake, with pool and table tennis, a swimming pool, and a basketball court.

Nambe Reservoir (about 20 miles north of Santa Fe via US 285 and NM 503; take turnoff to Nambe Falls). For boating information, contact, Nambe Pueblo (505-455-2550; 61 Np 102 east, Santa Fe, NM 87501).

Santa Cruz Lake Recreation Area (505-761-8700; Bureau of Land Management, 435 Montano Rd. NE, Albuquerque, NM 87107-4935). This small no-wake lake and recreation area near Española has a small-boat ramp and a 5 mph speed limit. Swimming is allowed only in the northeast picnic area.

Near Taos

At Eagle Nest Lake (east of Taos on the edge of the Enchanted Circle), Eagle Nest Marina (575-377-6941; 28386 NM 64, Eagle Nest, NM 87718) can give you information on boat rentals and activities.

Outside the Area

Abiquiu Lake (505-685-4371; Army Corps of Engineers; about 65 miles northwest of Santa Fe on US 84). This large, scenic reservoir behind Abiquiu Dam offers a little of everything, from canoeing and windsurfing to fishing and waterskiing. No boat rentals are available.

Heron and El Vado Lakes (near the town of Chama). These lakes are administered by the New Mexico State Parks Division (505-476-3355; 888-667-2757). Both have boat ramps and camping facilities. Heron is a no-wake lake, especially popular for small sailboats and Hobies. Waterskiing is allowed at El Vado. For further information, contact the Stone House Lodge (575-588-7274; HC 75, Box 1022, Los Ojos, NM 87551). Apr.–Nov., Stone House rentals include 24-foot pontoon boats with awnings and outboard engines, 20-foot Bass Buggies, and 14-foot fishing trollers, plus 17-foot canoes.

Storrie Lake (505-425-7278; 6 miles north of Las Vegas via NM 518). When it has sufficient water, this lake is one of the most popular windsurfing spots in the state. It includes a boat ramp and courtesy dock but no boat rentals. Recent years have been dry.

For more information on ramps, rentals, and activities, contact the New Mexico Parks and Recreation Division (505-827-7173; 888-NM-PARKS; www .emnrd.state.nm.us/nmparks). For new and used boats, motors, parts, and accessories and a full-service shop, contact High Country Marine (505-471-4077; 27736 W. Frontage Rd., Santa Fe, NM 87505).

WINDSURFING

Clear weather and strong breezes wafting across easily accessible lakes combine to make for some fine windsurfing. The most popular nearby lakes are Cochiti (505-465-0307) near Santa Fe, Eagle Nest Lake State Park (575-377-1594) near Taos, and Storrie Lake State Park (505-425-7278) and Abiquiu (505-685-4371) outside the area. Lakes may be affected by prolonged drought, however, so be sure to check on conditions before you go. At most lakes, the strongest winds tend to come up in the afternoon, whipping up whitecaps and whisking surfers across the water at dizzying speeds. Watch out for thunderstorms, though; they sometimes blow in with the afternoon winds.

For more information on these and other windsurfing lakes, see "Water Sports."

YOGA

See also "Fitness Centers" in this chapter.

Santa Fe

Body (505-986-0362; 333 Cordova Rd., Santa Fe, NM 87501). Daily yoga classes, workshops, child care, café, massage, and body treatments. Signature Vinyasa classes for the serious practitioner, plus hatha, ashtanga, kundalini, yoga to Indian music—what a menu!

Santa Fe Community Yoga Center (505-820-9363; 826 Camino de Monte Rey, Santa Fe, NM 87505-3977). A complete nonprofit yoga network with bargain prices with instructors of various lineages; prenatal, men's, and children's classes; and meditation. Flow, restorative, qigong. The emphasis is on defining the correct level for the practitioner.

White Iris Yoga Studio (505-819-0681; 1701 Callejon Emilia, Santa Fe, NM 87501). Instructor Gail Ackerman and her associates teach classes in Iyengar yoga mornings and evenings. Call for a complete schedule.

Yoga Moves (505-989-1072; 825 Early St., Santa Fe, NM 87501). Yoga plus swing dance; kids acting classes.

TIN
WITH MARBLES
30% OFF

Shopping

ANTIQUE, BOUTIQUE, AND UNIQUE

SANTA FE AND TAOS are both cities where cultures converge, and as such they have always been centers of trade. Santa Fe, of course, sits at the end of the Santa Fe Trail; Taos is perched on the Rio Grande, at the northernmost point of the eight Pueblos. The towns are places where people have always met and exchanged ideas and goods—both decorative and utilitarian.

The contemporary scene is no different—Taos and Santa Fe are shopping centers for Native American art and jewelry, for the painting of both local and international artists, and for the crafts of the entire world. The area presents unique shopping, whether in galleries and boutiques or in the more informal settings of vendors on the Plaza.

Shops and Markets
that will pique your interest

FLEA MARKETS AND MUSEUM SHOPS

The **Santa Fe Flea Market**, operated by Tesuque Pueblo, is a wonderful example of goods arrayed from as far away as Africa and as nearby as the studios of local artisans. This huge outdoor shopping arena is situated next to the Santa Fe Opera 10 minutes north of Santa Fe on US 84/285, open seasonally Fri.–Sun., 8 AM–5 PM. The shopper can browse for fine jewelry, leather, furniture, masks, and the occasional odd lot. Beneath a turquoise sky and within sight of the Sangre de Cristo Mountains, this is a relaxed place to shop, and it may still be possible to find a bargain, although caution must be applied when selecting goods. Bargaining is acceptable here.

There's more to discover in the shopping meccas of Taos and Santa Fe than any one guide can easily cover, so we focused on the best of southwestern arts and

LEFT: Jackalope is more than a store; it's an international bazaar.

Santa Fe Flea Markets

The Flea at the Downs (505-982-2605; I-25, exit 599, off Cerrillos Rd.). Three markets in one: vintage, artists and artisans, and growers market. Open May–June, Sat.–Sun. 9–4; July–Aug., Fri., Sat., Sun.; Sept.–Oct., Sat.–Sun. Shuttle from the Plaza.

Pueblo of Tesuque Flea Market (505-670-2599; 6 miles north of Santa Fe on US 84/285, exit 171). Known as the place to search out jewelry, art, rugs, and imports. Many shops in town have booths here. Open March–Dec., Fri.–Sun. 8–4.

Santa Fe Flea Market (505-982-2671; El Museo Cultural in The Railyard, 555 Camino de la Familia). Open Sat. 8–3, Sun. 10–4.

Also visit the Artisans Market, Sun. in the Farmers Market Building in The Railyard.

our favorite choices from the world bazaar. We kept an eye out for quality and value so that whatever your budget, you can find the right keepsake.

Remember that the closer you are to the main plazas, the higher the prices. Whenever you are buying, ask what materials were used to make the craft item you're considering. Don't assume everything for sale here is made locally. Find out where the item came from. You may want to drive out to the pueblos (see "Pueblos" in chapter 4, *Culture*) to buy handmade Indian pottery, jewelry, and other crafts directly from the artists.

A word about bargaining: Haggling over prices of artist-made goods is not a widely accepted practice in New Mexico. Much time and work go into the creation of a pot, a carving, or a piece of jewelry, and artists know the value of their work. Specifically, bargaining with vendors under the Palace of the Governors portal is not encouraged. All goods sold here are guaranteed locally Native made. However, if you have talked to the artist and feel he or she is receptive, a diplomatic discussion of price may be appropriate. Also remember that shop hours may vary with the amount of traffic. It's always wise to call ahead if you're making a special trip.

Millicent Rogers Museum Gift Shop sells reliably gorgeous and authentic wares.

While prices may be slightly higher, museum shops at the Palace of the Governors and the Wheelwright Museum in Santa Fe, as well as the Millicent Rogers Museum in Taos, offer a good selection of rugs and jewelry that may be relied on as authentic. And museum shops frequently do not charge tax.

ANTIQUES

Santa Fe

Antique Warehouse (505-984-1159; 530 S. Guadalupe St., Ste. B, Santa Fe, NM 87501, at The Railyard). Spanish colonial antiques, including hard-to-find architectural elements, doors, unusual tables, and gracious benches.

Clairborne Gallery (505-982-8019; 608 Canyon Rd.). Owner Omer Clairborne, a respected expert on Spanish colonial antiques, travels the world in search of items for his shop. Antiques from Mexico, Spain, Guatemala, the Philippines, and South America are featured.

Things Finer (505-983-5552; La Fonda Hotel, 100 E. San Francisco St., Santa Fe, NM 97501). Nestled in the classic Pueblo Deco lobby of the La Fonda Hotel, Things Finer is a treasure trove of jewelry, antiques, silver, miniatures, and rare icons from Russia. The staff will also do appraisals on items you bring in.

Taos

Antiquarius Imports (575-776-8381; 487 NM 150, Arroyo Seco, NM 87514). Antique Persian and tribal rugs, kilims, gypsy textiles, African arts, prayer rugs, and naturally dyed carpets, at reasonable prices.

BOOKS

Santa Fe and Taos are both towns full of writers—and readers. Most stores have sections emphasizing publications on the arts, history, and culture of the region. Secondhand-book stores are the perfect place to discover a treasure, and all shelves invite some browsing before buying. Keep in mind that most museums and historic sites listed in chapter 4, *Culture*, have excellent bookshops specializing in local and regional writers as well.

Santa Fe

Alla Spanish Language Books (505-988-5416; 102 W. San Francisco St., upstairs). In keeping with the history of the region, Alla is devoted to books in Spanish—with about 20,000 general titles and more than 2,000 books for kids. Also Spanish-language records and tapes.

Ark Books (505-988-3709; 133 Romero St., off Agua Fria, west of downtown). This New Age bookstore is a complete environment for browsing, with comfortable chairs, a pleasant atmosphere, statues, and crystals galore. Six rooms of books specialize in healing, world religions, relationships, mythology, and magic. You can also buy music and shop for an extensive collection of tarot cards, jewelry, incense, and accoutrements that may be useful on the path to enlightenment. A splendid place for a relaxing browse.

Books & More Books (505-983-5438; 1341 Cerrillos Rd.). This spacious used bookstore attracts browsers all day. The art section is excellent, as are the southwestern books, fiction, poetry, religion, New Age, and natural sciences. Good finds on children's classics.

Collected Works Bookstore (505-988-4226; 202 Galisteo St., Ste. A, Santa Fe, NM 87501). This is the place to go if you are in the mood to read something—but don't yet know what. A fine selection of current fiction and memoirs greets you at the entrance. Also extensive southwestern books—from local guidebooks to the history and literature of the region. This "new" location is more spacious than the old San Francisco Street shop with the plus of a central fireplace, coffee bar, and pastries from Harry's Roadhouse. Longtime owner Dorothy Massey is a great supporter of local writers, and there's usually a signing or event going on.

Dumont Maps & Books of the West (505-988-1076; 314 McKenzie St., Santa Fe, NM 87501). Formerly Parker Books, Dumont continues to offer a fine selection of antiquarian maps as well as rare and out-of-print western and Americana books.

Garcia Street Books (505-986-0151; 376 Garcia St., Ste. B, Santa Fe, NM 87501). A good display of new titles by regional authors, as well as general interest titles plus quality literature; books on art, architecture, and style; and an excellent collection of affordable paperback classics. Specializes in fast special orders. A small bookshop with a good eye.

Photo-Eye Books & Prints (505-988-5152; 370 Garcia St., Santa Fe, NM 87501). Calling itself the "world's foremost online photography book store," the sampling on display here is a knockout.

Taos

Brodsky Bookshop (575-758-9468; 226 Paseo del Pueblo Norte). An almost "legacy" intimate shop with a wide range of western and southwestern fiction and nonfiction, general interest titles, and used books—plus maps and cards. The scent of the old days wafts through.

G. Robinson Old Prints & Maps (575-758-2278; 124-D Bent St.). Need an 1885 hand-colored map of Alaska or an 1830 steel-engraved map of Tierra del Fuego? This is the place. Some maps are expensive, but many are available for less than $100. The perfect spot to find a gift for those who have everything.

Moby Dickens Bookshop (575-758-3050; 124-A Bent St.). The go-to bookshop in Taos. A browser's heaven, with several rooms of irresistible volumes of current fiction and nonfiction, as well as as the requisite cat. The store continues upstairs, and this second floor is not to be missed. A good selection of journals and blank books to record your time in Taos, plus a small yet well-selected music section.

CHILDREN'S SHOPS

Kids do love to shop, whether spending their hard-earned pennies, their allowance, or their parents' money! However, shopping with children doesn't have to be a stressful experience or even an advanced case of the gimmes. The stores listed here are small and stocked with toys that can educate as well as entertain.

Santa Fe

Doodlet's Shop (505-983-3771; 120 Don Gaspar Ave.). A shop like none other, packed with toys that appeal to both kids and grown-ups, Doodlet's stocks treasures from chocolate sardines to tin mermaids. Browse and be amused by postcards, stickers, teacups, Victoriana, charms, and miniatures.

Horizons—The Discovery Store (505-983-1554; 328 S. Guadalupe St.). Science and natural history play a part in the fascinating displays here of everything in the world around us, from magnets to dinosaurs. A visit to the store is a trip to a minimuseum—books, globes, and guides all help stimulate learning in both children and adults.

Marcy Street Card Shop (505-982-5160; 75 W. Marcy St.). With a little browsing, you can find a card, witty or wise, to chime with the mood you have in mind. Especially great assortment of Christmas and Valentine's Day cards. Shop early for best selection.

Taos

Tiovivo (575-758-9400; 226 Ranchitos Rd.). What feels like acres of everything a toy store should be to enchant young patrons. Kites hang from the ceiling, an erector-set Ferris wheel turns, and there are enough stuffed animals to stock the most exotic menagerie. Also books, games, kits, and toys for all ages. Plenty of parking.

Twirl Toystore and Playspace (575-751-1402; 225 Camino de la Placita). Those who say there are not enough activities for kids in Taos have not been to Twirl. Part playground, part activity and crafts center, and mostly just the most magical toy store–for all ages—you have ever seen, Twirl gives kids the world from their point of view.

CLOTHING

Santa Fe style—or a southwestern style of dressing—combines traditional elements with individual taste to create a timeless look. It emphasizes longer skirts, luscious fabrics, and lots of accessories. For men, it combines western shirts and boots with the decorative bolo tie. Historically, the look comes from western dress, fiesta costumes, and Native American styles. It is also contemporary and fashionable, mixing elements together. It may take years to create your own look. Start by shopping in Santa Fe and Taos for items that are uniquely you—and don't be afraid to try unusual combinations, colors, and styles you'd never have dared wear before, as you go. As one turquoise-and-velvet-clad doyenne of Santa Fe declared, "I don't worry about styles. These clothes have been good for 400 years; they'll be good for another year."

Contemporary

Santa Fe
Chico's (505-984-1132; 328 S. Guadalupe St.; 505-989-7702; 135 W. Palace Ave.). Although we do not usually mention chain stores, we'll make an exception here. Chico's clothes for women are sporty yet comfortable, featuring go-anywhere relaxed styles in nonwrinkling fabrics. Bold prints mix well with basics here, and the costume jewelry collection provides the perfect finishing touches. Excellent for the traveler's wardrobe.

Lucille's (505-983-6331; 223 Galisteo St.). Specializing in imports, this store is hung from floor to ceiling with racks of soft loose dresses and separates, many designed in ethnic fabrics. This is the place to find the perfect outfit that won't bust the budget, or the colorful, unusual accessory for a special event. A favorite of the well-dressed Santa Fe woman, and one where larger-sized fashions are available.

Origins (505-988-2323; 135 W. San Francisco St.). One of the best wearable-art shops in the country, Origins is an Aladdin's cave of treasures. Fabrics from around the world mingle with designer clothing and one-of-a-kind art creations. Explore the store to discover tribal arts, antique jewelry, fantasy hats, embroidered shawls, and the new gold-and-antiques room. Find the perfect outfit for the opera or your class reunion. The owner's motto is: "We feature forever dressing," and that is true. I am still wearing (and getting compliments on) a hand-made antique Pendleton jacket I "invested" in more than 20 years ago.

Sign of the Pampered Maiden (505-982-5948; 123 W. Water St.) To be completely honest, the Maiden would be my first choice Santa Fe shop to put together the perfect outfit, be it a spring dress with a little jacket or the most fashionable sweater and skirt for fall. A bit on the pricey side, but not forbiddingly so, at least not for that one perfect outfit. Shop here and you are guaranteed to look like a class act, and not only in Santa Fe.

Spirit Clothing (505-982-2677; 109 W. San Francisco St.). This pricey, high-end boutique carries clothes from European, Japanese, and American designers. If you must distinguish yourself and have the bank account, this is the place to get the best money can buy.

Zephyr Clothing (505-988-5635; 125 E. Palace Ave.). Unique pieces of women's clothing in velvet, silk, wool, and rayon. The coats are specially designed for sale in the store. The place to find that one-of-a-kind.

Taos

Artemisia (575-737-9800; 117 Bent St.) Tucked away around a corner, find delectable velvet jackets, hand-dyed linens, deluxe silks and cottons, style-setting one-of-a-kind scarves, shawls, sweaters, and accessories to treasure forever. Splurge, decorate your life, make a statement, and take home a piece of wearable art.

Francesca's Clothing and Jewelry Boutique (575-776-8776; 492 NM 150, Arroyo Seco; 575-737-0300; 1018 Paseo del Pueblo Norte). Voted the favorite shop of Taos women, packed with colorful and relaxed pieces to mix and match in unusual ways. Perfect for après-ski fun. Totally geared to the Taos imagination and look, perhaps best characterized as something of a "gypsy-cowgirl-nostalgia princess."

Spotted Bear (505-758-3040; 127 Paseo del Pueblo Sur). One of the most extraordinary clothing stores anywhere, Spotted Bear is worth a pilgrimage. Women's clothing here is exotic and exquisite, from velvet animal-print scarves to amusing flowered hats. There are dresses of hand-painted silk and vintage designer outfits, as well as unique raincoats in rich materials. Choose your era, from a period look to right-now metallic and faux leopard. If you shop here, it's guaranteed no one else will be wearing anything at all resembling your outfit. And you can do very well on the sale racks, especially if you are short in stature.

Leather

Santa Fe

Desert Son (505-982-9499; 725 Canyon Rd.). Custom leatherwork for men and women, including boots, moccasins, and a particularly good selection of belts. The store also features bags and hats in western and other styles.

Overland Fine Sheepskin & Leather (575-758-8820; 1405 N. NM 522; also at 505-986-0757, 74 E. San Francisco St.). Shearling coats to see you through the coldest winters, plus hats, slippers, mittens, and more. Imported fine Italian leathers and gorgeous beaded leather jackets. Find something fine to fit the budget—belts, gloves, slippers, wallets—or splurge on a lifetime purchase. Items sold here will never go out of style. Look for the spring sales, starting around Valentine's day.

Shoes

Santa Fe

Back at the Ranch Cowboy Boots (505-989-8110; 209 E. Marcy St.). Don't be surprised if your jaw actually drops here at the fabulous selection of wild and fanciful cowboy boots in designs from peacock to retro. You'll be forgiven if this is where you bust the budget.

Boots & Boogie (505-983-0777; 102 E. Water St.) Choose from among 350 pair of handmade boots on display or create your own custom footwear, your choice of design, heel, and leather (they have dozens), hand tooled in Texas. Prices start from $600 and go all the way to five figures; average cost is $1200 to guarantee you'll be kicking it and taking names for a long time to come. Formerly located in Santa Fe Village.

Goler Fine Imported Shoes (505-982-0924; 125 E. Palace Ave.). If shoes have personalities, then these range from the saucy to the chic to the downright elegant, in materials from leather to brocade. Upscale shoes from everywhere on the fashion map.

Don't walk away from northern New Mexico without a fabulous new pair of boots.

On Your Feet (505-983-3900; Sanbusco Market Center, 530 Montezuma St.). For comfortable shoes that look good and cute shoes that feel good, this is the place for both men and women. Also fabulous socks.

Santa Fe Boot Company (505-989-1168; 60 E. San Francisco St.). The right boots are certainly necessary to a cowboy, and they are also the basis for a Santa Fe–style outfit. Luckily, Santa Fe Boot Company offers both working boots and boots that work well with your wardrobe. A large selection includes trusted brand names.

Street Feet (505-984-3131; La Fonda Hotel, 100 E. San Francisco St.). Street Feet has shoes galore from Italy and South America, as well as Canadian boots. You'll also find stylish clothing, with an emphasis on soft fabrics, tunics, jackets, and sweaters, including leggings, bags, scarves, and belts.

Taos

The Good Sole (575-737-5000; 1033 Paseo del Pueblo Sur). Name brands in comfort and practicality for men and women—Keen, Clark, Ecco. Essential footwear for the active Taoseño.

Steppin' Out (575-758-4487; 120 Bent St.). Two floors of fine leather goods, from shoes to belts to handbags, is the last word in style. Some high-end waterproof boots make bad weather not only endurable but a chance for chic. Also a selection of gracious soft clothing.

Southwestern

Santa Fe

Double Take at the Ranch (505-820-7775; 321 S. Guadalupe St.). Delightful array of classic cowboy and cowgirl wear as well as western kitsch and memorabilia. This place is a palace packed with pawn jewelry, knockoffs of vintage cowboy shirts, fiesta skirts, fringed leather jackets, and anything else you need to indulge your western whim and rodeo queen fantasy. You'll also find items of décor to add western flair to your surroundings. This shop is incredible!

Montecristi Custom Hat Works (505-983-9598; 322 McKenzie). Get a hat as individual as you are, made to order at Montecristi. They feature western hats, Dick Tracy–style fedoras, and a few ladies' styles. Prices may be intimidating, but the hats will last a lifetime.

Vintage

Santa Fe

Act 2 (505-983-8585; 839 Paseo de Peralta). "Affordable retail therapy" is the way this boutique advertises itself. Good stock of fashionable bargains and treasures, often designer labels marked way down. Truly a place to enhance or build a wardrobe. If it's your lucky day, you'll feel blessed indeed. Look for the colored tag specials.

Double Take (505-989-8886; 321 S. Guadalupe St.). Santa Fe's premier resale shop, this store has an extensive well-chosen stock, from wardrobe basics to more exotic items. Also an excellent selection of children's clothing, much of it in mint condition. Hit it first and often!

Kowboyz (505-984-1256; 345 West Manhattan Ave.) Died and gone to cowboy heaven. Thousands of bargain flannel shirts, used boots, fringed buckskin jackets and vests, hats. Get the look at a better price here than anywhere else. Parking lot, too.

FURNISHINGS AND RUGS

Santa Fe

Arius Tile (505-988-8966; 1800 Second St.). Since 1972, Arius Tile has provided Santa Fe with original hand-glazed and hand-painted tiles, both individual designs and as parts of larger mosaics. A beautiful collection of Judaica, as well as Virgin of Guadalupe designs may be found here.

Artesanos Imports Co. (505-471-8020; 1414 Maclovia). The largest distributor of Mexican tile in the United States, Artesanos features cheerful tiles of birds and flowers that also enliven many local kitchens and bathrooms. Consider individual tiles as wall hangings or trivets.

Design Warehouse (505-988-1555; 101 W. Marcy St.). This is where the locals shop for sleek contemporary design in home furnishings and accesories from candles to couches, lunch boxes to beds. Has an excellent selection of modern glass and dinnerware.

El Paso Import Company (505-982-5698; 419 Sandoval St.). For the home decorator looking to add a touch of the warmth of old Mexico, this is the place to shop. El Paso Import sells rustic chairs, tables, sideboards, and a wide variety of painted wooden furniture. The store also features pots, pot stands, ceramic candleholders, trunks, ironwork lamps, hardware for doors, and old spurs.

Heriz Oriental Rug Services (505-983-9650; 1201 Don Diego Ave.) is owned by Shahin Medghalchi, who lovingly restores rugs and sells carpets old and new. The store features Navajo, Persian, and Afghani rugs, along with custom furniture. Prices are reasonable, and you receive service that caters to your taste and budget.

Seret & Sons Rugs and Furnishings (505-980-3027; 224 Galisteo St.) Ira Seret has been importing from Afghanistan for more than 40 years. In the main showroom on Galisteo, see carved wood and custom-covered couches, chairs, and chaises fit for a scene from the Arabian Nights.

Southwest Spanish Craftsmen (505-988-1229; 314 S. Guadalupe St.). Traditional look. This is the showroom for the oldest furniture company in the Southwest, founded in 1927. Although the company specializes in southwestern styles, they work with the customer and have designed everything from English desks to Italian beds. Wood, finish, and texture can all be chosen; books of design help the customer select something individual and beautiful. Work is done painstakingly by local artisans.

Taos Furniture (505-988-1229; 217 Galisteo). This showroom/workshop features furnishings for home and office in a variety of southwestern-based styles, including durable ponderosa pine furniture, plus a wide selection of handcrafts.

Taos

Country Furnishings of Taos (575-758-4633; 534 Paseo del Pueblo Norte). You want local? We got local. Unique and appealing folk art furniture painted by local artists. Home accessories, jewelry, and a panoply of gifts by some of the state's top craftspeople.

Starr Interiors (575-758-3065; 117 Paseo Del Pueblo Norte) Step into Starr and bring home the aura of the Southwest. Known for hand-crafted Zapotec Indian weavings, this shop also features benches, tables, and *trasteros* (cabinets) hand-carved and hand-painted by Taos artisans. Oaxacan masks and more. A reliable décor source since 1974.

GALLERIES

Santa Fe and Taos each have enough galleries to engage the most avid art enthusiast. Here are a few personal favorites, but space does not permit a complete listing. Your best bet is to set aside time for browsing and visit those that call to you. Friday evenings are the traditional time for gallery openings. Check the *Santa Fe New Mexican*'s Friday "Pasatiempo" section for times and places. See also "Posters" in this chapter.

Contemporary Art

Santa Fe

These fine-art galleries feature recent paintings, sculpture, and prints in both representational and abstract styles. Some focus on southwestern-inspired work; others are nonregional.

Jane Sauer Gallery (652 Canyon Rd.; 505-995-8513).Innovative, mesmerizing textile arts and mixed media.

Shidoni Foundry and Galleries (505-988-8001; Shidoni Lane, off Bishop's Lodge Rd., 5 miles north of Santa Fe). A must-visit. This eight-acre sculpture garden in the lush Tesuque River Valley is internationally known. Bronze pourings are on Saturday afternoons; call for times. Open year-round.

Turner Carroll Gallery (505-986-9800; 725 Canyon Rd.). A fresh, distinct aesthetic characterizes the well-selected, sometimes startling work displayed here, much from Eastern Europe.

Waxlander Gallery (505-984-2202; 622 Canyon Rd.). A strong sense of color characterizes the largely sculptural work of the 10 or so New Mexico contemporary artists featured in a 150-year-old adobe.

Taos

The Fenix Gallery (575-776-8167; 228-B Paseo del Pueblo Norte). A small, excellent gallery with paintings, prints, and sculpture mostly by Taos artists of national and international repute. Director Judith Kendall has an eye for work that's nonrepresentational but "with a lot of content." Also featured are the expressionistic landscapes of Alyce Frank.

New Directions Gallery (575-758-2771; 107-B North Plaza). Some of the deepest and most challenging contemporary art is on display here, including the work of Taos artists Larry Bell and the late sculptor Ted Egri.

Parks Gallery (575-751-0343; 110 Paseo del Pueblo Norte). High-quality, imaginative contemporary painting, photography, sculpture, prints, and jewelry. Eye-opening, thoughtful work by standouts such as the late Melissa Zink.

Santa Fe

Davis Mather Folk Art Gallery (505-983-1660; 141 Lincoln Ave., a block north of the Plaza). One of the best collections of New Mexico animal woodcarvings and Mexican folk art. Owner Davis Mather delights in recounting how he discovered the work of Felipe Archuleta, the New Mexico artisan who popularized the whimsical animal carvings in the 1960s.

Montez Gallery (505-982-1828; 125 E. Palace Ave., Ste. 33, Sena Plaza courtyard). Excellent New Mexico folk art by a large group of *santeros*, many of whom have worked in the Smithsonian Institution. *Santos, retablos, bultos*, tinwork, furniture, paintings, pottery, weavings, and jewelry from $3 to $3,000.

Near Santa Fe

Chimayó Trading and Mercantile (505-351-4566; NM 76 at Chimayó). Chimayó weavings, New Mexico folk art, Indian art, pottery and jewelry, antiques and furniture. Open daily.

Galeria Ortega and Ortega's Weaving Shop (505-351-4215; 53 Plaza de Cerro, Chimayó). Watch Andrew Ortega, a seventh-generation weaver, at work in his studio. Authentic 100 percent woolen blankets, rugs, coats, vests, and purses made in the Chimayó weaving style. This is an excellent place to find a "lifetime" garment. Also Santa Clara Pueblo pottery and southwestern books. Snacks are available at the adjoining Café Ortega.

Find chile, milagros, and much more at the old trading post in Chimayó.

High Road Marketplace Artists' Co-Op & Gallery (505-689-2689; 1642 State Road 76, Truchas). Traditional and contemporary arts and crafts by more than 70 northern New Mexico artists, from whimsical sage dolls to tinwork and fine wood-carving. A good overview introduction to traditional arts and contemporary inter-pretations of those traditions. A nonprofit community store.

Theresa's Art Gallery (505-753-4698; NM 76 between Española and Chi-mayó). A small welcoming gallery operated out of the home of Theresa and Richard Montoya, artists who paint Spanish colonial folk art. They also carry wood carvings, *retablos* and *bultos* made by area artists, Santa Clara Pueblo pottery, and more. Reasonably priced.

Taos

Act 1 Gallery (575-758-7831; 226 N. Paseo del Pueblo Norte). Features local folk artists as well as jewelry, ceramics, and pastels.

Martinez Hacienda (see "Historic Buildings and Sites" in chapter 4, *Culture*). Quality New Mexico folk art, from carvings and paintings to tinwork.

Millicent Rogers Museum (see "Museums" in chapter 4, *Culture*). *Santos, retablos*, tinwork, and Rio Grande and Chimayó weavings.

Native American Art

Santa Fe is an international center for the sale of Native American art and antiqui-ties. Most Native American artisans from the Southwest make pottery and jewelry, but there are also traditions of weaving, basket making, carving, and painting. Some of these artists have international reputations.

Most potters tend to work within the context of their own pueblo's traditions, though they usually find room for innovation. Each pueblo's pottery has distinctive designs, shapes, and colors, but traditional pottery is all made by the same labor-intensive process. The clay is gathered and cleaned by hand, and pots are shaped by the coil method, in which the artist winds a long, thin roll of clay into the desired shape. Paints and slips (thin clay soup painted on the outer surface of the pot to smooth it) are made by hand from plant and mineral materials, and the pot is fired in an outdoor kiln. Many hours and great skill are required to create even a small pot. The pueblos best known for their fine pottery are San Ildefonso, Santa Clara, San Juan, and Acoma, as well as the Hopi villages of northeastern Arizona.

If you want to buy an authentic traditional pot, be sure to ask whether it's handmade or slip-cast (commercially molded). Some artists buy slip-cast pots and paint them. These are fine decorator items, but they will never appreciate in value; a well-made hand-coiled pot will.

Jewelry making is also a fine art among the Pueblo Indians. They have been crafting fine turquoise and shell beads for many centuries. As with pottery, jewelry making by traditional methods is a painstaking, time-consuming process, and an artisan may apprentice for several years.

The Navajo (who are not a Pueblo tribe) are the acknowledged masters of sil-verwork, crafting the turquoise and silver jewelry and concha belts that epitomize the Southwest. The Hopi produce a unique kind of silverwork called overlay, char-acterized by angular geometric repeat patterns on rings, bracelets, necklaces, bolos, and more. The Zuni of west central New Mexico make the finest lapidary work, such as needlepoint and petit point, in which tiny bits of turquoise are indi-

A modern-day view of the Old Santa Fe Trail leading down toward the Plaza.

vidually shaped and inlaid precisely into silver settings. The Santo Domingo Pueblo natives are the most skilled creators of *heishi*, or finely carved beads made of shell.

If you're buying from artists who sell under the portal at the Palace of the Governors on the Santa Fe Plaza, it is good to know that this area is reserved only for New Mexican Indians and that all items must be made by hand, either by the seller or by members of his or her family. In shops, clerks should be able to provide information on who made an item and something of its tradition. Following are some shops and galleries that specialize in Native American art. If you have time, though, we suggest you visit the pueblos (see "Pueblos" in chapter 4, *Culture*). Also included below are some reputable shops that deal in Native American antiquities; most of these offer contemporary artwork as well.

Santa Fe

Keshi: The Zuni Connection (505-989-8728; 227 Don Gaspar Ave.). Keshi carries a fine selection of Zuni fetishes—small stone carvings in the shapes of totem animals—as well as Zuni jewelry, sold with integrity. That's important, because Zuni wares are easily and commonly copied.

Morning Star Gallery (505-982-8187; 513 Canyon Rd.). One of Santa Fe's most reputable dealers in antique Indian art: pottery, weavings, clothing, basketry, blankets, kachina dolls, and more.

Niman Fine Arts (505-988-5091; 125 Lincoln Ave.). The exclusive representative for Dan Namingha, a Tewa-Hopi artist with a growing international reputation. Namingha's paintings, mixed-media pieces, and sculptures evoke a powerful spiritual response in many people, and he's also become a spokesman for Native cultures worldwide.

Palace of the Governors Print, Book and Photo Archive Shop (505-988-3454; 100 Palace Ave.). All authentic, Indian-made artwork in all media, plus a wide variety of books on the Southwest. No state sales tax charged here.

Price-Dewey Galleries (505-982-8632; 53 Old Santa Fe Trail). This gallery features historic Southwest Indian and Hispanic art and old Navajo textiles as well as classic and modern furniture.

The Rainbow Man (505-982-8706; 107 E. Palace Ave.). Indian trade blankets are the passion of owners Bob and Marianne Kapoun. Their eight-room shop is a little museum of western art and memorabilia. Blankets, pawn jewelry, Edward S. Curtis photographs, railroad items, Indian art and fine crafts, and contemporary Hispanic folk art.

Taos

R. B. Ravens (505-758-7322; 4146 NM 68, Ranchos de Taos, south of Taos in St. Francis Church plaza). Even if your budget can't handle an antique Navajo weaving, you'll enjoy viewing the museum-quality Pueblo, vintage Navajo, and Rio Grande textiles here. The beautiful adobe building also houses antique Indian jewelry, paintings by Taos Founders, pottery, kachina dolls, and pre-Columbian art. An excellent selection of books on Navajo textiles.

Taos Drum Showroom (575-758-3796; 803 Paseo del Pueblo Norte). Treat yourself to at least a browse of fine handmade drums of all sizes and sounds, rattles, lamp shades, and other genuine artifacts. You will be tempted to bring home a piece of the Southwest.

Photography

Santa Fe

Andrew Smith Gallery, Inc., Masterpieces of Photography (505-984-1234; 122 Grant Ave.). Acclaimed as the world's leading gallery selling 19th- and 20th-century masterworks, both European and American, this "house of photography" is always worth a look. Ansel Adams, Edward Curtis, Laura Gilpin, and contemporary photographers of the western landscape.

Monroe Gallery of Photography (505-992-0800; 112 Don Gaspar Ave.). Following 9/11, Sidney Monroe moved his fine photography gallery from lower Manhattan to Santa Fe. Excellent shows of historical 20th-century photography and the photographers who made that history. Always exciting exhibits.

Traditional Art

Santa Fe and Taos attracted artists from the East Coast and Europe in the early decades of the 20th century. The painting movements they started became known as the Santa Fe School and the Taos moderns. Today their works are in great demand, and many artists who live here continue to work in the style popularized by these earlier artists. Most of the galleries below also carry traditional paintings and sculptures of artists of the greater West.

Santa Fe

Gerald Peters Gallery (505-954-5700; 1011 Paseo de Peralta). This international gallery features classic western and Taos Society of Artists as well as contemporary paintings, sculpture, and photography. Peters is known for his O'Keeffes. Think of a fine museum where everything is for sale.

The Owings Gallery (505-982-6244; 76 E. San Francisco St., on the Plaza). Owings shows 19th- and 20th-century American art, including western, traditional, and contemporary paintings, watercolors, and original graphics. Stieglitz Circle, Ashcan School, Taos Society of Artists, and Santa Fe moderns all have their place here.

Taos
Total Arts Gallery (505-758-4667; 122-A Kit Carson Rd.). For more than 40 years, this six-room gallery has presented a cross section of fine art that embraces traditional and contemporary artists of national and international repute.

World Art and Gifts

Santa Fe
Fourth World Cottage Industries (505-982-4388; 102 W. San Francisco St., upstairs). Imports from Central and South America in a range of prices. Casual cotton and wool garments for men and women add a bit of ethnic chic to any wardrobe. The store also has art hangings, pottery, masks, and Guatemalan handwoven fabric.

Glorianna's Beads (505-982-0353; 55 W. Marcy St.). Exotic beads tell tales of trade and travel, and there are strands and strands of everything from amber to crystal to glass at Glorianna's. Also bead books and other crafts information.

Guadalupe's Fun Rubber Stamps (505-982-9862; 114 Don Gaspar Ave.). "Our store reflects the quirky times we live in," is the motto. Stamp your own creative mark on the world by choosing from hundreds of imaginative and outrageous rubber stamps. Also pads, inks, and handmade icons.

Jackalope (505-471-8539; 2820 Cerrillos Rd., about 3 miles south of downtown). Jackalope's motto is "Folk Art by the Truckload," and its wealth includes handmade furniture from Mexico, folk art imports, famous chile lights, and more than two acres of irresistible pottery from around the world. With a patio restaurant, greenhouse, prairie dog village, tiny carousel, and occasional entertainment—from mariachis to puppet shows—Jackalope is an enchanted world unto itself. Plenty of inspiration for souvenir buying.

Maya (505-989-7590; 108 Galisteo).For years, Maya has lent its distinct voice to the realm of Santa Fe fashion. This could be one of the best places to find distinctive accessories. An international boutique, Maya features clothing and jewelry from around the world, as well as Oaxacan animal carvings, Huichol bead and yarn art, and carvings from Tibet. The Day of the Dead items are charming, if a bit scary, and there is one of the best earring selections in town. Clothing in sensuous fabrics is well chosen.

Pachamama Gallery (505-983-4020; 223 Canyon Rd.). An entrancing collection of antiques and traditional folk art from Latin America in a wide range of prices. Specializes in magical and religious objects such as *santos, retablos*, and *milagros*, as well as furniture, masks, jewelry, toys, baskets, and musical instruments. So much fun!

Susan's Christmas Shop (505-983-2127; 115 E. Palace Ave.). Santa himself couldn't do better than this dazzling array of handmade Christmas ornaments from New Mexico, Mexico, and beyond. Incredibly fanciful and ornate ornaments for all. Look for seasonal changes: hearts on Valentine's Day and collector-quality decorated eggs for Easter.

FX/18 (575-758-8590; 140 Kit Carson Rd.). Whimsical sculptures, retro items, silver jewelry, and dining and household wares with a playful touch. The store shows the work of younger cutting-edge local jewelers, as well as locally made soaps, notecards, and gifts.

Taos Artisans Cooperative Gallery (575-758-1558; 107 Bent St.) Silverwork, tile, woven sculpture, watercolors, and acrylics from the hands of 14 local artists, priced for any budget.

Taos Blue (575-758-3561; 101 Bent St.). Saints and angels brush halos and wings in this gift shop specializing in objects with divine inspiration—from pottery to paintings on wood to luscious hand-knit sweaters. The place to find a unique gift by a local craftsperson.

JEWELRY

Santa Fe

James Reid, Ltd. (505-988-1147; 114 E. Palace Ave.) offers breathtaking concha belts and belt buckles in silver and gold, in both traditional and contemporary designs. High end and awesome.

Luna Felix, Goldsmith (505-989-7679; 116 W. San Francisco St.). Designer Luna Felix pioneered the Etruscan revival look in fine jewelry—lavish stones in neoclassical, almost architectural, settings. A renowned goldsmith, her name is synonymous with the romantic in jewelry. Rings and earrings are particularly compelling in this collection.

Ortega's on the Plaza (505-988-1866; www.ortegasontheplaza.com; 101 W. San Francisco St.). This venerable trader has a first-class selection of Indian jewelry, emphasizing traditional designs in turquoise and silver. Also pottery, kachinas, and some elegant velvet clothing.

Palace of the Governors Portal (Palace Ave., entire north block of the Plaza). One of the best places in town to shop for traditional Indian jewelry is beneath the portal of the historic Governors Palace. Artists and artisans assemble from the surrounding pueblos and as far away as the Navajo Reservation to sell traditional silver and turquoise jewelry, as well as small pots and other items. Prices are reasonable, and there is a special pleasure in buying from the jeweler or a family representative. Earrings, necklaces, bolo ties, and rings are in particular abundance, and a tiny bracelet makes a special baby present. Vendors are assigned slots daily by lottery, so if you find something you love, buy it—it may be difficult to trace later.

Silver Sun (505-983-8743; 656 Canyon Road). Dazzling array of turquoise treasures. A very reliable place to make a purchase. Don't be put off by the Canyon Road brand. You can't go wrong on quality or price—just commit to what you can't live without. Bargain racks in the back can provide some real finds.

Sissel's Discount Indian Jewelry (505-471-3499; 541 S. Guadalupe St.). Turquoise and silver jewelry, from fetish necklaces to bolo ties, at a discount price. This is the place to adorn yourself with squash blossom necklaces, earrings, and belts without emptying your wallet.

Tin-Nee-Ann Trading Co. (505-988-1630; 923 Cerrillos Rd.). The trading company is a quintessential old-fashioned curio shop, with great deals on Indian jewelry, from earrings to squash blossom necklaces. Also features kachinas, pottery, and sand paintings.

Taos

Artwares Contemporary Jewelry (575-758-8850; 129 N. Plaza). Known for its stylized Zuni bears, executed in precious metals and used to adorn earrings, necklaces, and pins. There is fine lapidary work, and a mix of Native American and contemporary-style jewelry in a reasonable price range.

KITCHENWARE

Santa Fe

Las Cosas Kitchen Shoppe & Cooking School (505-988-3394; DeVargas Center). Probably the best-equipped, most reasonably priced, and friendliest cookware shop in town.

Nambe Outlet Store (505-988-5528, 924 Paseo de Peralta; 505-988-3574, 112 W. San Francisco St.). Nambe (nam-BAY) ware is a secret metal alloy that does not include silver, lead, or pewter. It shines like sterling silver yet can be used for cooking and retains heat or cold for hours. Nambe dishes, platters, trays, plates, and bowls are cast at a foundry in Santa Fe. The pieces make classic wedding or housewarming gifts.

Taos

Monet's Kitchen (575-758-8003; 124 Bent St.). A nicely apportioned kitchen shop with espresso makers, woks, pottery, aprons, and table linens. Some gourmet foods and coffees as well, for a complete gift basket.

Taos Cookery (575-758-5435; 113 Bent St.). Besides featuring general kitchenware, Taos Cookery also represents many local potters. Among the most eye-catching designs are the multicolored productions of Ojo Sarco Pottery, whose husband-and-wife team creates dishwasher- and microwave-safe pottery emblazed with patterns taken from the New Mexico landscape.

MALLS

Santa Fe

Baca Street Arts: The Soho of Santa Fe (Baca Street just west of Cerrillos Rd.). Not exactly a mall, this area is the up-and-coming hip new neighborhood of Santa Fe, with artists at work in their studios and galleries and an energy that begs exploration. Check out Liquid Light Glass, the studio of Elodie Holmes (505-820-2222; 926 Baca St.) and grab a light, creative lunch on the patio at Counter Culture Café (930 Baca St.).

Design Center (no phone; 418 Cerrillos Rd.). A rich collection of cafés, furniture stores, import shops, galleries, and home design studios, as well as ethnic eateries. Great browsing turf.

DeVargas Center (505-982-2655; www.devargascenter.com; 564 N. Guadalupe St.). The oldest mall in Santa Fe is a shopping center for residents in the northern half of town. It has refurbished recently, and it's just the right size. It has about 50 stores, with Ross Dress for Less, CVS, Office Depot, Starbucks,

The General Store at Arroyo Seco has everything you didn't realize you needed.

Albertson, and Sunflower groceries, as well as the popular Java Joe Café. The mall also has jewelry stores, movie theaters, pizza, and ice cream.

Sanbusco Market Center Mall (505-989-9390; 500 Montezuma St.). In the renovated historic railyard area, Sanbusco has a pleasant indoor arcade atmosphere. It features high-end clothing boutiques such as Bodhi Bazaar as well as REI and shops selling beauty products and home accessories. Despite the loss of anchor Border Books, it's still an interesting browse.

Santa Fe Place Mall (505-473-4253; 4250 Cerrillos Rd.). Once called Villa Linda Mall, Santa Fe Place Mall is the largest in Santa Fe, with 110 stores, including Dillard's. It has movie theaters, a video arcade, a post office, a public library branch, and a food court with carousel.

Santa Fe Premium Outlets (505-474-4000; 8 miles south of Santa Fe Plaza at 8380 Cerrillos Rd.). With more than 40 outlet stores just south of Santa Fe, Santa Fe Premium Outlets offers the shopper good prices on many name brands. You'll find shoes from Bass and Nine West, leather goods by Coach and Samsonite, housewares from Dansk, as well as books, children's clothing, and more.

POSTERS

Santa Fe

The Santa Fe Opera, Chamber Music Festival, Santa Fe Indian Market, and Santa Fe Spanish Market all publish quality art posters each year that become collectors' items. In particular, the Chamber Music Festival's Georgia O'Keeffe poster series remains popular. Some southwestern artists and photographers also publish their work as posters. The following shops are in the Plaza area:

Fox Gallery: 505-983-2002; 217 W. Water St.

Posters of Santa Fe: 505-982-6645; 111 E. Palace Ave.

Posters of the West: 505-820-1221; 107 Don Gaspar Ave.

Taos
Final Touch Frame Shop: 575-758-4360; 800 Bond Dr.

Total Arts: 575-758-4667; 122-A Kit Carson Rd.

TEXTILES AND FIBERS

Santa Fe
Handwoven Originals (505-982-4118; 211 Old Santa Fe Trail). Handwoven clothing and painted silk are the hallmarks of this store. Much of the work is done by local artists and designers. Features shawls, skirts, vests, jackets, hats, and scarves.

Santa Fe Weaving Gallery (505-982-1737; 124 Galisteo St.). The gallery shows clothing designed by 25 nationally recognized fiber artists. Fabrics include handwoven chenille, cotton knots, silk appliqué, and painted wool and silk. Take home some art you can wear.

Taos
Twining Weavers & Contemporary Crafts, Ltd. (575-758-5040; 103 Bent St.). The stock here includes handwoven wool rugs, pillows made from hand-dyed yarns, Guatemalan cotton runners, place mats, napkins, and baskets from around the world. They will work directly with the customer to customize colors and designs.

Near Taos
Arroyo Seco Mercantile (575-776-8806; 488 NM 150). Vintage textiles, including quilts, Saltillo weavings and Indian trade blankets, toys, gifts, *santos*, books, and garden ornaments. A shopping experience in an 1895 general store.

If Time Is Short

THE MORE TIME YOU SPEND IN NEW MEXICO, the more you will want to see. If your time is limited, however, you won't want to miss these attractions. The suggestions here are but a few personal favorites, each with its own distinctive flavor. If you must make your visit brief, try to come back soon and create your own list of favorites.

Lodging

Santa Fe

The Bishop's Lodge Ranch Resort & Spa (505-629-4822; 800-768-3586; 1297 Bishop's Lodge Rd., Santa Fe, NM 87504). Honeymoon, anniversary, family vacation: this is the place to relax and find complete serenity.

Inn on the Alameda (505-984-2121; 304 E. Alameda). The charms of a small European hotel.

Taos

Inn on the Rio (575-758-7199; 910 Kit Carson Rd.). A true home away from home, at reasonable prices. A real find.

Mabel Dodge Luhan House (575-751-9686; 800-846-2235). 240 Morada Lane, Taos, NM 87571. Set on five acres at the edge of a vast open tract of Taos Pueblo land, this rambling three-story, 22-room adobe hacienda *is* Taos history. Savor time standing still in the elegant home of Taos's most notorious patron of the arts.

Cultural Attractions

Santa Fe

Georgia O'Keeffe Museum (505-995-0785; 313 Read St.). View the evolution of the artist's vision in an elegant setting she would have approved.

Museum of International Folk Art (505-827-6350; 706 Camino Lejo). You simply cannot visit Santa Fe and skip this rich, colorful treasure trove.

Santuario de Chimayó (505-351-4889; in Chimayó, 26 miles northeast of

LEFT: Charm and comfort abide at Inn on the Rio.

You can stay cozy at the fireside at Santa Fe's intimate Inn on the Alameda.

Santa Fe on NM 76). Nowhere can you get a better understanding of the spirit of northern New Mexico than at this holy shrine.

Taos
Harwood Museum (575-758-9826; 238 Ledoux St.). Excellent overview of the Taos Modern painters, plus the spectacular new Agnes Martin wing.

Martinez Hacienda (575-758-0505; 2 miles south of the Plaza on NM 240). The best place to get a feel for Spanish colonial life is at this well-preserved hacienda.

Millicent Rogers Museum (575-758-2462; 4 miles north of Taos on NM 522). The best all-around collection of Native American jewelry, pottery, painting, and textiles, including the Martinez family's collection of Maria's pottery.

Recreation
To Relax
Bandelier National Monument (505-672-3861; 46 miles west of Santa Fe). Hike and climb amid cliff dwellings and view village ruins and ceremonial kivas through Frijoles Canyon.

Rafting the **Rio Grande Gorge**, specifically, the Taos Box (see chapter 8, *Recreation*), can be an unforgettable whitewater adventure.

Ojo Caliente Hot Springs (505-583-2233; Ojo Caliente). With four kinds of mineral waters and a variety of heated pools, this is the place to soak and unwind.

Ten Thousand Waves (505-982-9304; Ski Basin Rd., Santa Fe). Pamper yourself in this spectacular Japanese spa with private tubs overlooking the city.

Santa Fe

Guadalupe Cafe (505-982-9762; 422 Old Santa Fe Trail, Santa Fe). Excellent home-style New Mexico cooking where the chile is good and hot and the portions are huge. Do not make the mistake of asking for your chile "on the side."

The Pink Adobe (505-983-7712; 406 Old Santa Fe Trail, Santa Fe). Can't go wrong with steak dunigan and gypsy stew. This classic restaurant has returned to its former glory since founder Rosalea Murphy's family reentered the kitchen. You can try 'em all, but you'll come back here. Like coming home.

Taos

Dragonfly Café & Bakery (575-737-5859; 402 Paseo del Pueblo Norte, Taos) Any day that begins with brunch on the patio here is a good day. Whoa! Knockout fresh-baked pastries and coffee cakes.

Love Apple (575-751-0050; 803 Paseo del Pueblo Norte, Taos). Locally sourced smallish menu includes steak, vegetarian, New Mexican offerings; funky-romantic candlelit former chapel is the real Taos deal.

Rancho de Chimayó (505-351-4444; around the bend from Santuario de Chimayó). A beautiful renovated 1880s ranch house that lives and breathes the traditions of northern New Mexico. A must for first-time visitors. Dine al fresco on the terrace. Well recovered from the kitchen fire.

Taos Diner (575-758-2374; 908 Paseo del Pueblo Norte, Taos). Hang with the locals! My go-to place for salads, huevos rancheros smothered in red chile, and the best burger, locally sourced.

Information

PRACTICAL MATTERS

HERE IS A MODEST ENCYCLOPEDIA of useful information about the Santa Fe and Taos area. Our aim is to case everyday life for locals and help ensure that vacation time goes smoothly for visitors. This chapter covers the following topics:

AMBULANCE, FIRE, POLICE, AND HOSPITALS

Emergency Numbers
The general emergency number (fire, police, ambulance) for Santa Fe and Taos is 911. Other emergency numbers are as follows:

Santa Fe
Crisis Intervention: 505-820-6333
Esperanza Shelter: 505-474-5536
Landlord-Tenant Hotline: 800-348-9370
New Mexico Suicide Intervention Project: 505-820-1066
Poison Control: 800-222-1222
Rape Crisis Center: 505-721-7273

LEFT: Texas Red's is the place to go in Red River.

Taos
Ambulance: 575-758-1911
Fire: 575-758-3386
Poison Control: 800-222-1222
Police: 575-758-2217
Sheriff: 575-737-6485

State Police
Española: 505-753-9318
Santa Fe: 505-827-9300
Taos: 575-758-8878

Hospitals
Española
Española Hospital: 505-753-7111; 1010 Spruce St.

Los Alamos
Los Alamos Medical Center: 505-662-4201; 3917 West Rd.

Santa Fe
Christus St. Vincent Hospital: 505-983-3361; 455 St. Michael's Dr.

Taos
Holy Cross Hospital: 575-758-8883; 1397 Weimar Rd.

BANKS

Most banks in Santa Fe and Taos are linked electronically to nationwide automatic teller systems. Here is a list of telephone numbers and addresses of some of these banks' main offices.

Santa Fe
Bank of America (505-473-8211; main office at 1234 St. Michael's Dr.). Linked to Plus, MasterCard, Maestro, Lynx, Pulse, Visa, and Bank Mate systems.
First National Bank of Santa Fe (505-992-2000; main office on the Plaza). Linked to Lynx, Plus, Pulse, and Bank Mate systems.
First State Bank (505-992-8444; main office at 201 Washington Ave.). Linked to Bank Mate, Plus, Pulse, Lynx, Cirrus, and Discover Novus systems.
Wells Fargo (505-984-0500; 241 Washington Ave.).

Taos
Centinel Bank of Taos (575-758-6788; 508 Paseo del Pueblo Norte). Linked to Cirrus, Lynx, and Pulse systems.
First State Bank of Taos (575-758-6600; main office at 120 W. Plaza). Linked to Plus, Pulse, Bank Mate, Cirrus, Discover Novus, MasterCard, and Lynx systems.
Peoples Bank (575-758-8331; main office at 1356 Paseo del Pueblo Sur). Linked to Cirrus, Lynx, Pulse, and Money systems.

Local chambers of commerce and visitors bureaus are usually a quick and convenient way of getting information about the specific area you want to visit:

Santa Fe

Santa Fe Convention and Visitors Bureau: 505-955-6705; www.santafe.org; 201 W. Marcy St., Santa Fe, NM 87504-0909.

   Santa Fe County Chamber of Commerce: 505-988-3279; sfccoc@nm.net; www.santafechamber.com; 8380 Cerrillos Rd., Santa Fe, NM 87507-4418.

Taos

Taos Association of Bed and Breakfast Inns: http://taos-bandb-inns.com/taos _lodging.

   Taos County Chamber of Commerce: 575-751-8800; www.taoschamber.com; 515 Gusdorf Rd., Taos, NM 87571.

Taos Area

Angel Fire Chamber of Commerce: 575-377-6661; 800-446-8117; askus@angel firechamber.org; www.angelfire chamber.org; Centro Plaza, 3407 NM 434, Angel Fire, NM 87710.

   Eagle Nest Chamber of Commerce: 575-377-2420; 50 W. Therma Dr., Eagle Nest, NM 87118.

   Red River Chamber of Commerce: 575-754-2366; 800-348-6444; rrinfo@red rivernewmex.com; www.redrivernm.com; 100 E. Main St., Red River, NM 87558.

CLIMATE AND WEATHER REPORTS

Santa Fe and Taos are blessed with a healthful, dynamic, high-desert climate. The air is dry all year, and at 7,000 feet (the approximate elevation of both cities), nights are always cool. There are 300 days of sunshine a year.

   Sound wonderful? It is. But you'll enjoy it more if you take a few precautions. Bring and use sunscreen (with a protection level of at least 30), lip balm, and skin lotion. Be sure to take it easy when you first arrive to give your body a chance to adjust to the altitude. To keep your energy up, eat foods high in carbohydrates. Go easy on alcohol, tranquilizers, and sleeping pills. And drink lots of water.

   You can get information on road conditions by calling the state police at 505-827-9300 or New Mexico Road Conditions at 800-432-4269 or the 511 hotline. Your best bet is to go to www.nmroads.com, which is updated frequently and gives information on road closures as well as driving conditions. You can reach the National Weather Service in Albuquerque at 505-243-0702.

GUIDED TOURS

There are a number of delightful and informative sightseeing tours in the Santa Fe–Taos area. Local cabdrivers can usually be persuaded to drive you around, adding colorful histories that only a cabbie might know. For more organized, detailed tours, consider the following:

Aboot About Santa Fe (505-988-2774; 624 Galiseto, #32). Tour guides Alan and Carla Jordan will take you to places in and near the Santa Fe Plaza that are reputed to be haunted. Reservations are required. $10 adults; senior discounts.

Afoot in Santa Fe (505-983-3701). Tours, conducted by longtime guide Charles Porter, gather at 207 and 211 Old Santa Fe Trail.

Custom Tours by Clarice (505-438-7116) offers luxury transportation, charters, and special events as well as tours of Santa Fe for $10 per person.

Fiesta City Tours (505-983-1570). Run by Frank Montaño, a former Santa Fe city councilor, these tours focus on downtown historic sites. Tours depart from the corner of Palace and Lincoln on the northwest corner of the Plaza at 10 AM, noon, 2 PM, 4 PM, and 6 PM. Historic Walks of Santa Fe (505-986-8388) departs from the La Fonda Hotel daily at 9:45 and 1:15; and the Plaza Galeria at 10 and 1:30. Cost is $10 per person.

Loretto Line Open Air Trolley Tram City Tours (505-983-3701). Departure times are 10 AM, 11 AM, noon, 1 PM, 2 PM, and 3 PM. Meet in the Loretto Chapel area, 207 Old Santa Fe Trail. Arrive at least 15 minutes before departure time to purchase your tickets for $15 from the bus driver. The tour lasts approximately 1.25 hours.

Recursos de Santa Fe (505-982-9301). This nonprofit organization specializes in educational tours under Royal Road Tours, which include excursions to archaeo-

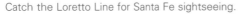

Catch the Loretto Line for Santa Fe sightseeing.

logical sites, lectures in Georgia O'Keeffe country, and visits to the homes and studios of local artists.

Santa Fe Detours (505-986-0038). First-rate walking tours of the downtown area with guides who are longtime residents and know local history and anthropology. Motorized tours will pick you up at your hotel at 9 AM. For walking tours, meet under the T-shirt tree next to the Burrito Co. Cafe at 107 Washington Ave. Reservations are required. Stop by the Santa Fe Detours office (54½ E. San Francisco St. above Häagen-Dazs on the Plaza) for a discount. They also offer a hotline for unique area B&Bs and lodging.

Santa Fe Ghost and History Tours (505-986-5002). Includes the paranormal.

Santa Fe Southern (505-989-8600). For a taste of the Santa Fe region circa 1890, the railway offers a ride aboard a passenger train to Lamy, 25 miles to the southeast; catered lunch in Lamy is available on certain days. The train departs from Santa Fe every Mon., Thurs., and Sat. at 10:30 AM at the Santa Fe Railyards, six blocks southwest of the Plaza. $32–55 adults; $18–42 ages 3–13; $27–50 ages 60 and over; under 2 are free.

Santa Fe Spy Tours (www.santafespytour.com). By appointment.

Taos

Artours (575-758-4246; 800-582-9700; http://artoursltd.com;). Artours is the company of Marcia Winter, whose great-grandfather was O. E. Berninghaus, one of the founding members of the Taos art colony. She specializes in small, customized group tours of art museums, artists' studios, and private collections.

Taos Historic Walking Tours (575-758-4020). Arsenio Cordova is a sixth-generation Taoseño with a wealth of information on the history of the Taos region. May–Sept., he offers one foot tour daily. During the rest of the year, appointments must be made in advance. $15 per person.

DISABILITY SERVICES

To obtain a copy of a booklet that identifies handicapped-accessible facilities, contact the Governor's Committee on Disability at 505-827-6328; 491 Old Santa Fe Trail, Lamy Building, Room 117, Santa Fe, NM 87501-2753. For further information, contact City of Santa Fe, Community Services Division at 505-992-9862. Out-of-state handicapped visitors can obtain a temporary placard for handicapped parking by calling the New Mexico Motor Vehicle Division at 888-683-4636. Capital City Cab Co. (505-438-0000) offers disabled people a 75 percent discount on fares with a coupon available from City Hall. You must have proof of American Disabilities Act qualification to receive a 21-day visitors pass. Your best bet for information on accessibility and parking in Taos is the Taos County Chamber of Commerce (575-751-8800; www.taoschamber.com; 515 Gusdorf Rd., Ste. 6, Taos, NM 87571).

LATE-NIGHT FOOD AND FUEL

If the munchies hit or your fuel gauge drops perilously low in the wee hours, there are places you can go. Santa Fe in particular has an abundance of convenience stores, restaurants, and gas stations that stay open 24 hours a day.

INFORMATION

Convenience Stores and
Gas Stations
Allsup's: 505-988-3862; 305 N.
Guadalupe St., Santa Fe and 505-
758-0037; 507 Paseo del Pueblo Norte,
Taos.

    Carrow's: 505-471-7856; 1718 St.
Michael's Dr., Santa Fe.

    Denny's: 505-471-2152; 3004
Cerrillos Rd., Santa Fe.

    Dunkin' Donuts: 505-983-2090;
1085 S. St. Francis Dr., Santa Fe.

    Giant Service Station: 505-473-
9744; 2691 Sawmill Rd., Santa Fe.

Restaurants
The Kettle: 505-473-5840; 4250 Cerrillos Rd. at Villa Linda Mall, Santa Fe.

    Walgreen's: 505-474-3507; 3298
Cerrillos Rd., Santa Fe.

LOCAL GOVERNMENT: CITY HALLS AND ZIP CODES

Santa Fe, New Mexico's capital, is the
seat of Santa Fe County, which is
headed by a five-member county com-

Along the "low road" to Taos

mission. Taos is the seat of Taos County, which is headed by a three-member
county commission. The two other major cities in the region with sizable local gov-
ernments are Española and Los Alamos. In addition, there are 11 Indian pueblos
in the area located on reservations. Politically and legally, each pueblo is a sovereign nation led by a tribal governor and a tribal ruling council. Each also has its
own police force. For general information, call the following numbers or write to
the city or county clerk, in care of the city or county in question, or to the tourist
information centers at the pueblos.

Town or Pueblo	Telephone	Zip Code
Cochiti Pueblo	505-465-2244	87072
Española	505-747-6100	87532
Los Alamos County	505-663-1750	87544
Nambe Pueblo	505-455-2036	87747
Ohkay Owingeh	505-852-4400	87566
Picuris Pueblo	575-587-2519	87553
Pojoaque Pueblo	505-455-2278	87506
Rio Arriba County	505-753-7019	87532
San Felipe Pueblo	505-867-3381	87001
San Ildefonso Pueblo	505-455-3549	87506
Santa Clara Pueblo	505-753-7330	87532

Santa Fe	505-955-6521	87501
Santa Fe County	505-986-6280	87501
Santo Domingo Pueblo	505-465-2214	87052
Taos	575-751-2000	87571
Taos County	575-737-6380	87571
Taos Pueblo	575-758-1028	87571
Tesuque Pueblo	505-983-2667	87506

MEDIA

For current information about events in Santa Fe (music, arts and culture, business, nightlife, family activities, and more), go to www.santafe.com.

Magazines and Newspapers

Journal Santa Fe (505-988-8881; www.abqjournal.com; 328 Galisteo St., Santa Fe, NM 87501). A branch of the statewide *Albuquerque Journal*, this morning newspaper includes a section published daily and is distributed in northern New Mexico.

The Magazine (505-424-7641; 320 Aztec St, Ste. A,, Santa Fe, NM 87507). A monthly magazine of the arts with regional, national, and international perspectives.

New Mexico Magazine (505-827-7447; www.nmmagazine.com; Lew Wallace Building, 150 Old Santa Fe Trail, Santa Fe, NM 87501). A general-interest monthly published by state government, covering New Mexico culture, history, and travel.

The best way to find out what's going on is to read the paper beside the Santa Fe River.

Santa Fe New Mexican (505-986-3082; www.santafenewmexican.com; 202 E. Marcy St., Santa Fe, NM 87501). A general-interest daily distributed in northern New Mexico. Morning paper.

Santa Fe Reporter (505-988-5541; 132 E. Marcy St., Santa Fe, NM 87501). A general-interest weekly published each Wed. and distributed free of charge throughout Santa Fe and vicinity. Read for entertainment and film listings.

Taos News (575-758-2241; www.taosnews.com; 226 Albright St., Taos, NM 87571). A weekly newspaper covering local news and human interest. Comes out every Thurs.

Radio Stations

KSFR-FM 90.7 (505-428-1527). Santa Fe; community radio, arts, culture, jazz, classical, local talk, and weather.

KTAO-FM 101.9 (575-758-5826). Taos; adult rock and local news.

Television Stations

The major television stations are located in Albuquerque.

KASA FOX TV Channel 2 (505-246-2285). Albuquerque; old movies and sitcoms.

KCHF TV Channel 11 (505-883-1111). Santa Fe; religious.

KNME TV Channel 5 (505-277-2121). Albuquerque; public.

KOAT TV Channel 7 (505-884-7777; 505-988-2923 Santa Fe Bureau). Albuquerque; ABC affiliate.

KOB TV Channel 4 (505-243-4411; 505-988-3678 Santa Fe Bureau). Albuquerque; NBC affiliate.

KRQE TV Channel 13 (505-243-2285). Albuquerque; CBS affiliate.

REAL ESTATE

If owning a home in the Land of Enchantment sounds like a dream come true, then you might be interested in a little housing information.

If you're shopping for real estate in the Santa Fe or Taos areas, you can get information in a variety of ways. For a list of realtors, consult the Yellow Pages or contact the chambers of commerce. The **Santa Fe County Chamber of Commerce** (505-988-3279) is located at 8380 Cerrillos Rd., Santa Fe, NM 87507. The mailing address for the **Taos Visitor Center** (575-758-3873; 800-732-8267) is 1139 Paseo del Pueblo Sur, Taos, NM 87571. Both organizations will send lists of their Realtor members.

If you're thinking about buying property here, it's a good idea to study local zoning laws, building permits, restrictive covenants, and so forth. Also see "Local Government: City Halls and Zip Codes" in this chapter.

ROAD SERVICES

Here is a list of some 24-hour emergency road services in the Santa Fe–Taos region.

Santa Fe
A-1 Towing: 505-983-1616

A-Jack Towing: 505-438-6042

Flores Wrecker Service: 505-471-5271

Taos
AA-1 Wrecker Service: 575-758-8984

AC Towing & Transport Service: 575-758-1111

Española
Holmes Wrecker Service: 505-753-3460

Los Alamos
Knecht Automotive: 505-662-9743

RPM Automotive Towing: 505-662-7721

Bibliography

FOR THE TRAVELER WHO ENJOYS READING about a region as well as visiting it, we've put together a list of some of the many books that have been written on the Santa Fe–Taos area. (For information on Santa Fe–Taos booksellers, see "Bookstores" in chapter 8, *Shopping*. See also "Libraries" in chapter 4, *Culture*.)

Autobiographies, Biographies, and Reminiscences

Berke, Arnold. *Mary Colter: Architect of the Southwest*. New York: Princeton Architectural Press, 2002. 320 pp., $35.

Cabeza de Baca, Fabiola. *We Fed Them Cactus*. Albuquerque: University of New Mexico Press, 1954, 1994. 186 pp., $9.95.

Chavez, Fray Angelico. *But Time and Chance: The Story of Padre Martinez of Taos 1793–1867*. Santa Fe: Sunstone Press, 1981. 171 pp., $11.95.

Church, Peggy Pond. *The House at Otowi Bridge: The Story of Edith Warner and Los Alamos*. Albuquerque: University of New Mexico Press, 1959. 149 pp., $9.95.

Cline, Lynn. *Literary Pilgrims: The Santa Fe and Taos Writers Colonies 1917–1950*. Albuquerque: University of New Mexico Press, 2007. 184 pp., $19.95.

Horgan, Paul. *Lamy of Santa Fe*. New York: Noonday Press, 1975. 523 pp., $17.95.

Luhan, Mabel Dodge. *Winter in Taos*. Taos: Las Palomas de Taos, 1935. 237 pp., $14.95.

Magoffin, Susan Shelby. *Down the Santa Fe Trail and into Mexico: The Diary of Susan Shelby Magoffin, 1846–1847*. Lincoln: University of Nebraska Press, 1982. 284 pp., $6.95.

Russell, Marian. *Land of Enchantment: Memoirs of Marian Russell Along the Old Santa Fe Trail*. Albuquerque: University of New Mexico Press, 1954. 163 pp., illus., index, $10.95.

Cultural Studies

Bullock, Alice. *Living Legends of the Santa Fe Country*. Santa Fe: Lightning Tree—Jene Lyons Publishers, 1978. 96 pp., illus., $7.95.

Chavez, Fray Angelico. *Origins of New Mexico Families: A Genealogy of the*

LEFT: At Bandelier, you can visit ancient cave dwellings.

National Park Service photo, courtesy Bandelier National Monument

Spanish Colonial Period. Revised edition. Santa Fe: Museum of New Mexico Press, 1992. 441 pp., $33.

Dickey, Roland F. *New Mexico Village Arts*. Albuquerque: University of New Mexico Press, 1990. 266 pp., $24.95.

Edelman, Sandra A. *Summer People, Winter People: A Guide to the Pueblos in the Santa Fe Area*. Santa Fe: Sunstone Press, 1986. 32 pp., index, $4.95.

Gibson, Arrell Morgan. *The Santa Fe and Taos Colonies: Age of the Muses, 1900–1942*. Norman: University of Oklahoma Press, 1983. 345 pp., illus., index, $13.95.

Julyan, Robert. *The Place Names of New Mexico*. Albuquerque: University of New Mexico Press, 2000. 385 pp., $21.

Kutz, Jack. *Mysteries and Miracles of New Mexico: Guidebook to the Genuinely Bizarre in the Land of Enchantment*. Corrales, NM: Rhombus Publishing Co., 1988. 216 pp., $7.95.

Lynn, Sandra D. *Windows on the Past: Historic Lodgings of New Mexico*. Albuquerque: University of New Mexico Press, 1999. 209 pp., $24.95.

Morrow, Baker H., and V. B. Price. *Anasazi Architecture and American Design*. Albuquerque: University of New Mexico Press, 1997. 214 pp., $29.95.

Poling-Kempes, Lesley. *Valley of Shining Stone: The Story of Abiquiu*. Tuscon: University of Arizona Press, 1997. 272 pp., $24.99.

Steele, Thomas J. *Santos and Saints: The Religious Folk Art of Hispanic New Mexico*. Santa Fe: Ancient City Press, 1974. 220 pp., index, $12.95.

Trimble, Stephen. *Talking with the Clay: The Art of Pueblo Pottery*. Santa Fe: School of American Research Press, 1987. 116 pp., $22.95.

Weigle, Marta. *Brothers of Light, Brothers of Blood: The Penitentes of the Southwest*. Santa Fe: Ancient City Press, 1976. 300 pp., $12.95.

Weigle, Marta, and Kyle Fiore. *Santa Fe and Taos: The Writer's Era 1916–41*. Santa Fe: Ancient City Press, 1982. 229 pp., illus., index, $16.95.

Weigle, Marta, and Peter White. *The Lore of New Mexico*. Albuquerque: University of New Mexico Press/American Folklore Society, 1988. 523 pp., $37.

Wilson, Chris. *The Myth of Santa Fe: Creating a Modern Regional Tradition*. Albuquerque, University of New Mexico Press, 1997. 409 pp., $35.

Literary Works

Anaya, Rudolfo A. *Bless Me Ultima*. Berkeley, CA: Tonatiuh–Quinto Sol International, 1972. 247 pp., $11.95.

Bartlett, Lee, V. B. Price, and Dianne Edenfield Edwards, eds. *In Company: An Anthology of New Mexico Poets After 1960*. Albuquerque: University of New Mexico Press, 2004. 542 pp., $39.95.

Bradford, Richard. *Red Sky at Morning*. New York: Harper & Row, 1968. 256 pp., $8.95.

Cather, Willa. *Death Comes for the Archbishop*. New York: Vintage, 1927. 297 pp., $8.95.

Crawford, Stanley. *Mayordomo: Chronicle of an Acequia in Northern New Mexico*. New York: Anchor Books Doubleday, 1988. 231 pp., $8.95.

Hillerman, Tony, ed. *The Spell of New Mexico*. Albuquerque: University of New Mexico Press, 1976. 105 pp., $9.95.

Horgan, Paul. *The Centuries of Santa Fe.* Santa Fe: William Gannon Publishers, 1956. 363 pp., index, $9.95.

Nichols, John. *The Milagro Beanfield War.* New York: Ballantine Books, 1974. 629 pp., $5.95.

Niederman, Sharon. *Return to Abo: A Novel of the Southwest.* Albuquerque: University of New Mexico Press, 2005. 300 pp., $24.95.

Waters, Frank. *The Man Who Killed the Deer.* New York: Farrar Rinehart, 1942. 217 pp., $3.95.

Local Histories

Chauvenet, Beatrice. *Hewett and Friends: A Biography of Santa Fe's Vibrant Era.* Santa Fe: Museum of New Mexico Press, 1983. 248 pp., illus., index, $16.95.

DeBuys, William. *Enchantment and Exploitation: The Life and Hard Times of a New Mexican Mountain Range.* Albuquerque: University of New Mexico Press, 1985. 394 pp., index, illus., $15.95.

Gregg, Josiah. *The Commerce of the Prairies.* Lincoln: University of Nebraska Press, 1967. 343 pp., index, $9.95.

Hemp, Bill. *Taos Landmarks & Legends.* Los Alamos, NM: Exceptional Books Ltd., 1996. 134 pp., $19.95.

Hordes, Stanley. *To the End of the Earth: A History of the Crypto-Jews of New Mexico.* New York: Columbia University Press, 2005. 499 pp., $40.

Horgan, Paul. *Great River: The Rio Grande in North American History.* Austin: Texas Monthly Press, 1984. 1,020 pp., index, $14.95.

Jenkins, Myra Ellen, and Albert H. Schroeder. *A Brief History of New Mexico.* Albuquerque: University of New Mexico Press, 1974. 87 pp., illus., index, $8.95.

Price, V. B. *The Orphaned Land: New Mexico's Environment Since the Manhattan Project.* Photography by Nell Farrell. Albuquerque: University of New Mexico Press, 2011. 362 pp., $23.

Rudnick, Lois Palkin. *Utopian Vistas: The Mabel Dodge Luhan House and the American Counterculture.* Albuquerque: University of New Mexico Press, 1996. 401 pp., $19.95.

Simmons, Marc. *New Mexico: An Interpretive History.* Albuquerque: University of New Mexico Press, 1988. 207 pp., $10.95.

Tobias, Henry. *A History of the Jews in New Mexico.* Albuquerque: University of New Mexico Press, 1990. 294 pp., $19.

Photographic Studies

Brewer, Robert, and Steve McDowell. *The Persistence of Memory: New Mexico's Churches.* Santa Fe: Museum of New Mexico Press, 1991. 152 pp., $39.95.

Cash, Maria Romero. *Built of Earth and Song: A Guide to New Mexico Churches.* Santa Fe: Red Crane Press, 1993. $11.95.

Clark, William, Edward Klanner, Jack Parsons, and Bernard Plossu. *Santa Fe: The City in Photographs.* Santa Fe: Fotowest Publishing, 1984. 72 pp., $14.95.

Gregg, Andrew K. *New Mexico in the 19th Century: A Pictorial History.* Albuquerque: University of New Mexico Press. 196 pp., index, $15.95.

Nichols, John, and William Davis. *If Mountains Die: A New Mexico Memoir.* New York: Alfred A. Knopf, 1987. 144 pp., $19.95.

Taos Morada, traditional chapel of the Penitente brotherhood

Robin, Arthur H., William M. Ferguson, and Lisa Ferguson. *Rock Art of Bandelier National Monument.* Albuquerque: University of New Mexico Press, 1989. 156 pp., index, $29.95.

Varjabedian, Craig, and Michael Wallis. *En Divina Luz: The Penitente Moradas of New Mexico.* Albuquerque: University of New Mexico Press, 1994. 130 pp., $25.

Warren, Nancy Hunter. *Villages of Hispanic New Mexico.* Santa Fe: School of American Research, 1987. 109 pp., $18.

Wilson, Chris, and Stefanos Polyzoides, eds. *The Plazas of New Mexico.* Photography by Miguel Gandert. San Antonio: Trinity University Press, 2011. 337 pp., $48.

Recreation

Anderson, Fletcher, and Ann Hopkinson. *Rivers of the Southwest: A Boater's Guide to the Rivers of Colorado, New Mexico, Utah, and Arizona.* Boulder, CO: Pruett Publishing Co., 1982. 129 pp., illus., index, $8.95.

Kaysing, Bill. *Great Hot Springs of the West.* Santa Barbara, CA: Capra Press, 1984. 213 pp., illus., index, $10.95.

Matthews, Kay. *Cross-Country Skiing in Northern New Mexico: An Introduction and Trail Guide.* Placitas, NM: Acequia Madre Press, 1986. 96 pp., maps, $7.95.

Pinkerton, Elaine. *Santa Fe on Foot: Walking, Running and Bicycle Routes in the City Different.* Santa Fe: Ocean Tree, 1986. 125 pp., illus., maps, $7.95.

Santa Fe Group of the Sierra Club. *Day Hikes in the Santa Fe Area.* Santa Fe: Sierra Club, 1997. 192 pp., index, $8.95.

Ungnade, Herbert E. *Guide to the New Mexico Mountains.* Albuquerque: University of New Mexico Press, 1988. 235 pp., index, $10.95.

Travel

Chronic, Halka. *Roadside Geology of New Mexico.* Missoula, MT: Mountain Press Publishing Co., 1987. 255 pp., index, $11.95.

Fugate, Frances L., and Roberta B. Fugate. *Roadside History of New Mexico.* Missoula, MT: Mountain Press Publishing Co., 1989. 483 pp., index, $15.95.

Niederman, Sharon. *Signs & Shrines: Spiritual Journeys Across New Mexico.* Woodstock, VT: The Countryman Press, 2012. 256 pp., $19.95.

Blacker, Irwin. *Taos.* Cleveland, OH: World Publishers, 1959. A fictional account of the 1680 Pueblo Indian Revolt that drove the Spaniards out of New Mexico for 12 years.

Boyd, E. *Popular Arts of Spanish New Mexico.* Santa Fe: Museum of New Mexico Press, 1974. A color photographic study of the entire spectrum of Hispanic art in the Land of Enchantment.

Hackett, Charles Wilson. *Revolt of the Pueblo Indians of New Mexico and Otermín's Attempted Reconquest, 1680–1682.* Albuquerque: University of New Mexico Press, 1942.

Henderson, Alice Corbin. *Brothers of Light: The Penitentes of the Southwest.* New York: Harcourt, Brace, 1937. One of the best treatments of the Penitente phenomenon.

Kendall, George. *Narrative of the Texan–Santa Fe Expedition.* Albuquerque: University of New Mexico Press, 1844. Illus., maps. Outlines the beginning of the conflict between Texas and New Mexico that is still evident today, mostly in attitudes.

Knee, Ernest. *Santa Fe, New Mexico.* New York: Chanticleer Press, 1942. An unpretentious, classic photographic study of authentic old Santa Fe charm accompanied by text.

Robertson, Edna. *Artists of the Caminos and Canyons: The Early Years.* Santa Fe: Peregrine Smith, 1976. A study of the turn-of-the-20th-century artists in Santa Fe and Taos.

Ross, Calvin. *Sky Determines.* Albuquerque: University of New Mexico Press, 1948. A unique book that covers New Mexico history, weather, art, landscape, and more.

Spivey R. *Maria.* Flagstaff, AZ: Northland Press, 1979. About the famous San Ildefonso Pueblo potter.

Glossary

FOR THE MOST PART, Spanish pronunciation is phonetic. That is, it sounds the way it looks—with a few exceptions: *ll* sounds like "yuh"; *j* sounds like "h"; *qu* sounds like "k"; and *ñ* sounds like "ny." There are also a few tricky rules—for example, double *r*'s are trilled, and *d* is often pronounced "th"—but we'll leave these details for Spanish classes. Following, then, are reasonable pronunciations and short definitions for Spanish words (and a few other terms) that are commonly used in the Santa Fe–Taos area.

acequia (ah-SEH-kee-ya)—irrigation ditch.

Anasazi (an-a-SAH-zee)—Navajo word meaning "ancient strangers," used to refer to the peoples who inhabited such places as Chaco Canyon, Mesa Verde, and Bandelier National Monument A.D. 900–1300.

arroyo (a-ROY-oh)—dry gully or streambed.

arroz (a-ROSS)—rice.

banco (BONK-oh)—adobe bench, usually an extension of an adobe wall.

bizcochitos (biz-koh-CHEE-tose)—cookies.

bulto (BOOL-toh)—traditional Hispanic, three-dimensional carving of a saint.

burrito (boo-REE-toh)—flour tortilla usually wrapped around a filling of beans, meat, cheese, and sauce.

canales (ka-NAL-ess)—gutters, rainspouts.

cantina (kan-TEE-na)—saloon or barroom.

capirotada (ka-pi-ro-TA-da)—bread pudding.

carne (KAR-ne)—meat.

carne adovada (KAR-ne ah-do-VA-da)—meat chunks (usually pork) marinated in red chile sauce.

carne asada (KAR-ne ah-SA-da)—roast beef.

carnitas (kar-NEE-tas)—strips of beef or pork marinated in green chile.

carreta (ka-RET-ah)—wagon.

casita (ka-SEE-ta)—cottage; one-room guesthouse.

LEFT: Hoodoos at Kasha-Katuwe Tent Rocks National Monument near Cochiti Pueblo.

chicharrones (chick-a-ROH-nees)—crispy fried pork rinds.

chile (CHEE-leh)—sauce made from either red or green chile peppers, used for seasoning most foods in northern New Mexico.

chile relleno (CHEE-leh re-YEH-no)—crisp, batter-fried green chile pepper stuffed with chicken and/or cheese.

chimenea (chee-me-NEH-ya)—chimney.

chorizo (cho-REE-so)—spicy Mexican sausage.

concha (KON-cha)—belt of inscribed silver plates originally made by the Navajo Indians.

con queso (cone KEH-so)—with cheese.

corbel (kor-BELL)—wooden beam support, usually ornately carved.

curandera (coor-an-DEH-ra)—female Hispanic healer who uses a combination of herbal and other folk remedies.

empanada (em-pa-NAH-da)—fried pie stuffed with seasoned, chopped meat and vegetables or fruit, then sealed and deep-fried; in northern New Mexico, often filled with piñon nuts, currants, spices, and wine.

enchilada (en-chi-LA-da)—flour tortilla filled with cheese, chicken, or meat and covered with red or green chile.

fajitas (fa-HEE-tas)—small strips of highly seasoned, charbroiled meat eaten in a rolled tortilla with guacamole and sour cream.

farolito (far-oh-LEE-toh)—paper bag containing a glowing candle, often displayed in rows around Christmastime to symbolize the arrival of the Christ Child.

flan—caramel custard covered with burned-sugar syrup, a traditional northern New Mexican dessert.

fry bread (not "fried bread")—*sopaipillas* made by the Pueblo Indians.

guacamole (gwok-a-MOLE-eh)—a thick sauce or paste made with a mix of mashed avocados and salsa.

hacienda (AH-see-EN-da)—a large estate, dwelling, or plantation.

heishi (HEE-she)—jewelry made of tiny, hand-carved shell beads.

horno (OR-no)—beehive-shaped outdoor oven for the making of bread, originally brought from Spain.

huevos (WEH-vose)—eggs.

huevos rancheros (WEH-vose ran-CHEH-ros)—fried eggs with red chile sauce, cheese, and lettuce.

jalapeño (HALL-a-PEN-yoh)—small hot pepper.

kachina doll (ka-CHEE-na)—a small wooden doll representing a Hopi spirit, usually carved from cottonwood.

kiva (KEE-va)—circular underground chamber used by the Pueblo Indians for ceremonial and other purposes.

kiva fireplace—traditional adobe fireplace, usually small, beehive shaped, and placed in a corner.

latillas (la-TEE-ahs)—network of thin wooden strips placed over beams or vigas just beneath the roof.

luminaria (loo-mi-NA-ree-ah)—hot, smoky bonfire made of pitchy piñon pine to celebrate the Christmas season.

nachos (NA-chos)—tortilla chips covered with a mix of beans, cheese, and chile, baked and served as hors d'oeuvres.

natillas (na-TEE-ahs)—vanilla custard, a traditional northern New Mexican dessert.

nicho (NEE-cho)—recessed niche in an adobe wall for holding a statue or other ornament.

panocha (pan-OH-cha)—wheat flour pudding.

placita (pla-SEE-ta)—patio.

pollo (PO-yo)—chicken.

portal (por-TALL)—covered patio or sidewalk with supports and fixed roof.

posada (po-SA-da)—resting place or inn.

posole (po-SOLE-eh)—a hominy-like corn stew.

pueblo (PWEB-loh)—a Native American communal village of the Southwest consisting of multitiered adobe structures with flat roofs around a central plaza.

quesadillas (KEH-sa-DEE-yas)—lightly grilled tortillas stuffed with chicken, beef, or beans.

reredos (reh-REH-dose)—carved altar screen for church.

retablo (reh-TAB-loh)—traditional Hispanic painting of a saint on a wooden plaque.

ristra (REES-tra)—string of dried red chiles, often hung on front porches.

salsa (SAL-sa)—traditional northern New Mexican hot sauce composed of tomatoes, onions, peppers, and spices.

santero (san-TEH-roh)—artist who depicts saints.

santo (SAN-toh)—a painted or carved representation of a saint.

sopaipilla (so-pie-PEE-ya)—Spanish popover. These "little pillows" puff up when fried, providing convenient hollows to fill with honey or butter.

taco (TA-koh)—folded corn tortilla usually filled with beans, meat, cheese, tomato, and lettuce.

tamale (ta-MAL-eh)—cornmeal stuffed with chicken or pork and red chile, wrapped in corn husks and steamed.

tapas (TAP-ahs)—appetizers.

tortilla (tor-TEE-ya)—thin pancake made of cornmeal or wheat flour.

tostados (tos-TA-dos)—corn tortillas quartered and fried until crisp, usually eaten as hors d'oeuvres.

trastero (tras-TER-oh)—wooden, freestanding closet or chest of drawers dating from the 17th century; usually ornately carved.

vigas (VEE-gas)—heavy ceiling beams usually made of rough-hewn tree trunks, traditional in Southwest architecture.

zaguan (zag-WAN)—long, covered porch.

Index